GOLDEN KICKS

Bloomsbury Sport

An imprint of Bloomsbury Publishing Plc
50 Bedford Square
London
WC1B 3DP
UK

1385 Broadway
New York
NY 10018
USA

www.bloomsbury.com

BLOOMSBURY and the Diana logo are trademarks of Bloomsbury Publishing Plc

First published in 2016
© Jason Coles, 2016

British Library Cataloguing-in-Publication Data
A catalogue record for this book is available from the British Library.

Library of Congress Cataloguing-in-Publication data has been applied for.

ISBN: Hardback: 9781472937049
ePub:9781472937056
ePDF: 9781472937063

10 9 8 7 6 5 4 3 2 1

Typeset in Trade Gothic by RK Design
Printed and bound in Italy by Printer Trento

To find out more about our authors and books visit www.bloomsbury.com. Here you will find extracts, author interviews, details of forthcoming events and the option to sign up for our newsletters.

GOLDEN KICKS THE SHOES THAT CHANGED SPORT

JASON COLES

BLOOMSBURY
LONDON · OXFORD · NEW YORK · NEW DELHI · SYDNEY

CONTENTS

FOREWORD // 8

INTRODUCTION // 9

A STAR IS BORN
CONVERSE ALL STAR – 1917 // 10–13

IT RUNS IN THE FAMILY
J.W. FOSTER & SONS RUNNING PUMPS – 1924 // 14–17

THE REBEL WITH A RACKET
DUNLOP GREEN FLASH 1555 –1934 // 18–21

JESSE VS THE NAZIS
GEBRÜDER DASSLER SPORTSCHUHFABRIK 'WAITZER' SPIKES –1936 // 22–25

A GIANT OF THE GAME
PRO-KEDS ROYAL – 1949 // 26–29

THREE GOLDS WON, THREE STRIPES GONE
KARHU HELSINKI SPIKES – 1952 // 30–33

BANNISTER'S PLAN B
G.T. LAW & SON RUNNING SPIKES –1954 // 34–37

THE GERMANS' RAIN
ADIDAS ARGENTINIA – 1954 // 38–41

NOT JUST FOR CHICKENS
NEW BALANCE TRACKSTER – 1960 // 42–45

BIRTH OF THE CONQUEROR
ONITSUKA TIGER CORSAIR/NIKE CORTEZ – 1962 // 46–49

THE SILENT SALUTE
PUMA SUEDE – 1968 // 50–53

THE BATTLE OF MEXICO CITY
ADIDAS WELTREKORD – 1968 // 54–57

FROM A FLOP TO 'THE FLOP'
ADIDAS SPECIAL – 1968 // **58–61**

A SUPERSTAR IS BORN
ADIDAS SUPERSTAR – 1969 // **62–65**

THE SPIRIT OF THE SWOOSH
NIKE PRE MONTREAL RACER – 1969 // **66–69**

WHEN PELÉ CROWNED THE KING
PUMA KING – 1970 // **70–73**

THESE BOOTS WERE MADE FOR DANCING
ADIDAS BOXING BOOT -1970 // **74-75**

ISN'T STAN SMITH A SHOE?
ADIDAS STAN SMITH – 1971 // **76–79**

MR BOWERMAN'S WAFFLES
NIKE MOON SHOE – 1972 // **80–81**

CLYDE STYLE
PUMA CLYDE – 1972 // **82–85**

GRACE VS GUTS
LE COQ SPORTIF ARTHUR ASHE – 1975 // **86–89**

A NEW ERA
VANS STYLE #95 ERA – 1976 // **90–93**

DOUBLE JEOPARDY
ONITSUKA TIGER (ASICS) RUNSPARK – 1976 // **94–95**

THE MESSENGER
ADIDAS ORION – 1980 // **96–97**

TEEN ANGEL VS SUPERBRAT
DIADORA BJÖRN BORG – 1980 // **98–101**

FEEL THE FORCE
NIKE AIR FORCE 1 – 1982 // **102–103**

GIRL POWERED
REEBOK FREESTYLE – 1982 // **104–107**

LIKE BUTTER ON STUDS
ADIDAS COPA MUNDIAL – 1982 // **108–109**

DRINK BEER AND TRAIN LIKE AN ANIMAL
SAUCONY DXN – 1983 // 110–111

BATTLEFIELD LA
NIKE ZOOM RUNNING SPIKES – 1984 // 112–115

THE LEGEND BEGINS
NIKE AIR JORDAN I – 1984 // 116–119

WIMBLEDON GOES BOOM BOOM
PUMA BORIS BECKER – 1985 // 120–123

MCENROE GETS CROSS
NIKE AIR TRAINER – 1986 // 124–127

AS GOOD AS GOLD
ADIDAS GRAND SLAM – 1988 // 128–131

PUMP UP AND AIR OUT
REEBOK THE PUMP – 1991 // 132–135

NO HALF MEASURES
VANS HALF CAB – 1992 // 136–139

MR BOWERMAN'S WAFFLES
PUMA DISC – 1993 // 140–141

SKIPPY'S NEW BOOTS
ADIDAS PREDATOR – 1994 // 142–145

KING OF THE HILL
FILA THE HILL – 1994/95 // 146–147

MESMERIZING
REEBOK SHAQNOSIS – 1995/96 // 148–151

THE ANSWER'S QUESTION
REEBOK THE QUESTION – 1996 // 152–155

THE LAST VAULT
ASICS GYM ULTRA – 1996 // 156–159

GOLD AND BOLD
NIKE GOLD RUNNING SPIKES – 1996 // 160–163

DAVID WHO?
NIKE AIR ZOOM M9 – 1999 // 164–167

THE WARRIOR
ADIDAS EQUIPMENT RUGBY – 1999 // **168–171**

DREAMTIME
NIKE RUNNING SPIKES – 2000 // **172–175**

KOBE'S MIXED KICKS
NIKE/REEBOK/CONVERSE/VARIOUS MODELS – 2002 // **176–179**

MICHAEL SCHUMACHER'S SHOE MAKER
PUMA SPEED CAT/FUTURE CAT – 2004 // **180–181**

NO LIMITS
OSSUR/NIKE FLEX RUN NIKE SOLE – 2006 // **182–185**

FROM CLOWNING TO CROWNING
PUMA COMPLETE THESEUS II – 2008 // **186–189**

THE MASTER BLASTER'S CENTURY OF CENTURIES
ADIDAS 22YDS LITE IV – 2012 // **190–193**

SEVENTH HEAVEN
NIKE ZOOM VAPOR 9 TOUR – 2012 // **194–197**

THE PROJECT
NIKE ZOOM VICTORY ELITE – 2012 // **198–201**

ACE OUTTA COMPTON
NIKE NIKECOURT FLARE – 2015 // **202–205**

BLOOD, SWEAT & CLEATS
SIDI WIRE CARBON AIR VERNICE – 2015 // **206–209**

MESSI'S MIDAS TOUCH
ADIDAS MESSI 15 – 2016 // **210–213**

NO SWEAT
UNDER ARMOUR CURRY II – 2016 // **214–217**

BIBLIOGRAPHY & SOURCES // 218

PHOTO CREDITS // 219

INDEX // 220–223

ACKNOWLEDGEMENTS // 224

When I was first approached by Horst Dassler to endorse adidas' flagship tennis shoe, I never imagined that over forty years later it would be one of the most popular and best-selling of all time. So popular in fact, that many fans don't even realize that I'm an actual person, not a shoe! Over the years I've been amazed and humbled at the way it has stood the test of time. Echoing the stories of so many of the most popular sports shoes covered in *Golden Kicks*, it was born as a performance shoe and the choice of not just myself, but many professional tennis players, and over time has become an iconic lifestyle shoe in its own right and the favorite of millions of people across the globe. Although it now comes in countless styles and colors, it remains essentially the same simple, comfortable shoe that I wore when I won Wimbledon, back in 1972.

As you're about to discover, *Golden Kicks* is full of fascinating stories about the shoes that athletes of all kinds have worn during the greatest moments in sporting history. Not just the ones that involved winning trophies and championships, but also those that won hearts and minds. From Jessie Owens and Adi Dassler embarrassing Hitler in 1936, to Lionel Messi celebrating his fifth Ballon d'Or in boots made with platinum in 2016, whether you're a casual sports fan or a passionate 'sneakerhead', I'm sure, like me, you'll enjoy reading and sharing these anecdotes.

We all take our shoes for granted - it's part of their job - but I hope after reading *Golden Kicks*, next time you put on those simple white shoes with the green heel tab (or whatever your favorite sneakers happen to be), you might appreciate just a little more, the stories that you're quite literally wearing on your feet.

The man, the shoe.
Stan Smith

INTRODUCTION

I have to come clean. My passion for sports shoes is a relatively new thing in my life. I wish I could say I've been crazy about them for decades, but despite having worn them from when I first started walking, and building a career with agencies and brands that marketed and sold them, until a few years ago I'd never really given them much thought. They were just things I put on my feet until they wore out and were replaced with another pair. But something happened that changed all that when I discovered the story of a feud between two brothers from a tiny village in Bavaria.

The more I learned about brothers Rudi and Adi Dassler, the founders of Puma and adidas, the more I fell in love with the wonderful stories behind the shoes they created and how their battle shaped the sports world. And when I'd learned all I could about the Dasslers, I moved on to the stories of their fellow pioneers, people like Phil Knight and Bill Bowerman of Nike, the Foster family of Reebok, Kihacharo Onitsuka of ASICS and William Riley of New Balance. Enthralling stories of passionate people who poured their devotion into making shoes so that athletes could perform better and achieve more. What struck me most was that they almost appeared to instill life into their creations. They were so much more than just pieces of canvas or leather stitched to rubber. Many seemed to have 'lives' of their own, becoming as legendary as the athletes who wore them, and then 'retiring' to live the rest of their days as streetwear.

Sports shoes quickly became an obsession and I immersed myself into sneaker culture. As my head filled with their stories, I couldn't go anywhere without looking at everyone's feet. It got so bad that when I met people, my first instinct was to look at what shoes they were wearing rather than their faces. Whatever they were — Stan Smiths, Suedes, Jordans or All Stars — I would find myself asking if they knew the story behind them. Naturally, at first I got some funny looks, but once they heard it, they were hooked and wanted to know more. Their reactions made me realize that even diehard sports fans and dedicated sneakerheads didn't know the sporting origins of the brands and shoes they loved and wore everyday. I just had to put these stories down on paper. And that's how the book you now hold in your hands was born. Sadly there were so many stories I couldn't possibly fit them all into one book. If I've missed out any of your favourites, please forgive me and let me know. I'll try to get them into book two!

Yours shoely,

Jason

Website: www.goldenkicksbook.com // Twitter: @goldenkicksbook // Facebook: goldenkicksbook // Instagram: goldenkicksbook

FOREWORD & INTRODUCTION_9

A STAR IS BORN

1917 CONVERSE CREATE THE ALL STAR

CONVERSE ALL STAR

We start with the Granddaddy of them all and the sports shoe arguably most deserving of the title, 'Greatest of All Time'. A shoe so iconic that it became more of a symbol for basketball than the ball itself; a shoe so universally acclaimed that at one point in its glorious history 60 per cent of Americans owned a pair. It is, of course, the Converse All Star, more affectionately known as 'Chucks' or 'Connies'.

Founded in 1908 in Malden, Massachusetts, by Marquis Mills Converse, the Converse Rubber Company began life manufacturing waterproof overshoes. Being a seasonal product, the company couldn't keep its workers busy all year round and so in 1915 it began making tennis shoes. With basketball steadily increasing in popularity, Converse developed a new shoe to meet the rising demand, and in 1917 the All Star was born.

Two things happened that were to ensure the shoe's destiny. The first was the entry of the United States into the First World War. The US army needed fit young men and, in the belief that the coming battles would first be won on the sports fields, physical activity and participation in sports were encouraged, increasing the need for sports shoes. The second thing that put the All Star on its path to greatness was the arrival at Converse of Charles Hollis 'Chuck' Taylor.

Legend has it that in 1921 Taylor walked into the Converse office complaining of sore feet. He was an experienced journeyman basketball player who played for the Boston Celtics and for industrial league team, the Akron Firestone Non-Skids. His complaint was that the current version of the All Star hurt his feet. Recognizing that his playing experience could be beneficial to the product and that he was a natural salesman, Converse immediately hired him. He recommended a number of improvements including greater flexibility, and in 1934 became the first person to have his name added to a sports shoe when a heel patch he suggested was added to provide better ankle support. The iconic patch still bears his signature to this day. Taylor never received a commission, however, and remained simply a salaried employee of the company, although it is rumoured that he made full use of the company expense account.

Taylor toured the country as both salesman and ambassador. His white Cadillac, its boot filled with shoes, became a welcome sight as he drove from city to city, hosting clinics in school and college gymnasiums. Working with local coaches, he taught basic basketball skills and then used his charm with the nearest sporting goods stores to encourage them to sell more of his signature shoes.

In 1922, he began the *Converse Basketball Yearbook*, in which he named his selection of the best players, teams and coaches of the year. His picks were highly respected because he only selected players and teams he had actually seen play. This meant he often included talent from less heralded schools and colleges where sports journalists never went, making the book compulsory reading for coaches and talent spotters.

Taylor's efforts to grow the game were effective, and as basketball grew in popularity so did the All Star. When the game debuted as a medal sport in the 1936 Olympics, it was All Stars that Team USA wore on the way to winning the first of seven consecutive gold medals. In 1939, when the first ever NCAA Championship game took place, both teams were wearing Chucks, and a year later the New York Rens won 88 straight games in a single season to take the first professional basketball championship, again, in All Stars. When Wilt Chamberlain scored a still record 100 points in single game he did in, yes, you guessed it, All

Opposite All wearing Converse All Stars, the United States Olympic basketball team celebrate their victory over France in the final of the 1948 London Olympic Games, their second of what would be seven consecutive Olympic gold medals.

Stars. To cap it all the real seal of approval came when they were named official sports shoe of the Olympic Games in 1938, remaining so all the way until 1968.

By the time of Taylor's death in 1969 he had left an incredible legacy: the game had never been so popular and it was estimated that 90 per cent of college and professional basketball players were wearing All Stars, helping Converse to take an 80 per cent share of the entire US sports shoe market.

Sadly, the early 1970s were not to be so kind. At the height of their popularity, Converse were dealt a blow they wouldn't recover from by the entry of adidas and Nike into basketball. More advanced shoes like the Superstar and the Blazer made the All Star look like a relic, both in appearance and performance. Chucks began to be a rare sight on court, and in 1979 Tree Rollins held the sad honour of being the last ever NBA player to wear a pair of All Stars in a game.

However, the late 1970s and 1980s saw a revolution in fashion, with young people starting to dress in sportswear outside the gym. Until 1971, Converse sold the All Star in only two colours, black and white, but recognizing this change, it began to offer more colours and styles. As its popularity increased so did the range of colours, almost 500 at one point. Already a sporting icon, the All Star began a new life as a cultural one.

In 2015, 98 years after its birth, Converse introduced the Chuck Taylor All Star II, an all-new version that stayed true to the original's classic look but refreshed it with new technologies fit for the twenty-first century. Reflecting Converse's membership of the Nike family, the company having being bought by the Oregon-based giants in 2003, the new All Star featured a Nike Lunarlon sock liner to improve its cushioning and arch support and a perforated micro suede liner to provide better breathability. It was also lighter, more durable and offered better ankle and instep support.

Although All Star II brought Chucks right up to date, the world is still in love with the original. As American as 'Old Glory', its classic style and simplicity, unchanged since 1949, means that a pair of All Stars is sold every 43 seconds. It's staggering to think that in 2017 the All Star celebrates its 100th anniversary, and while it may not grace the courts of the NBA anymore, it will probably grace the streets well beyond its 150th.

....

Right Converse 'Chuck Taylor' All Star II., (Converse, Inc).

IT RUNS IN THE FAMILY
1924 PARIS OLYMPIC GAMES

J.W. FOSTER & SONS RUNNING PUMPS

The story of British runners Harold Abrahams and Eric Liddell, immortalized in the 1981 film *Chariots of Fire*, is a tale of two men whose determination helped them to overcome barriers and achieve their dreams of Olympic glory. A lesser known but parallel tale is that of Joseph Foster, a shoemaker who shared a similar determination in wanting to make the best athletic running shoes possible, and played a key role in Abrahams' and Liddell's success.

While the Foster family were to be forever associated with running, their story starts not on the running track, but on a cricket pitch. In 1862, Samuel Foster, the latest in a long line of Nottinghamshire shoemakers, received a special guest in his workshop who was to change his and his family's destiny. That guest was Samuel Biddulph, star player of Nottinghamshire County Cricket Club. He had a problem he needed Foster to solve. Although better known as a wicketkeeper, he had developed a new bowling action that could only work with good grip, but the hobnails on his shoes weren't up to the job, especially on hard ground. Thinking the problem through, Foster realized that the answer was spikes. Working with a blacksmith, he produced a pair of shoes with short flat-headed nails in the sole that would bite into the ground, providing the bowler with plenty of grip. They worked well. So well that in 1863

Biddulph was taken on by the groundstaff of the MCC at Lord's, giving Foster's shoes a showcase that brought them much attention and led many cricketers to seek out a pair.

For 20 years Foster continued to make shoes for cricket and additionally golf and football, when in 1890 he welcomed another significant guest to his workshop, his grandson Joseph Foster. Joseph was a keen runner and on seeing his grandfather's sports shoes realized that with a little modification, they could give him an advantage on the track.

Apprenticing himself to his grandfather, Joseph was determined to learn all he could about shoemaking and began to experiment and evolve the shoes, customizing them for running and finding ways to reduce their weight. In 1898, he finally perfected the shoes he called 'Running Pumps'. Incredibly light and made of the strongest and softest leathers, they boasted six one-inch spikes for perfect grip. At every race he attended, Joseph was surrounded by customers keen to purchase a pair of his shoes and, as other runners began to set personal bests

---

Right Great Britain's Harold Abrahams breaks the tape to win the 100m gold medal at the 1924 Paris Olympic Games wearing J.W. Foster & Sons Running Pumps.

and smash records while wearing them, demand became so high that he had to move out of the bedroom that had served as his workshop and move next door to create the world's first sports shoe factory.

Dubbed the 'Olympic Works', athletes came from far and wide to visit J.W. Foster's and be fitted for a pair of his now famous Running Pumps. Strongly believing in an ethos based on the idea that each pair of shoes had to be custom made to suit each specific athlete, Foster even made shoes to suit specific races. From lightweight models that would only last a single race to models designed for use only at a specific track, no effort was spared in order to make shoes that would give the runner wearing them an advantage.

It was this advantage that made Foster's creations appeal to elite athletes and they began to be seen wherever British athletes competed. However, it was on the feet of Harold Abrahams and Eric Liddell at the 1924 Paris Olympic Games that they earned the addition of the word 'Famous' to their name. With Abrahams winning gold in the 100m and Liddell gold in the 400m while wearing them,

the shoes quickly became a household name.

Joseph Foster's legacy, however, was to be far greater than just the Running Pumps. After his death in 1933, his sons James and William took over the business and expanded the company's football and rugby ranges, but remained true to their father's mission of creating shoes designed for athletes. Their boots could be found on the feet of top players from across the country and such was their fame that when the legendary Moscow Dynamo made their first trip to the West in 1945, their first stop was Bolton, to the Olympic Works to be personally fitted with new boots.

The family business continued to thrive but in the 1950s disagreements between the generations over the company's direction led to a split, and James' and William's sons Joe and Jeff left to form their own company. With the rise of adidas and Puma, Foster's began to decline but for Joe and Jeff it was a different story. The company they founded continues to thrive to this day. You probably know it better as Reebok.

Left J.W. Foster & Sons Running Pump (Reebok Archive).

THE REBEL WITH A RACKET
1934 WIMBLEDON CHAMPIONSHIPS

DUNLOP GREEN FLASH 1555

Fred Perry and the Dunlop Green Flash was a match made in Wimbledon. Both British icons and products of the 1930s, they each brought a new approach and style to tennis after years of status quo. Despite leaving legacies that were to last for many years, both suffered periods during which they fell from grace, but re-emerged to be once more revered.

Born in 1909, the son of a cotton spinner and left-wing politician from Stockport, Fred Perry's family moved to London when he was nine. Educated at Ealing Grammar School, he began playing tennis on public courts near his family's housing estate. A far cry from the public schools and country clubs his contemporaries hailed from, and marking him out as an outsider to the upper echelons of tennis. When he won a place on the Davis Cup team in 1933, a team member remarked, 'As we've got to have the bloody upstart, we might as well knock him into shape and try to get the best out of him.' Their attitude towards this working-class gatecrasher was clear.

Perry was to have an impact on tennis that would change it both on and off the court. Although he is now remembered as Great Britain's greatest tennis player, in the 1930s when tennis was almost exclusively the domain of the British establishment, his rise to fame was as

warmly welcomed as a fox is in a chicken coop.

First hitting the shelves in 1929, the same year that Fred Perry first qualified for Wimbledon, the Green Flash was his tennis shoe of choice. It was, in fact, almost 100 years after its makers Dunlop created one of the first dedicated sports shoes. Originally called 'sand shoes' (for wearing on the beach) they later became known as plimsolls (because the canvas and rubber bond looked like a ship's plimsoll line) and were among the very first sports shoes. They were cheap and functional, but as people become more fashion-conscious in the post-war 1920s, a shoe with a touch more style was needed.

Dunlop's answer was the Green Flash. Unlike later versions, the original was almost all white with only 'flashes' of green on the toe box and the thin stitching on the upper. Its moulded rubber sole featured a herringbone pattern designed to give extra grip on grass. Essentially, it was the next step in the evolution of the humble plimsoll.

Fred Perry was undaunted by his reception among the tennis establishment and saw the snobbery he faced as motivation to do better. His approach would hold him in good stead. Playing at Wimbledon in 1934, the crowd was noticeably cold towards him. Being mostly made up of traditional tennis gentry, the presence of a player

who wasn't a 'gentleman' was almost offensive to them. A bachelor lifestyle, his clear ambition and the fact he wasn't afraid to indulge in a little gamesmanship also did little to endear him to fans. Resolute despite the hostility, Perry advanced through the tournament. Given the crowd's dim view of him, his opponent in the Men's Singles final seemed fated for him.

Joining Perry in the final was Australian Jack 'Gentleman' Crawford. The very model of a gentleman amateur, Crawford had an almost demure style which contrasted with Perry's more physical game, making him the favourite of the crowd and officials. Nevertheless, Perry's steel saw him through to win his first Wimbledon title 6–3, 6–0, 7–5. But even victory wasn't enough to win him any favour. The disdain with which his win was met was clear when his All England Lawn Tennis & Croquet Club members tie, awarded to all new Champions, was dismissively left draped over a chair in the dressing room instead of being presented to him personally. Making matters worse, in the changing room Perry overheard an official boast that he had given the winner's champagne to the defeated Jack Crawford, describing him as 'the better man'.

Opposite Fred Perry wearing Dunlop Green Flash on the way to winning his third consecutive Wimbledon Men's Singles Championship in 1936.

Below Dunlop Green Flash
c. 1975 (Wimbledon Museum).

If his lack of pedigree wasn't enough of a problem, his attitude to the amateur principles that tennis held dear made things even worse. The International Lawn Tennis Federation (ILTF) had decreed that tennis should be played purely for sport, not profit, meaning it was forbidden for Perry or any other player to be paid to play or make endorsements. This meant that by the rules, he wasn't allowed to receive any money from Dunlop for wearing Green Flash. Perry made no secret of the fact he wanted to monetize his fame, leading to frequent clashes with the ILTF.

Perry's attitude to training was also looked upon with suspicion. He was determined to make tennis a physical game and practised relentlessly. He also trained with Arsenal Football Club most mornings and played in weekly friendly matches. At a time when training and preparation were seen as 'ungentlemanly', his approach was deemed uncouth, and so despite winning again in 1935 and 1936, Perry was still seen as 'the bloody upstart'. In the 1935 final, the crowd were noticeably warmer to him, but that had more to do with the nationality of his opponent, Baron Gottfried von Cramm. Even an aristocratic background wasn't enough to win over a crowd, who, after the Great War, were hostile to anyone who was German. When Perry faced him again in the 1936 final, the crowd's sentiment towards the German remained the same.

Both finals were great examples of Perry's style of psychological warfare. In the 1935 final, knowing it would irritate Von Cramm no end, he played with the lining of his trouser pockets pulled out. He also played with a bright white racket, believing it would distract his opponent. And in the 1936 final his demolition of Von Cramm in less than 45 minutes was, in part, because the Wimbledon masseur had mentioned that he had treated the German player for a groin strain. Knowing the injury would impair his opponent's movement, Perry deliberately played wide forehand shots.

Disillusioned with the ILTF, Perry made the decision to leave Britain after his last Wimbledon win and to the horror of the establishment joined the professional circuit. Professionalism was so abhorred in Britain that he was immediately made an outcast, barred from using ILTF associated clubs and stripped of his honorary All England Club membership. Perry remained undaunted. If his own country could turn its back on him, he could do the same, and in 1938 he became an American citizen. With players who turned professional effectively not existing as far as the ILTF was concerned, Perry was essentially written out of British tennis history.

As a result it was many years before Fred Perry began to receive the kind of recognition a three-times Wimbledon Champion deserved. The 78-year wait for a new British Men's Singles Champion, that ended with Andy Murray's victory in 2013, meant that the esteem Perry was held in grew with each passing year and, thanks to Dunlop keeping it alive, so too did his association with the Green Flash. By the 1970s, the Green Flash was as much a British icon as Perry, and despite having largely disappeared from tennis courts it had become hugely popular as streetwear.

The tennis establishment too had begun to appreciate Perry's achievements and in 1984 he was invited to the All England Lawn Tennis & Croquet Club to celebrate the 50th anniversary of his first singles triumph with the unveiling of a bronze statue of himself. They also renamed the Somerset Road entrance to the grounds as the Fred Perry Gates.

At the height of its popularity during the 1970s, according to Dunlop a million pairs of Green Flash a year were sold. The shoe had evolved since being worn to victory by Perry, featuring a padded collar and tongue for added comfort, an insole made of sponge, eyelets for greater ventilation and a few more splashes of green. But things weren't so rosy in the 1980s. The advent of new technologies, like Nike's Air and Reebok's Pump systems, began to make the Green Flash look its age and by the 1990s they were rarely seen on the streets. But much like Fred Perry in his later years, the same people who denigrated them came to love them once again. The craze in sneaker culture for reissues has elevated the Green Flash to the status of a fashion icon and it's now more likely to be found in boutiques than in sports shops.

Despite his death in 1995, like his shoes, Fred Perry is more celebrated today than he was in his prime. The establishment that once sneered at his background and cast him out of tennis now revere and invoke him and one of the most fitting tributes to his achievements currently stands in the club that once took his membership away. Today, welcoming fans to Centre Court and in pride of place at the heart of Wimbledon proudly stands that same bronze statue of Fred Perry, right where he belongs.

JESSE VS THE NAZIS
1936 BERLIN OLYMPIC GAMES

GEBRÜDER DASSLER SPORTSCHUHFABRIK 'WAITZER' SPIKES

Having set three world records and equalled a fourth in one day at Ann Arbour in Michigan in 1935, James 'Jesse' Cleveland Owens was already a superstar before he arrived in Germany for the 1936 Berlin Olympic Games. But it was in Berlin that year that he became a legend. The son of a sharecropper and grandson of a slave, he arrived in Berlin to scenes similar to the reception the Beatles would receive 30 years later, with a crush of girls waiting with scissors to cut off snippets of his clothes as souvenirs. Afraid of being mobbed, he had to be accompanied by guards whenever he left the Olympic Village.

The irony of his welcome was that at the time the German Chancellor was a certain Adolf Hitler, and the country was in the grip of the Nazi regime. The Berlin Games was intended to be a showcase of Aryan superiority, however, Hitler hadn't counted on the popularity and performance of a black American athlete, completely disproving a key part of Nazi dogma.

Another hindrance that Hitler could not have foreseen was the collaboration of one of his own countrymen, Adolf 'Adi' Dassler in Owens' triumph. The shoemaker brothers Adi and Rudolph 'Rudi' Dassler had realized that the best advertising for their running spikes was victory on the track, and recognizing that Owens was the greatest athlete of his

day, Adi was determined to get him to wear Gebrüder Dassler (Dassler Brothers) spikes.

Adolf and Rudolf Dassler had first opened their sports shoe factory in Herzogenaurach, Bavaria, in July 1924. A rebel from an early age, Adi Dassler defied convention and spent most of his spare time playing sports. He had a passion for physical activity, particularly long-distance running, javelin throwing, shot-putting and skiing. Elder brother Rudi was also a sports fan but, unlike Adi, had a mind for business from a young age and spent much of his time learning about shoe manufacturing from his father. Sadly for both of them the call for the mobilization of the German army in 1914 interrupted their plans and they both found themselves in the trenches of Flanders.

Both managed to survive the war and after his return home Adi spent days in the countryside, scavenging army equipment and utensils left by retreating soldiers that could be recycled. Strips of leather were used to make shoes and parachutes turned into slippers. In early 1920 he started a shoe business in a workshop on the site of his mother's former laundry and, with tuition from his father, he learned how to stitch shoes. His passion for sport meant that he was most interested in sports shoes and, starting with slippers for gymnastics, he also began to experiment with running

spikes. Rudi, who had tried a few other professions since the war ended, eventually decided to return to Herzogenaurach and join his brother. On 1 July 1924 the two founded Gebrüder Dassler Sportschuhfabrik (Dassler Brothers Sports Shoe Factory).

On the face of it the brothers had chosen the worst time to open a shoe business. The loss of the war had led to great hardship in Germany but the situation was ultimately beneficial for them as people found sport to be a distraction from the misery. Shaking off Germany's conservative ways, young people turned to sport as a way of becoming more modern and even deviant. Football, being the creation of the English, was seen as the most deviant of sports but quickly became the most popular and clubs sprang up all over Germany. Initially, the brothers struggled to make sales to retailers but found success when they convinced the sports club in their home town to place an order for shoes to be offered to members. The club placed such a large order the brothers had to work flat out for months to fulfil it. Word of the brothers' shoes soon spread and a visit from the coach

Opposite Jesse Owens crosses the finishing line to win the 1936 Berlin Olympic Games 100m final in white Gebrüder Dassler running spikes (Olympic Multimedia Library).

of the German athletics team, Josef Waitzer, to learn more about their running spikes gave the brothers direct access to the national team and turned into a lifelong friendship.

In 1929, Germany's economy was hit once more by a collapse of the world economy triggered by the Wall Street Crash. The economic climate and state of the German government led to the rise of Adolf Hitler and the Nazis, who appealed to the many suffering from the economic situation and still feeling humiliation at the loss of the war. As the Nazis grew in power, many Germans believed that anyone wishing to stay in business, whether they were sympathetic or not, had to consider party membership. In May 1933, three months after Hitler had seized power, the brothers registered their names. The rise of the Nazis unexpectedly increased demand for the Dasslers' shoes. Hitler regarded sport as a powerful instrument to encourage discipline and comradeship and also of great propaganda value. It would also help develop him an army of athletic young men and, under a programme of compulsory integration, Hitler tightened the country's sports infrastructure and all sporting clubs and federations were merged under the Nazi banner. Participation in sport was seen as a patriotic duty and millions of young people joined the Hitler Youth, which encouraged sporting activity as well as political education. Although not at all politically minded, and far from enthusiastic about Hitler and the Nazis, Adi decided that in order to build contacts with the sports clubs and youth of Herzogenaurach he should become a coach and supplier to the Hitler Youth movement, and joined in 1935.

Adi, aware that Jesse Owens was one of the finest athletes in the world, also saw in him a kindred spirit, not just as an athlete but because he worked part-time in a shoe repair shop when he wasn't training. Despite the prevailing political attitude toward 'non-Aryans' and fully aware of

the risks involved in providing German shoes to a foreigner who might possibly beat German athletes, Adi remained undaunted. From the moment Owens set foot in the Berlin Olympic Village, he set about getting his spikes in front of the American track star. He first spoke to his friend Josef Waitzer, with whom he had developed the shoes. Knowing the possible consequences, Waitzer was understandably reluctant, but agreed to get three pairs to Owens. Lightweight and made from calves' leather, they were unlike anything he had run in before. But it didn't take long for him to be convinced that they were the right shoes for him.

Owens won four gold medals in the Dassler spikes: the 100m, 200m, 4x100m relay and the long jump. So much for Aryan supremacy. While recent evidence appears to refute the long-held belief that Hitler snubbed Owens after his first victory, one of his closest advisors, Albert Speer, confirmed that Hitler 'was highly annoyed by the series of triumphs by the marvellous coloured American runner, Jesse Owens.'

Whether Hitler congratulated Owens or not, one person who most certainly did was his main rival in the long jump, Carl 'Lutz' Long, a man who could have been the poster boy for the Aryan ideal. Despite being soundly beaten by Owens he made possibly one of the most magnanimous and daring gestures in defeat when he warmly embraced and congratulated him, right in front of the Führer.

For the Dassler brothers, Owens winning in their spikes helped launch them into the stratosphere and their shoes began to sell far beyond Germany. His patronage was to literally save their business. At the end of the Second World War, when the invading US soldiers discovered that the Gebrüder Dassler factory had made Owens' gold-medal-winning shoes, instead of blowing it up they allowed it to remain standing. They were soon to become the company's best customers when the sports-mad occupying soldiers

began ordering baseball and basketball shoes, ensuring the company's survival in the harsh post-war climate.

Although he was given a rapturous welcome when he returned home to a ticker-tape parade in New York, segregation was still very much in place in America, and Owens found himself having to ride the freight elevator at the Waldorf Astoria hotel to reach the very reception arranged in his honour. The quadruple gold medallist didn't even receive the customary invitation to the White House following his victories, nor even a congratulatory telegram.

After Owens' death in 1980, it was left to a later President, Jimmy Carter, to confirm his place in American history, when he said of him, 'Perhaps no athlete better symbolized the human struggle against tyranny, poverty and racial bigotry. His personal triumphs as a world-class athlete and record holder were the prelude to a career devoted to helping others. His work with young athletes, as an unofficial ambassador overseas, and a spokesman for freedom are a rich legacy to his fellow Americans.'

A GIANT OF THE GAME

1949 GEORGE MIKAN JOINS THE LAKERS

PRO-KEDS ROYAL

Ever wondered what would have happened if Clark Kent had decided to become a basketball player and not a journalist? The result would probably have been George Mikan. A giant of a man and player, Mikan dominated every court he played on, not just with his size but with his skill, power and agility. One of the first stars of the NBA he was among the first players to endorse a range of products, but the one he became most famous for was the Pro-Keds Royal.

Born in June 1924 in Joliet, Illinois, Mikan's basketball career almost didn't happen after his high school coach told him that it just wasn't possible to play basketball in glasses. An athletic career seemed even less likely as he matured. By the age of 18 he was 6ft 10in tall, weighed 110kg (14½ stone) and, due to his large frame, had a slow awkward movement. Topping it off was the fact he was near-sighted and needed to wear thick glasses. But his life changed when he attended DePaul University in Chicago in 1942 and met Ray Meyer, a young basketball coach who felt that Mikan had potential. At the time Mikan must have appeared to others to be a lost cause. There were very few tall players in the game because the prevailing attitude was that they were just too clumsy and uncoordinated to be good at basketball. However, Meyer realized that instead of it being a hindrance, Mikan could use his size as a unique advantage and, in just a few months, transformed the young player by using a combination of on-court training, dancing lessons, jumping rope and boxing.

Meyer's coaching worked wonders. Playing for DePaul in the National Collegiate Athletic Association, Mikan commanded the courts. His size and sheer presence daunted his opponents and the ambidextrous hook shot he developed with his coach, coupled with his height, made him a scoring machine. His height also made him a great defensive player. He was able to jump so high that when the opposing team took shots he could easily knock their balls away before they got anywhere near the basket. His domination led him to win the College Player of the Year award two years running and he was named an All-American player three times. He led DePaul to the National Invitation Tournament title in 1945 and was named Most Valuable Player for scoring 120 points in three games. In one game, Mikan scored 53 of DePaul's 97 points in a win over Rhode Island, equalling the number of points scored by the entire opposing team and also setting the collegiate single-game scoring record.

Following the 1945/46 college season Mikan joined the Chicago American Gears for his rookie pro season and led the team to the World Basketball Tournament title. But when the Gears' owner pulled the team out of the league to start his own championship, which folded after only a month, Mikan was signed by the Minneapolis Lakers. It was with the Lakers that he started his successful relationship with Pro-Keds. Founded in 1916, like a number of other shoemakers at the time, Keds was the shoe manufacturing division of a brand of tyres, the United States Rubber Company. Since tyres and sports footwear were both made of rubber, companies like B.F. Goodrich and Dunlop were among the first sports shoe makers. The name Keds was chosen because the original choice, Peds, from the Latin word for foot, was already trademarked. Their range of canvas shoes was so popular, especially in basketball, that the company set up 'Pro-Keds' in 1949 to make sports-specific shoes. The first in the new range was the Royal, a canvas-based shoe in low- and hi-top versions, which apart from blue and red midsole stripes, looked very similar to the incredibly popular Converse All Star.

Recognizing Mikan's potential, Pro-Keds began an endorsement relationship with him and it was immediately successful. In 1949, the Basketball Association of America and National Basketball League merged to form the NBA and Mikan was the star of the new league. The Lakers reached the play-offs with a 51–17 record, with Mikan averaging 27.4 point per game and taking the top-scoring title. After

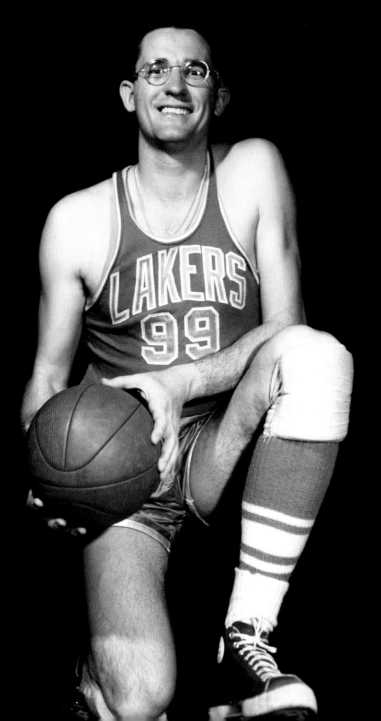

breezing through the play-offs the Lakers beat the Syracuse Nationals in the finals, winning 6-4 to become the first ever NBA Champions.

In the 1950/51 season, Mikan's dominance started to have an impact beyond the scoreboard after the Lakers played the Fort Wayne Pistons in a landmark game in NBA history. Such was Mikan's superiority that the Pistons decided that the only way to win the game was to deny him the ball. To that end, when they took a 19-18 lead, the Pistons spent the rest of the game passing the ball around but not making any attempt to score. The plan worked and the score stayed 19-18, still the lowest score ever in an NBA game. It also had the bizarre effect of making Mikan a record breaker. Having scored 15 of the Lakers 18 points, he set an all-time NBA game score of 83.3 per cent. Records aside, the NBA realized that something had to be done to stop 'Mikan blocking' becoming the norm, eventually introducing the shot clock, which forced a team in possession to attempt a shot within 24 seconds or else lose possession of the ball.

The nascent NBA was keen to use the appeal of the Lakers' No. 99 to bring more fans to the game. His fame and his approachable manner had been inspired by his hero Babe Ruth, who was famed for making time for his fans, and made him a natural promoter for the sport. He would usually arrive the day before a game to make appearances, meet fans and sign autographs at specially arranged promotional events. But, while Mikan was always a team player, on one occasion his fame caused a little resentment. Before a game between the Lakers and the Knicks at Madison Square Garden the billing read: 'Geo. Mikan vs Knicks'. Before the game Mikan walked into the locker room to find his teammates sitting around still wearing their street clothes. Mikan was puzzled until one of his teammates joked, 'They're advertising you're playing against the Knicks, so go play them. We'll wait here.' But with Mikan being far from an egotist his teammates quickly accepted his fame.

His appeal also made him a target for brands wanting him to endorse their products and a whole range of items from ironing boards to chewing gum became officially endorsed by Mikan, although his closest association remained with Pro-Keds. He became synonymous with the company and wherever they were advertised Mikan's endorsement would be the headline.

The 1951/52 season saw yet another rule change that was a result of Mikan's dominance. Because of his height Mikan was able to swat the opposing side's balls away from the basket easily and so to stop his 'goal-tending' the NBA decided to widen the foul lane under the basket from 6 feet to 12 feet. Players were only allowed in the foul lane for three seconds and, by widening it, players like Mikan were forced to defend from twice the distance. Clearly aimed at stopping Mikan, it was dubbed 'The Mikan Rule'. While it did have the effect of lowering his score average Mikan still led the Lakers to the NBA title that year.

Despite the rule changes, Mikan remained the NBA's best player and the Lakers took the title again in the 1952/53 and 1953/54 to win a 'three-peat' and their fifth title. However, Mikan was beginning to lose his edge. His average had dropped and the injuries he had sustained, including 10 broken bones, were beginning to take their toll. Despite having gained a reputation for his Superman-like ability to play through pain, it was getting more difficult. Approaching 30 and with a growing family, Mikan announced his retirement. Without him the Lakers suffered and while they made the play-offs they failed to reach the 1955 finals. Halfway through the 1955/56 season, Mikan couldn't bear seeing his team lose and made a return but his time away had affected his performance and at the end of the season he quit for good. He retired as all-time leading scorer, with 11,764 points and averages of 22.6 points, 13.4 rebounds and 2.8 assists in 520 NBL, BAA and NBA games.

Mikan's performances in Pro-Keds were legendary and would go on to provide a great legacy for the brand. It would continue to play an integral role in basketball through to the 1970s, appearing on the feet of top players like Kareem Abdul Jabbar, Bob Love, Jo Jo White, Lou Hudson, Willis Reed and Nate Archibald. Its connection with a number of players from New York made it one of the first sports shoes to cross over and become a cultural icon. The 69er model, in particular, became very popular in the Bronx and Harlem, earning the the nickname 'uptowns' and when hip hop pioneers like Afrika Bambaataa and the Rock Steady Crew began wearing them, they became the most desirable shoes on the block.

In contrast, Mikan's career after basketball was a difficult one. After a failed attempt at running for Congress he returned to the Lakers as coach only for the team to endure one of the worst seasons in its history. He then decided to concentrate on his law career, specializing in corporate and real estate law. He remained involved with basketball, however, and in 1967 became the first commissioner of the American Basketball Association, a rival league to the NBA. In the mid-1980s, with the Lakers having moved to California, he successfully led a bid to return basketball to Minneapolis when the Minnesota Timberwolves were awarded an NBA franchise for the 1989/90 season.

In his senior years Mikan suffered diabetes and kidney problems that led to his leg being amputated below the knee. When his medical insurance was cut off he found himself with severe financial problems that led him to fight a legal battle against the NBA, protesting againt the small pensions the NBA gave those who retired before the game's boom in the mid-1960s. Sadly, complications from his diabetes eventually led to his death in 2005.

The death of a man who was a giant beyond just his size was felt throughout the game. Mikan remains celebrated as one of basketball's greatest players and a pioneer of the modern game. The fact that his domination resulted in rules that are still the cornerstone of the sport speaks volumes about his performances. Mikan's later successor with the Lakers, Shaquille O'Neal, was so inspired by him that he felt compelled to pay for his funeral, saying of Mikan, 'Without number ninety-nine, there is no me.'

Left Pro-Keds Royal (Bata Shoe Museum, Northampton Museum Collection).

THREE GOLDS WON, THREE STRIPES GONE

1952 HELSINKI OLYMPIC GAMES

KARHU HELSINKI SPIKES

Watching Emil Zátopek run could only be accurately described as uncomfortable. With his head rolling, his arms flailing, loud panting and a pain-wracked face, he looked more like a man enduring agony at the back of the field than a winner. And yet, there has probably never been a runner in the history of the sport who lived life and achieved success so gracefully.

Born in Czechoslovakia in 1922, Zátopek arrived at the 1952 Olympic Games in Helsinki with a formidable reputation. He had won the 10,000m in the previous Olympic Games in London lapping all but two of the field, and in the interim had broken the 10,000m world record five times. But no one would have predicted what his next achievement would be.

The Helsinki Games brought Zátopek together with a brand that was almost as famous as he was in distance running and for which Helsinki was home turf. Founded in 1916, the Finnish shoemaker Karhu (Finnish for 'bear') started out making sporting equipment from locally sourced birch wood which, due to its strength and light weight, was perfect for making javelins, skis and discuses. But the company became famous for its running spikes and first came to prominence with the success of 'The Flying Finns', a group of Finnish athletes who dominated distance running in the 1920s. Most famous of these was Paavo Nurmi, winner of

five gold medals in the 1924 Paris Olympics, all of which were won wearing Karhus. The shoes were renowned for their good quality and their robustness, so much so that during the Second World War Karhu was called upon by the Finnish army to produce boots, camouflage uniforms, tents, rucksacks and skis for the war effort.

A soldier in the Czech army at the time, Zátopek was given time to train and to build endurance. Admiring the Finnish reputation for hard training, he modelled his training programme on Paavo Nurmi's techniques, initially undertaking his exercises wearing heavy army boots. But he soon began to form a more structured plan based around sprints and longer runs, bridged by recovery periods that were purposely too short to allow full recovery and so increased his stress tolerance. A day's training included five 200m sprints, twenty 400m runs, then five more 200m sprints. Finding that it translated to results, he trained even harder, increasing to fifty 400m runs, and then gradually up to an astounding one hundred 400m runs a day. Without even realizing it, he had in effect created interval training, the method that is now standard for most athletes.

Zápotek's belief in good training was something he shared with Karhu's founder, Arno Hohental. Encouraging his employees to train during their lunch breaks, his enlightened

approach bore fruit when two Karhu employees won gold medals in the 5,000m and the javelin at the 1932 Los Angeles Olympics.

Despite his almost inhuman training regime, Zátopek's humanity was something that many admired. With distance runners usually being quite literally 'distant', Zátopek's genial manner made him friends on and off the track, something he prized more than his success. Fiercely loyal to friends, when a teammate was forbidden to compete by the Czech communist authorities because his father was a political prisoner, Zátopek put his career on the line and refused to race. After a stand-off, the authorities relented and his friend was able to compete.

As was expected, in Helsinki Zátopek won the 10,000m easily. The 'Czech Locomotive' was simply unbeatable despite the best efforts of French runner Alain Mimoun, who could not match his relentless pace. Just two days later he was ready for the 5,000m, but this time it was far from a one-horse race. In what is often hailed as the most dramatic of his Olympic wins, going into the last lap the race could have been won by any of four runners. Heading into the final turn, Zátopek was in fourth place behind a wall of shirts with the race looking lost but, digging deep, he headed out to lane two and surged past Schade, Chataway and Mimoun

Left Emil Zátopek leads the marathon at the 1952 Helsinki Olympic Games wearing Karhus.

in one fell swoop to take the lead on the straight. Sprinting like a pursued octopus, the others crumbled behind him and to the delight of the ecstatic crowd, who cheered him like a Finn, he crossed the finish line to take the gold and repeat his London double.

By coincidence, the women's javelin final was taking place at the same time as the men's 5,000m. The winner was Dana Ingrova-Zátopková. Born on the same day in the same year as Zátopek, she was better known to him as Mrs Zátopek. Giving his reaction when he learned of her gold medal, Zátopek said, 'At present, the score of the contest in the Zátopek family is 2-1. This result is too close. To restore some prestige I will try to improve on it in the marathon.' Given his well-known sense of humour, no one was sure whether he was joking or not, however, it soon became clear he was absolutely serious. No one had ever tried the 'triple' before, let alone won it, but Zátopek was undaunted, believing that despite never having run a marathon, if he pushed hard enough anything was possible.

For the 10,000m and 5,000m Zátopek had worn adidas shoes but for the marathon he decided to wear the famed Karhus sported by his hero Paavo Nurmi. During the race Zátopek's strategy was simple. Great Britain's Jim Peters was the favourite and so his plan was to run with him. After

15 kilometres, seeing that Peters was suffering from fatigue, he casually asked the world record holder if the pace was too slow. Thinking he was playing mind games, Peters agreed that it was too slow. When Zátopek asked if he was sure, Peters replied 'yes', thinking he could keep pace with the Czech until his energy returned. It turned out to be a bad decision. Thankful for the seemingly benign advice, Zátopek increased his pace while Peters, after an effort to stay in touch, later collapsed. For the last five miles of the race, Zátopek was serene. His usually agonized face was instead smiling and relaxed and he greeted the crowds and joked with photographers and policemen. He entered the stadium to the cheers of 80,000 people, many chanting his name. He crossed the line to win the race by two and a half minutes, far enough ahead of second-placed Reinaldo Gorno that he was already on his lap of honour on the shoulders of the Jamaican 4x400m relay team when Gorno finished. He had beaten the Olympic record by an incredible six minutes and became the first, and to date the only man, to win the treble.

For Karhu, Zátopek winning the treble in their shoes and on their home soil was a dream come true. In total 15 gold medals were won in Karhus. As well as new customers, Karhu's dominance gained the attention of Adi Dassler, founder of a new company called adidas. Like Karhu, he used strips of leather to add extra side reinforcement to his shoes. After settling on three strips, he realized that they made them recognizable even at a distance. But having launched adidas as 'the brand with the three stripes' in 1948, he was perturbed to see Karhu also used three stripes, especially after their success in Helsinki. As trademark law was still in its infancy, Dassler decided to approach Karhu directly to agree an amicable solution and invited them to Frankfurt for a discussion. There they made an agreement that would change both brands forever when, for the equivalent of €1,600 and two bottles of whisky, Karhu agreed to cede the three stripes to adidas.

Zátopek returned to Czechoslovakia as a national hero. But after suffering from a hernia while training for the 1956 Melbourne Olympics (well, he was carrying his wife at the time), he nearly missed the Games entirely because he needed an operation. In the event, he made it to Australia but could only manage sixth in the marathon. After his retirement in 1957 his apartment in Prague became a destination for international athletes from all over the world hoping to meet him and hear his stories. All were greeted warmly and asked to stay for lunch or dinner.

Sadly, in his twilight years, having put the agony of training and competition behind him, Zátopek's life was to become heartbreakingly harsh. Having become influential in the Communist Party he was vocal in his support for democratic reform. But, following the Soviet Union's invasion during the 1968 Prague Spring, he was told to become a propagandist for the Soviet-backed regime or suffer the consequences. Characteristically, he steadfastly refused. Forced to do menial jobs like cleaning toilets and emptying bins, he was later sent to a uranium mine for seven years, his exceptional achievements a distant memory from another life.

In 1990, Czechoslovakia held its first free elections in 44 years and Zátopek returned to normal life. But the years in the mine had taken their toll and in November 2000, after suffering a stroke, he died aged 78 from a virus complicated by pneumonia and a weakened heart rate. The athletics world mourned him deeply and posthumously awarded him its highest honour, the Pierre de Coubertin medal. Today, Zátopek is not only regarded as the greatest runner of all time but also as one of those rare athletes whose extraordinary achievements were surpassed only by his character and integrity.

BANNISTER'S PLAN B
1954 AAA & OXFORD UNIVERSITY TRACK MEET

G.T. LAW & SON RUNNING SPIKES

The four-minute mile. For hundreds of years it was a mythical target that was considered beyond the realms of human performance, but on 6 May 1954, a 25-year-old medical student named Roger Bannister achieved sporting immortality by becoming the first man to surpass it. While it was a day that went down in history, as far as Bannister was concerned, it was one that shouldn't have happened in the first place. Originally planning to win the 1,500m at the 1952 Helsinki Olympic Games, at the time Bannister had his whole life mapped out in front of him. He would win the gold medal, retire gracefully from athletics and settle down in to life as a neurologist. But when he only managed to come fourth, he was forced to resort to Plan B.

The disappointment of Helsinki forced Bannister to put his retirement plans on hold. Feeling that he had to do something to justify all the training he had done, he decided to set his sights on a completely different goal; becoming the first man to run a mile in less than four minutes. While many had got near it, as Bannister had found on his first two attempts, breaking it was a different

matter. His date with destiny would begin on the morning of 6 May 1954 when he started his day by preparing his running spikes. Unlike most athletes of the day, Bannister hadn't been fitted for his shoes and instead had chosen an 'off the shelf' pair of G.T. Law & Son spikes. At the time there were only two shoemakers a self-respecting British athlete would consider, G.T. Law or J.W. Foster & Sons. Priced at a considerable £5, which amateur rules insisted competitors pay themselves, they were handmade from ultra-thin kangaroo leather, making them some of the lightest available, weighing in at only 4½oz. Wary of the spikes picking up cinder ash from the track and robbing him of precious tenths, Bannister ground them down with a grinding wheel at a hospital laboratory to make them thinner and then applied a coating of graphite to make them even less adherent.

As he travelled on the train from London to Oxford the windy weather gave him cause for concern. When he arrived at the Iffley Road track at 4.30 p.m. the wind speed was 25mph, making a sub-four-minute race look almost impossible and with the race starting at 6 p.m., it looked like the attempt was off. But just half an hour before the scheduled start, with a bit of encouragement from his pacemakers, Chris Brasher and Chris Chataway, Bannister

decided he would run. As if waiting for his decision, the wind calmed.

As 3,000 spectators looked on, six men lined up at the start. Alan Gordon and George Dole from Oxford University and four British Amateur Athletic Association runners – Bannister, his pacemakers Brasher and Chataway and Tom Hulatt. A seventh man, Nigel Miller, arrived straight from a lecture as a spectator and only discovered when he read the programme that he was due to run in the race. When running kit couldn't be found for him he was forced to drop out, reducing the field to six.

A false start by Brasher riled Bannister but served to fire him up for the restart. Brasher took the front and led the first lap in 58 seconds and then the half-mile in 1:58. Bannister was immediately behind and shouting at him to increase the pace, Chataway just behind him. Now in the zone, Bannister began to relax, later revealing he almost didn't hear the splits and didn't feel any strain despite the pace. At the beginning of the second lap Chataway took the front and maintained the pace with 3:01 at the bell. He continued to lead around the front turn until they reached the back straight when the time came for Bannister to make his move. Knowing he had to produce a last lap of under 59 seconds, he pounced to begin his finishing kick.

Opposite An exhausted Roger Bannister achieves the first sub four-minute mile in G.T. Law & Son running spikes.

With Brasher and Chataway having done their jobs, it was now down to him and he felt a mixture of anguish and elation, knowing that the moment of a lifetime had come. As he crossed the line he leapt at the tape and finished in just under 59 seconds, collapsing as he did so into the arms of the waiting crowd and his friend, the Reverend Nicholas Stacey.

Having given it his all, Bannister was in a state of complete exhaustion and on the verge of a blackout as a result of acute anoxia caused by a lack of oxygen. Emphasizing how much Bannister had put into his final kick, his heart rate was measured at 155, astounding for a man whose resting heart rate was only 40. Despite his exhaustion, as he recovered he sensed his achievement and later said, 'I knew I had done it, even before I heard the call.'

The stadium announcer that day was Bannister's friend Norris McWhirter, who went on to edit and publish *The Guinness Book of World Records*. He deliberately delayed the announcement of the results to raise the crowd's excitement before finally declaring, 'Ladies and gentlemen, here is the result of event nine, the one mile: first, number 41, R.G. Bannister, Amateur Athletic Association and formerly of Exeter and Merton Colleges, Oxford, with a time which is a new meeting and track record, and which, subject to ratification, will be a new English Native, British National, All-Comers, European, British Empire and World Record. The time was three ...' but the crowd drowned out the rest of his announcement in complete elation. Bannister had set a new record time of 3 minutes 59.4 seconds, making him the first man in recorded history

to break the four-minute mile. Although Bannister had intended to keep his record attempt as low-key as possible, fortunately Norris McWhirter had alerted the media before the race and the BBC sent a cameraman to capture it. The now priceless footage was rushed back to London and broadcast to the nation that evening.

As often happens in athletics, once a new record is set, it lives a celebrated but short life. Only 46 days later Bannister's record was broken by his rival, the Australian John Landy, with a ratified time of 3 minutes 58.0 seconds. But, later in 1954, the pair raced each other for the first time at the Empire Games in Vancouver in a race that came to be known as the 'Miracle Mile'. This time it was Bannister who was victorious after coming from 15 yards down, surprising Landy with a sprint off the final bend and winning with a time of 3 minutes 58.8 seconds.

Despite holding the record for such a short period of time, Bannister is still revered for having done it first. Making his performance even more remarkable is how relatively little training he did for it. Being a medical student he was only able to train during his lunch breaks and only ran 35 miles a week, a figure that even recreational runners exceed today. Also often overlooked is that Bannister's time was set on a cinder ash track, which would be between one and one and a half seconds slower than a modern running track.

On the 50th anniversary of the event Bannister was asked whether he looked back on the sub-four-minute mile as his greatest achievement. He proudly replied that he saw his 40 years of practising as a neurologist and some of the new procedures he introduced as far more significant.

THE GERMANS' RAIN
1954 WORLD CUP FINAL

ADIDAS ARGENTINIA

On paper the 1954 World Cup Final should have been over before it began. Hungary, the dominant force in football in the early 1950s, were to face West Germany, a team that had only just been allowed to return to international competition after the Second World War. Having not lost once in 32 matches, Hungary looked to be the overwhelming favourites. But they hadn't counted on two things that were on West Germany's side that day: the weather and Adi Dassler.

In a further twist, if it hadn't been for an argument between the West German team coach Josef 'Sepp' Herberger and Adi Dassler's brother Rudi, it's possible that history could have been very different. Herberger had been in charge of the German national team since 1948 and, with excellent connections within the German football league, he was a useful friend to the brothers, acting as an agent and consultant.

However, after 25 years of successfully running Gebrüder Dassler together the relationship between brothers Adi and Rudi Dassler ended in acrimony. Their opposing characters had increasingly caused rifts between them. Rudi grew frustrated at Adi's obsessive tinkering with shoes and aloofness to business matters. At the same time Adi had grown increasingly disturbed by his brother's brashness.

The rise of the Nazis had also played a part in their disagreements. While both were party members, Rudi was more approving and optimistic about Nazi plans to make Germany great again, whereas Adi was more cautious and reasoning.

The size and close proximity of the Dassler family also increased tensions. With the brothers' parents, Adi, Rudi, their wives and five children all living in one house, it was overcrowded and in the factory the two brothers each attempted to assert themselves as leader of the company. Rudi and his wife Friedl became convinced that Adi and his wife Käthe were planning to oust them and what was previously just tension sometimes boiled over into full-blown arguments. One night, during an allied bombing raid, the Dasslers took refuge in the family's shelter. Rudi and Friedl were already in the shelter when Adi and Käthe arrived. Adi was in a foul mood and, as he joined them, he said 'Here are the bloody bastards again'. Although he was referring to the Royal Air Force bombers, Rudi was convinced the comment was directed at him and his family.

Rudi's resentment towards Adi grew even further when Hitler called for the mobilization of all Germany in order to end the war more quickly. Adi was declared exempt due to his being required at Gebrüder Dassler, however, Rudi

was seen as non-essential and was drafted. Such was his resentment that he wrote to Adi, saying, 'I will not hesitate to seek the closure of the factory so that you will be forced to take up an occupation that will allow you to play the leader and, as a first-class sportsman, to carry a gun.' Adi, however, remained safely in Herzogenaurach.

The resentment between the two continued after the war. When Rudi returned to Herzogenaurach he was arrested by American soldiers who believed he was a high-ranking Nazi having been drafted into the SS and was under suspicion of performing counter-espionage and censorship. The Americans told him that his arrest had come about as the result of a denunciation. He was in no doubt as to who he believed the source was. When the two brothers had to defend themselves before the local denazification committee, suspicions between the two became part of court proceedings and on Rudi's part quickly turned into outright accusations.

When Rudi was questioned about the wartime activities of Gebrüder Dassler, he used the opportunity to implicate his brother and reported that the requisitioning of their factory for weapons manufacturing had been organized solely by Adi and that he would have opposed it. This infuriated Käthe and she wrote her own account of the

quarrels between the two brothers, insisting Adi had gone out of his way to help and exonerate his brother despite his malevolent attitude and that the political speeches Rudi alleged that Adi held in the factory were in fact held by Rudi. Her statement led the denazification committee to lower Adi's wartime classification to 'Mitläufer', a member of the party who did not actively contribute to the Nazi regime. This was effectively a clearance and allowed Adi to continue to run the family business.

Although the court case ended with no further action, the two families could no longer live together and Rudi and his family left the Dassler home and moved across the river Aurach to the other side of town. Believing the company would fail without him, Rudi took control of a small shoe factory they owned and left Gebrüder Dassler to his brother. The two brothers registered separate companies, Adi first registered the name 'Addas', which was refused, as it was too similar to an existing children's shoe company, before settling on 'adidas'. Rudi registered 'Ruda' but later changed it to his childhood nickname 'Puma'.

Not only did the split tear the Dassler family in two, it also split the town of Herzogenaurach in half with the river Aurach acting as the divide. It became known as 'the town where people always looked down' because they were careful to note which shoes someone was wearing before starting a conversation.

Herberger was keen to remain friends with both brothers, and so made sure that some of his players wore Puma boots while others wore adidas. But, as his relationship had originally begun with Rudi, he remained a more frequent visitor to the Puma factory. However, when Herberger decided he wanted to charge for his consultancy services, things changed. Rudi was incensed by the coach's request that Puma pay him 1,000 marks per month for his services. How dare he ask to be paid for what he saw as favours? Rudi's response was simple: he expressed his deep disappointment in Herberger and bid him farewell. Not one to dwell, Herberger immediately headed over to the adidas factory, where Rudi's brother Adi happily accepted his terms. Puma boots quickly disappeared from the national side's team kit and Adi Dassler was welcomed as part of the West German team entourage. At the 1954 World Cup in Switzerland he was ever present at Herberger's side.

Having reached the final with an impressive 6-1 thrashing of Austria in the semi-final, their task looked nigh on impossible. They were to face Hungary, a team that hadn't lost for four years. In 1953 Hungary had taught England, the inventors of the game, a lesson, beating them 6-3 at Wembley and just to make sure, thrashed them again 7-1 in Budapest the following year. They had also already beaten West Germany 8-3 in the preliminary rounds. Despite Herberger having saved his best side for the final, surely only a miracle could stop Hungary from winning?

In the months before the tournament Adi Dassler had been working on a new boot called the 'Argentinia'. His passion for South America and its cultures had led to one of his first boots being called the 'Samba' and the Argentinia continued what would be a long line of shoes with South

American themed names such as 'Santiago', 'Brasil', 'Chile 62' and 'Azteca'. What made the Argentinia special was its adjustable studs which, depending on the conditions of the pitch, could be modified with short studs for dry conditions or longer studs for muddy or slippery conditions. They were not a new idea and patents for screw-in studs had existed since the 1920s. However, Adi was sure his was the best system as the studs were much easier to replace than previous designs. What was also special about the boots was that they were light, weighing only 350g. Knowing the Hungarian's boots lacked long studs and at 500g, were heavier, and in the wet would get even heavier, Dassler and Herberger began to pray for a rainstorm. The fact that team captain Fritz Walter played his best in rain soaked heavy pitch conditions the Germans often called 'English football', only added to their hopes for a downpour.

On the morning of the final, the skies were clear and their hearts sank. But by the time they prepared to leave for the Wankdorf Stadium, both felt a tingle of excitement when it began to rain. When they reached the stadium the few drops had become a steady shower and as the team prepared for the match Herberger turned to Dassler and said 'Adi, stoll auf!' ('Adi, screw them on!'). Shod with their secret weapon rain studs, the West German team began the match with hope. But their hopes were immediately dented. After only six minutes, Ferenc Puskas put the Hungarians ahead. Two minutes later Zsoltan Czibor added a second thanks to a defensive mix-up. Yet another demolition looked on the cards. But then, as the rain came down harder, the tide began to turn, as Hungary's goals seemed only to make West Germany even more determined. After 11 minutes, Max Morlock pulled one back, poking the ball past Hungarian keeper Grosics. Eight minutes later, captain Fritz Walter, in his element in the conditions, fired in a corner that Helmut Rahn turned into the back of the

Hungarian net to make it all square at 2-2.

The second half began on a waterlogged pitch and the Germans felt they would have the advantage. The Hungarians pressed hard with German goalkeeper Toni Turek having to make save after save, but their defence held firm and the score remained deadlocked. Only six minutes before the final whistle, Helmut Rahn collected the ball on the edge of the German penalty area, sidestepped a Hungarian defender and shot low into the corner of the net. In Germany, the commentator Herbert Zimmerman's screams of 'TOOOOOR!' could have been heard as far away as Bern. Two minutes before the whistle, Hungary's Puskas appeared to equalize, but he was ruled offside. It was all over. West Germany's spirit had ended Hungary's unbeaten run in one of the greatest comebacks in history. Miracles could indeed happen. At home in Germany, euphoria swept the nation. Still mired in sadness and humiliation after the Second World War, the win became known as 'The Miracle of Bern' giving Germans a reason to celebrate and be proud. Indeed, many historians identify Rahn's goal as the moment Germany was reborn following the Nazi tyranny.

Returning home, Adi Dassler was hailed as one of the architects of the victory. The German press went so far as to title him 'The Nation's Cobbler' and his boots were lauded in newspapers across Europe as having made the crucial difference. A British tabloid even ran a story about the boots with the headline 'What a Dassler!' With Adi's name spread far and wide, orders came flooding in. However, even more importantly, adidas had been thrust into the lead in the battle with Puma and if there was one German not celebrating his country's victory, it was Rudi. Having introduced a football boot with adjustable studs two years before his brother, he must have been left wondering what might have been if he had accepted Sepp Herberger's offer.

Left adidas Argentinia, worn by
Max Morlock (adidas Archive).

NOT JUST FOR CHICKENS
1960 NEW BALANCE LAUNCHES THE TRACKSTER

NEW BALANCE TRACKSTER

The majority of the people you will read about in this book are athletes who reached the top in their respective sports. But just because you aren't one of the tiny percentage of people who make it to the Olympic Games doesn't make you any less of an athlete. Our personal finish lines lie in many different places and while many sports brands communicate that to their consumers, none have made that belief as core to their being as New Balance.

Founded in Boston in 1906, English immigrant and chicken farmer William Riley started the New Balance Arch Support Company having been inspired by his fowl. He had observed that their three-clawed feet gave them excellent support and believed that a similar flexible arch with three support points would provide people with greater comfort and 'new balance'. Feeling sure his arches could transform the working lives of people, such as policemen and postal workers, for whom walking was key to their professions, he made the goal of improving the comfort of walking and running the cornerstone of his new company.

Reflecting their quality, the arch supports were sold for a not inconsiderable $5, a price often greater than the shoes they were placed in. But they quickly won loyal customers and their reputation grew by word of mouth.

With the company growing rapidly, Riley needed help and in 1927 recruited Arthur Hall, a salesman who travelled around New Balance's home state of Boston organizing foot clinics, where he listened to visiting customers' needs and demonstrated the benefits of the product. It was the personal touch that customers enjoyed and remembered and this became another cornerstone of New Balance's approach to business.

Impressed by Hall, Riley asked him to become his partner in the company. Despite it being the middle of the Great Depression, by staying small the company managed to stay afloat while many of its competitors perished. Towards the end of the Depression Riley began to think about making not just supports but the shoes themselves, and designed and manufactured the first New Balance running shoe for a local running club, the Boston Brown Bag Harriers. They were made of kangaroo leather and had a crepe rubber sole. They proved a success and, in addition to running, Riley began to branch out into shoes for baseball, tennis and boxing.

Left The New Balance factory in Lawrence, Massachusetts, where shoes are still hand made in the USA to the highest levels of quality.

In 1951, William Riley retired, leaving Hall to run the business. Three years later Hall sold the company to his daughter and son-in-law, Eleanor and Paul Kidd, for $10,000. They brought new ambition and drive to the business but valued and wished to maintain the customer focus that Riley had fostered. Eleanor concentrated on customer service, while Paul focused on manufacturing. Although arch supports and prescription footwear remained their biggest-selling products, they grew increasingly interested in the manufacture of athletic footwear. With more and more athletes approaching the company for custom-made shoes, the direction the business should take seemed obvious.

In their basement at home, the Kidds experimented with designs for a new running shoe based on feedback from their customers. The result was the Trackster, the world's first high-performance running shoe. While previously most shoes used for running had evolved from older designs, the Trackster was a whole new concept and was specifically designed to meet the needs of runners. It was contoured to fit the shape of the human foot and had a soft leather upper and a saddle to help hold the shoe closely around the mid-foot. It also featured a ripple sole that had originally been designed for paratroopers' boots, providing excellent traction and cushioning the foot. It was also very flexible and therefore perfect for running. Another feature that set it apart from its competitors was the fact it was available in a range of widths to ensure the best fit. While retailers felt this complicated the buying process and meant they needed to keep more stock, the bespoke approach proved popular with customers.

Continuing Riley and Hall's philosophy that word of mouth was the best advertising, the Kidds promoted and sold the Trackster at athletics events, trade shows and coaching clinics. Through YMCA activity programmes it became the organization's unofficial shoe and when college track teams at MIT and Boston University adopted the Trackster, they were followed by colleges and schools all around the United States. They also received much attention when Kenneth Cooper, MD, the 'Father of Aerobics', praised the shoes in his 1967 book *Aerobics* and also wore them in a marathon.

The Trackster was such a leap forward in the evolution of running shoes that it would be the model that defined New Balance's approach to making sports shoes for decades to come. It also embodied the company's foresighted ethos of making the best shoes for all athletes. Not just the ones who win Olympic gold medals, but the rest of us, whose personal bests are achieved in the park and whose finish lines are our own front doors.

BIRTH OF THE CONQUEROR
1962 THE FOUNDING OF NIKE

ONITSUKA TIGER CORSAIR/NIKE CORTEZ

Many companies can claim to have started from humble roots but few can claim to have roots as humble as Nike, whose origins can be traced back to the boot of a green Plymouth Valiant owned by a young runner from Portland, Oregon, by the name of Philip 'Buck' Knight. He was a good runner, but by the standards of some of his record-breaking teammates on the track and field team at the University of Oregon, not a great one. However, what marked him out in the eyes of legendary team coach Bill Bowerman was his drive and determination, the fact he detested losing and that he was always the first one ready for his 6 a.m. training runs.

Bowerman was to play a huge role in Knight's life and would coach him both on the track and far away from it. Apart from regularly airing his dim views of the people who ran the American Athletics Union and those who 'sat on their butts watching life go by,' Bill Bowerman was known as a man of few words. Taciturn to a fault, he was once asked to reveal what the secret was to improving performance, Bowerman simply replied, 'Run faster.'

Running faster was something that Bowerman gave a lot of thought to. From training regimes to customizing running shoes for individual athletes, he spent much of his free time considering ways he could help his 'Men of Oregon', as he called them, to improve their performance. Much of his focus centred on footwear. In the 1960s adidas had a near monopoly on running spikes and this bothered Bowerman. He felt that they weren't well made, were too expensive and, most critically in his view, far too heavy. Lightness was a near obsession for him and having calculated how many strides his runners needed to cover a mile, he realized that by cutting just one ounce from the weight of their shoes, they would in effect have to carry 550 pounds less during a race. This led him to experiment with a number of alternative lightweight materials, from kangaroo skin to cod. Yes, cod!

Knight's graduation from Oregon was only the beginning of his relationship with Bowerman. Having enrolled at Stanford Graduate School of Business, it was during a small business management course in which he was assigned to write a term paper on starting a small business that he began to think about Bowerman's opinion of adidas's track shoes. His first pair of running shoes had been a much-cherished pair of adidas but after hearing a debate about whether the new cheaper cameras from Japan could ever topple the premium cameras from Germany, he began to consider if a low-cost Japanese manufacturer could do the same with running shoes and break the grip that adidas had on the market.

After Knight graduated, needing to earn a living, he put what he called his 'crazy idea' on hold for a while and began a career as an accountant. But, struck by the travel bug, Knight decided to go on a world tour. While in Japan, with the thought of knocking adidas off their perch still formenting in his mind, Knight decided to take a trip to Kobe, home of the Onitsuka company, one of Japan's oldest shoe manufacturers and the makers of a range of sports shoes called Tiger. The company had been founded in 1949 by Kihacharo Onitsuka in the hope of raising post-war youth self-esteem through athletics and by the 1960s had produced a wide range of sports shoes, including the Marathon Tabi, a split-toed running shoe, the Limber Up, a popular training shoe, and the Throw Up, an unfortunately named discus shoe. After a merger in 1977 it was to become better known by the name it still bears today – ASICS – an acronym for Onitsuka's mantra, the Latin phrase 'anima sano in corpore sano', 'a healthy mind in a healthy body'.

Opposite Bill Bowerman and Phil Knight
(second runner from the left), who would later
become the founders of Nike

Left & Below Onitsuka Tiger Corsair
(Northampton Museum) and Nike Cortez (Nike
Archive).

After making an appointment, Knight met with executives from the company, introducing himself as a representative of 'Blue Ribbon Sports', a name some say he made up on the spot, inspired by the blue ribbons on his bedroom wall, which he had earned from his running. Others claim the name was inspired by the Pabst Blue Ribbon beer he had been drinking the night before. Knight managed to convince Onitsuka that his firm was the ideal choice as their exclusive US distributor and asked him to send over some samples, with a promise to place an order after his 'partners' had looked at them. Returning to the US, Knight took out a loan from his father to pay for the samples and sent a few pairs to his former coach. To Knight's surprise, Bowerman was impressed with their quality and saw them as a potentially cheaper alternative to adidas for his athletes to train in. What surprised Knight even more was that Bowerman asked him to consider making him a partner in the new business. Feeling that there was no one he'd rather have on board, they shook hands on it and Blue Ribbon Sports was born.

The two founded the company on an investment of $500 each and purchased a thousand pairs of Tigers. Knight became the fledgling company's first salesman and his green Plymouth Valiant became a regular sight at high-school track meets across the Pacific Northwest as he sold the shoes from the boot of his car. The shoes sold well and a year after founding the company, Knight had sold $8,000 worth of shoes, which was immediately spent on ordering another 3,500 pairs. Still working as an accountant, Knight needed a full-time salesman and hired friend and fellow middle-distance runner Jeff Johnson for the job. Johnson opened the closest thing to a store that Blue Ribbon had when he turned his apartment into a place where customers could drop by to try on and buy shoes. He also frequently

attended track meets to sell them to athletes and often encountered adidas representatives, who laughed at his supposedly inferior Japanese shoes. Having to grit his teeth and bear it, it only provided him with even more motivation to one day beat the Germans at their own game.

While Knight juggled running Blue Ribbon and his day job as an accountant and Johnson was on the road, Bowerman was busy working on ways to make the Onitsuka shoes even better, focusing on how he could reduce their weight. He had built a prototype that was a hybrid of the best features of two existing models, Onitsuka's Mexico and Marup shoes. Featuring a nylon upper and an outsole made from a sandwich of dual-density foam and a wedge of EVA, it was light, comfortable and had good shock-absorbing qualities. When Bowerman shipped one of his prototypes held together with pins to Japan, the Onitsuka executives thought it was a wonderful idea and quickly put it into production.

When it came to naming the new shoe, the name Aztec was chosen in honour of the host city of the upcoming Mexico Olympic Games. When adidas released the Azteca Gold, they threatened to sue unless the name was withdrawn. With his characteristic dry wit, Bowerman suggested 'Cortez', after the Spanish conquistador who conquered the Aztec empire. The shoe immediately sold well and by 1971 helped Blue Ribbon to reach sales of $1 million.

Despite their success, Blue Ribbon's relationship with Onitsuka was becoming increasingly shaky. Suspecting that Onitsuka was looking to ditch Blue Ribbon, Knight 'borrowed' a dossier from a visiting Onitsuka executive's briefcase that revealed the Japanese company was indeed considering distribution deals with other companies. A 'spy' Knight had recruited from inside Onitsuka, following the generous gift of a bicycle, confirmed his suspicions and Knight knew the writing was on the wall. He decided that

the only way to assure Blue Ribbon's future was to launch its own brand of shoes. As they pondered on a name, Knight came up with 'Dimension Six', while Jeff Johnson suggested Nike, the name of the Greek goddess of victory, a thought that had come to him in a dream. It suggested a spirit of sportsmanship and also had a K in it, which they felt made it more memorable-like other brand names that included the K sound, such as Kodak, Xerox and Kleenex. After much discussion, and some reluctance from Knight, Nike was the name chosen, along with a 'Swoosh' logo designed by Carolyn Davidson, a graphic design student Knight knew from Portland State University, to whom he paid $35. Needing something quickly, Knight was initially unsure about it and said, 'I don't love it, but it will grow on me.' When the logo later became one of the most recognized in the world, Knight presented Davidson with a diamond ring engraved with the Swoosh, along with an envelope filled with an undisclosed amount of Nike stock.

Blue Ribbon's relationship with Onitsuka finally came to an end when an official from the Japanese manufacturer was visiting Blue Ribbon's Los Angeles store and discovered in the stockroom dozens of orange boxes containing Cortez shoes branded as Nike and boasting their new swoosh logo. Considering it a betrayal, Onitsuka took their case to court. However, the court decided that, as the shoe had been jointly developed by both companies, they could both continue selling it. While Nike kept the original Cortez name, Onitsuka renamed their version the similar-sounding Corsair. Now, armed with its own brand, a popular shoe and Bowerman busy developing innovative new models, the newly named Nike, Inc. set its sights on taking on the giants who dominated the industry and whose toppling had inspired them to start Blue Ribbon in the first place ... adidas.

PUMA CRACK/SUEDE

The 1968 Mexico Olympic Games are remembered for some of the most important athletic achievements in sporting history. But one of its most iconic moments was when politics and sport came together – and a pair of Pumas played a small part in one of the most important political statements in the history of civil rights, earning them a place in black history.

Still remembered as much for events that happened off the track as on it, the 1968 Games were controversial even before they opened. The 1960s was a time of segregation and social injustice in the United States, so much so that in the lead-up to the Mexico Olympics many black American athletes considered a boycott. But, realizing that the Games offered a chance to use their visibility to make a stand, they decided to use the global platform to highlight the injustices they faced as an underclass and to protest against 'the outdated bigots' they felt ran athletics and prevented athletes from monetizing their talent.

Black American athletes dominated the Games, winning numerous gold medals and breaking multiple records. In one of the event's most exciting races, Tommie Smith took victory in the 200m final ahead of Australian Peter Norman and compatriot John Carlos. Determined to put on a highly visible act of protest, Smith and Carlos decided to seize the opportunity that their gold and bronze medals presented them, in defiance of the death threats that protesting athletes had received from extremists in the United States.

After the race, Smith and Carlos headed to the podium for their medal ceremony. Receiving their medals shoeless, they wore only black socks to symbolize black poverty, and each placed a single black Puma Crack running shoe in clear view on the podium. While both had intended to bring black gloves, Carlos forgot his, leaving them behind in the Olympic Village, and it was second place finisher, Australian Peter Norman, who suggested Carlos wear Smith's left-handed glove. As 'The Star-Spangled Banner' rang out, Smith and Carlos, heads bowed, raised their gloved fists above their heads, a symbol of strength and unity. The gesture was met with complete shock. The anthem was silenced and a hush fell across the entire stadium. The iconic image of the gesture, complete with the Puma shoes, was seen across the world.

While the salute was intended as a protest against inequality, the presence of the Puma Crack on the podium had also been symbolic of the athletes' feelings towards the International Olympic Committee's (IOC) policy on brand endorsement. Olympic rules forbade payments to athletes but, after Puma had caused controversy by paying German athlete Armin Hary to wear Puma spikes for his 100-metre dash at the Rome Games in 1960, athletes began to realize that brands would pay them to wear their products. Although it was a strict violation of amateur rules, many athletes found it hard to balance a working life with training. Endorsements meant they could train without needing to worry about having a job. Highlighting what they felt was the hypocrisy of it all, many athletes pointed out before the Games that if all those who took payments from shoe companies were censured, the Mexico Olympics would have been a second-rate event.

Booed as they left the podium, public and political outrage towards the two athletes followed immediately. IOC President Avery Brundage ordered their expulsion, threatening to disqualify the entire US Track and Field team if Smith and Carlos weren't expelled. In the United States they were condemned and banned from the Olympics for life. To the criticism Smith retorted, 'If I win, I am American, not a black American. But if I did something bad, then they would say I am a Negro. We are black and

Opposite With their black gloves, socks and Puma Cracks, Tommie Smith and John Carlos's salute sends shockwaves across the world.

we are proud of being black. Black America will understand what we did tonight.'

Peter Norman, often thought to be not much more than a bystander during the event, was in truth just as much a part of the protest as Smith and Carlos. A devout Christian with an upbringing in the Salvation Army, he strongly believed in equality. Donning the badge of the Olympic Human Rights Project on his chest, he stood in complete solidarity with Smith and Carlos, proud to be part of their protest.

Criticizing Smith and Carlos for their actions, the IOC condemned them for using the Games to advertise their domestic political views. Things got even worse when they returned home. They were treated as pariahs by the US sporting establishment and they and their families were subjected to abuse and even death threats. Smith's mother died of a heart attack believed to be the result of the pressure from neighbouring farmers, who sent her manure and dead rats in the mail. His brothers in high school were kicked off their football team and another had his scholarship taken away. For his support, Peter Norman suffered too. He was shunned at home in Australia when the selectors purposely decided not to select him for the following Olympic Games in Munich, leading him to retire from the sport he loved.

Today, however, their protest is hailed as a landmark in sporting and civil rights history and the IOC recognize that: 'Over and above winning medals, the black American athletes made names for themselves by an act of racial protest'. Naturally the focus of the protest remains rightfully on the act itself, but often overlooked is the performance that got Tommie Smith to the podium. Crossing the line in 19.83, Smith didn't just break the previous world record, he demolished it by an almost unheard of three-tenths of a second.

Despite only playing a minor role in their protest, the Puma Crack became one of the symbols of their salute and is still inextricably linked to Tommie Smith and John Carlos' salute. Speaking about Puma and the shoes in his autobiography *Silent Gesture*, Smith said, 'I wore them when I won the gold medal, and they were sitting on the victory stand that night – I had taken them off, of course, as part of the silent protest. But it was important that I have them on the stand, because they helped me get there, during the race and long before. They were as important as the black glove and the black socks.' When Puma replaced the Crack with the very similar-looking Suede a few years later, it was the Suede that took on the mantle as the symbol of Puma's part in the protest, and over 30 years later it remains a potent reminder of Smith and Carlos' courage and defiance.

Left Puma Suede, Tommie Smith 68 – 40th
Anniversary Edition, signed by Tommie Smith
(Author's Collection).

THE BATTLE OF MEXICO CITY
1968 MEXICO CITY OLYMPIC GAMES

ADIDAS WELTREKORD

In the late 1960s the stakes for supremacy in the global sports shoe market had never been higher. At the 1968 Mexico City Olympic Games, with the world's attention focused on the gathered athletes, cousins Horst and Armin Dassler declared war on each other, making their fathers Adi and Rudi Dassler's disagreements look like a relative skirmish.

Having been sent to the Mexico City Games to represent their fathers' interests, the two cousins were keen to get as many athletes to wear their shoes as possible, which increasingly meant paying them. While their fathers Adi and Rudi Dassler abhorred the notion of payments, they grudgingly accepted this was the norm and both realized their sons were more adept at handling these new relationships than they were. Although Olympic and amateur rules forbade payments to athletes, the rivalry between adidas and Puma was fantastic for those determined to monetize their performances and 'under the table' deals to avoid the attention of the governing bodies became commonplace. Before and during the Games, many tried to play the two off against each other as both brands vied for their loyalty.

Armin's secret weapon in Mexico City was Puma rep Art Simburg. The American was already battle hardened,

having often been the victim of pranks that left him stranded at track meets when adidas people called his car rental company and hotel to cancel his reservations, a trick that Horst frequently enjoyed pulling on Armin.

adidas lacked Simburg's unrivalled network of contacts, which had helped him build an enviable stable of American Puma talent for the Games, including sprinters and gold medal contenders Tommie Smith, John Carlos and Lee Evans. However, Puma could have all the athletes they wanted, but if they didn't have any shoes to wear, they would be disgraced, and Horst's first salvo against his cousin threatened that very thing. Before the Games he had made a deal giving adidas exclusive rights to shoe sales in the Olympic Village. That meant Puma would have to pay an import tariff of $10 per pair to get their shoes through customs. In an attempt to avoid the extortionate tariff, Armin made sure that the Puma shipment, stamped AD, looked to anyone not in the know like an adidas shipment and arranged for documentation to be 'produced' confirming it. However, Horst was one step ahead and pre-warned the customs officials, who impounded the whole shipment, leaving Armin with the prospect of a Puma-less Olympics. To make matters worse, Horst encouraged the Mexican officials to raid Armin's hotel room and charge

him with forging false customs papers. Interrogated for hours, he argued that it was simply a mistake. He was firmly advised to leave the country. Thankfully for Armin, a bribe to the right person helped to get 50 pairs out of the customs depot but meant Puma shoes would be in short supply and would in effect have to be 'rationed'.

Horst's killer move came when two undercover policemen grabbed Puma's Art Simburg in the Olympic Village and took him to a prison cell, where he was given no reason for his arrest and wasn't allowed to make any phone calls. When Puma officials finally found him they were told he was being detained for doing business while travelling on a tourist visa. It took all the efforts of the US State Department to get him released five days later. During the Games, nothing was off limits to the battling cousins. Competitors recounted earning an extra $10,000 by running from Horst to Armin and another recalled switching to Puma just before winning a gold medal and Armin rewarding him with $6,000.

Opposite Bob Beamon smashes the World and Olympic long jump records at the 1968 Mexico City Olympic Games in the prophetically named adidas Weltrekord shoes.

One of the athletes that Puma had signed was Bob Beamon. Born in August 1946 in Queens, New York, Beamon's start in life made a career in athletics seem unlikely. His mother died of tuberculosis before his first birthday and he never knew his father. Raised by his stepfather until his imprisonment, he was then taken into the care of his maternal grandmother and spent his childhood growing up in New York's Jamaica district, an area beset by a culture of gangs, drugs and violence. After hitting a teacher during a fight at school, he was first sent to a juvenile correction centre and then to a reform school operated by the chillingly named Bureau for the Education of Socially Maladjusted Children. It was there that Beamon was introduced to sport, learning good discipline and how to focus his energy towards achievement on the track. By 1964, he was one of the top high-school jumpers in the country and was regularly breaking local and state records. The following year he set a national high-school triple jump record. After graduating, Beamon initially attended North Carolina A&T State so that he could be close to his ailing grandmother but after her passing, as the second-ranked long jumper in the country, he won a scholarship to the University of Texas-El Paso and joined its famed track and field team. However, Beamon was later suspended after he refused to compete against Brigham Young University, alleging it was a racist institution. Now without a coach, and with the 1968 Mexico City Olympics on the horizon, he turned to his friend and the joint world record holder Ralph Boston to help him train.

Ahead of the Games and in spite of a lack of coach, Beamon was one of the favourites for the gold medal, having won 20 out of 21 meets in 1968. Recognizing his potential, Art Simburg persuaded him to wear Puma. Beamon had always worn adidas but duly pulled on the pair of white Pumas that Simburg had given him. On the morning of 17 October Beamon attempted to qualify for the final but on his first two attempts he overstepped the marks and fouled his jumps. Turning to Ralph Boston again, he asked for his advice, to which Boston suggested he start his take-off way before the board. In doing so he qualified, jumping 8.18m on his last attempt.

On the day of the final Beamon faced the cream of long-jumping talent, including the defending Olympic champion, Briton Lynn Davies, and the joint world record holder, Ralph Boston. Known for his enjoyment of playing mind games with his rivals, Boston had warned Davies about trying them with Beamon, 'Don't get him riled up because he's liable to jump out of the f*****g pit.' Little did he know how prophetic his caution would be.

Conditions were perfect. Mexico City's elevation of 7,349ft meant the air was thin and the wind speed measured two metres per second, the maximum permissible by the rules for official records. As he prepared for his first attempt Beamon stood at the end of the runway and focused intently on the end pit. He rocked slightly and accelerated towards the board. Willing himself not to foul, when he reached the board he planted his right foot perfectly and leapt to the sky, rising as much as six feet above the pit according to the watching legend Jesse Owens. When gravity finally began to reassert itself, Beamon swung his legs forward and his arms backward as much as he possibly could to gain extra thrust and then landed

in a plume of sand. It had been a jump of shattering proportions, shocking not just the officials and his fellow competitors but many of the onlooking spectators who knew they had seen something very special.

As the judges began to attempt to measure the jump they realized that it had been so long that Beamon's landing point was beyond the limit of the electronic measuring equipment. As he waited for the length to appear on the scoreboard Beamon couldn't understand why it was taking so long. He knew it had been good and thought he might have broken the record by an inch or two. However, after a wait of almost 20 minutes, during which the judges had to resort to using an old-style measuring tape, the distance of 8.90m appeared on the scoreboard. Beamon had not just passed the world record, he had obliterated it by a margin of 55cm. Unused to metric measurements Beamon was still unaware of what he had achieved until he was told the distance in feet (29 feet 2½ inches). Realizing the enormity of what he had done, he collapsed and suffered a cataplectic seizure, a sudden weakness in the muscles brought on by sheer emotion. Another person who may have felt like having a seizure after the jump was Armin Dassler. With Beamon in Pumas it should have been one of their greatest moments, but as he sailed through the air, the three red stripes on his shoes were clear for all the world to see. The reason is still debated. Puma blame the 'rationing' that Horst's customs blockade caused for Beamon's feet being Puma-less, while adidas say that he just preferred their shoes. Whatever the reason, it was adidas that Beamon wore for the greatest jump the world had ever seen.

FROM A FLOP TO 'THE FLOP'
1968 MEXICO CITY OLYMPIC GAMES

ADIDAS SPECIAL

You may already know the story of Dick Fosbury. Hailed as a perfect example of the value of innovation, it is a tale told at thousands of business conferences and seminars across the world. And yet Fosbury's story is really more akin to a Forrest Gump-like tale of how a very average high-school athlete, desperate to stay on his school team, discovered a crazy new technique that not only kept him in the team but revolutionized an entire sport.

Born in March 1951 in Portland, Oregon, Dick Fosbury only became a high jumper because it was the sport he was least bad at. Having failed to make it on to his high school American football and basketball teams, he turned to athletics and found that the only discipline in which he stood a chance of making the team was the high jump. Tall for a teenager, his height of 1.93m was no advantage because it made it difficult for him to perform well using either the traditional scissors jump or the more modern straddle technique. While he preferred the scissors, his coaches discouraged him from using it because it was seen as old hat. But even when using the Western Roll, the technique his coaches encouraged, the best he could do was a mediocre 1.63m.

Despite describing himself as 'the worst jumper on our team, the worst jumper in the conference', Fosbury was determined not to quit, but knew he needed to do something different. Exhaustively trying all sorts of methods, he eventually found a technique that, to his surprise, actually worked. Starting his run diagonally to the bar and curving away from it before take-off in a J shape, he was able to lift his hips and transfer his weight to his upper body so that it caused his shoulders to go back, allowing him to thrust his body backwards over the bar. The new technique yielded better results and kept him on the team.

Over the next two years Fosbury honed his new technique and began to use it in competition. It was so different that it drew derisory comments from coaches, judges and the press, who deemed it inelegant, describing Fosbury as the 'world's laziest high jumper' and looking like 'a fish flopping in a boat', which led to the name 'The Fosbury Flop'. Indeed, it was so unorthodox that many judges weren't even sure that it was legal. But they were forced to concede that it was, since rules regarding which part of the body had to cross first had been removed, and stated

Opposite Wearing differently coloured pairs of adidas high jump shoes, Dick Fosbury performs the Fosbury Flop to win gold at the 1968 Mexico City Olympic Games..

Right adidas Special, worn by Dick Fosbury
(adidas AG / studio waldeck).

only that a jumper had to take off on one foot. Even so, despite the fact that it was within with the rules, not many in the sport took it seriously and few thought Fosbury would go far with it.

One of the doubters was Berny Wagner, Fosbury's coach at Oregon State University. He considered the flop to be 'a shortcut to mediocrity' and encouraged Fosbury to revert to the more conventional techniques. However, still interested in helping Fosbury improve, Wagner decided to film the technique. He set the bar at 1.98m and Fosbury flew over it. When Wagner reviewed the footage, he saw that he had cleared the bar by a good 15 centimetres.

Another person to realize the effectiveness of the flop was Adi Dassler of adidas. A former high jumper himself, he was intrigued by Fosbury's unique method. He got in touch with Fosbury and asked him numerous questions about his technique. A few weeks later a package arrived from Germany. It contained a pair of prototype shoes that Dassler had designed and made himself to fit Fosbury perfectly and to suit his flop technique. At a time when athletes were beginning to expect payment in return for wearing branded equipment, Fosbury, over the moon that someone would spend hours making a pair of spikes just for him, was adamant that he wouldn't accept any money.

Still refining his technique and carrying an injury to the heel of his jumping foot, Fosbury only narrowly qualified for the 1968 Mexico City Olympic Games. With many still doubting him and his method, however, he wasn't expected to be a medal contender. But, when he made it through to the final, even the doubters began to entertain the idea that he could leave Mexico City with a medal around his neck.

During the final his technique at first amused but then thrilled the crowd. Fosbury thrived on the attention and used it to heighten his focus. He didn't miss a single jump. When the bar was set at 2.18m there were only two others in contention, meaning a medal was assured. At 2.22m, only his fellow countryman Ed Caruthers still faced him. The bar was then set to 2.24m, an Olympic record height. Fosbury failed twice, but so did Caruthers. It would all come down to the final jump. Fosbury knew that if he succeeded and Caruthers failed, the gold medal was his.

Fosbury seemed to take an age preparing himself for his final jump. Rocking on his heels, looking down at the ground and clenching and unclenching his fists, it seemed as if he was drawing in power from the expectant crowd. He finally began his run, reached his jump point and sailed over the bar. It all rested on Caruthers. He failed, and the gold medal was Fosbury's. Or was it? As he waited for confirmation, incredibly the judges debated whether he was in breach of any of the regulations. After an agonizing wait they decided he was not, and Fosbury was crowned Olympic high jump champion.

Returning to the United States, Fosbury found that he had become an overnight sensation, but it was something he found hard to deal with. Not used to such attention, he struggled to maintain his training regime and failed to qualify for the 1972 Olympics in Munich, instead returning to university to pursue a degree in engineering. The move came at a cost, namely the end of his sporting career. In Fosbury's absence, Juri Tarmak won Olympic gold using the straddle, but it was to be the last high jump gold won using a technique other than the Fosbury Flop.

A SUPERSTAR IS BORN
1969 ADIDAS CREATES THE SUPERSTAR

ADIDAS SUPERSTAR

Horst Dassler, son of adidas founder Adi Dassler, was a frustrated man. He was full of ideas and ambitions for the future of his father's company, but his pleas for more say in the family business usually ended in rows with his mother Käthe, who ran the business while his father developed new shoes. But, with the company rapidly growing, a new plant was needed and, recognizing Horst's obvious talent, Adi and Käthe made a decision that would change the course of the company.

The village of Dettwiller in Alsace, France, was famed for its shoemaking traditions and it was there that the Dasslers decided to buy an ailing shoe manufacturing plant that could help meet the increasing demand for adidas shoes. Realizing the new plant would be the perfect opportunity to give their ambitious son more responsibility, Horst was sent to Alsace.

To his parents' delight, the plant was soon running well, but Horst was still frustrated. Greater responsibility had only increased his ambitions and desire for control. Knowing that his parents were not going to hand over the reins of the company any time soon, he decided to create his own empire from his outpost in France. His plan was to turn it into the heart of the company, developing and selling its own ranges independently of Germany. If his

plan worked, Horst would, in effect, be competing with his own parents.

His first move was to find a new centre of operations, which he found in nearby Landersheim in the shape of an old hunting lodge named the Auberge de Kochersberg. He renovated and expanded the property. He then assembled a crack team of loyal staff to run dedicated development, marketing and production departments. Famed for being a workaholic and barely needing sleep, he drove his staff hard but, realizing he had to earn their loyalty, ensured he looked after them. Being a networker before networking existed his list of influential friends grew rapidly and he gained a reputation for his exceptional hospitality. The Auberge's guest rooms, restaurant and wine cellars soon became a destination of choice for athletes, agents and sports officials. Just as Horst had planned, adidas France had become a fully-fledged subsidiary.

With his parents focused on Europe, Horst turned his attention to America. He was keen to develop adidas France products that he felt would appeal in this potentially huge market. Chris Severn, one of Horst's US advisors, had an idea of what one of those could be. He had noted that basketball shoes hadn't changed since the early 1900s and were mostly canvas based, like Converse's

All Star and Pro-Ked's Royal. Providing little support and poor grip, players often suffered injuries to their ankles and knees. Severn drew on his experience of playing basketball and wanted to create a basketball shoe that provided more stability, comfort and, above all, excellent traction. He also used knowledge gained while developing a new adidas tennis shoe (which would go on to be the Stan Smith). With basketball and tennis requiring similar physical demands, he knew a similar design would work in basketball. Severn worked closely with Horst Dassler and technicians at adidas France to develop what would be an entirely new concept of basketball shoe construction: a 'shell sole', which provided a superior sole profile to grip the court, better stability and was 30 per cent lighter. The finishing touch was the addition of what would become the shoe's defining feature – a 'shell toe' – which was designed to slow down wear and tear in the forefoot area. Named the 'Supergrip', it was launched in 1964, accompanied by a hi-top version called the 'Promodel'.

Initially, the new shoe was a tough sell. Players and

Opposite Kareem Abdul-Jabbar signs for adidas with Chris Severn (left) and Horst Dassler (right) alongside (Chris Severn).

coaches eyed it suspiciously – having worn canvas all their lives, they assumed that leather was heavy and inflexible. But they did appeal to one coach, Jack McMahon, of the San Diego Rockets. With three of his players out due to injuries caused by slipping, he liked the idea of a shoe that might prevent those types of injuries and convinced his team to try the new shoes. They loved them, and because they were in scarce supply, didn't want to wear them out in practice and so would save them as their 'game shoes'. By the end of the season, players from other teams had noticed their unusual new shoes and Severn received numerous enquiries about them. Many came from Boston Celtics players, the leading team in the league and after they won the title in 1969 wearing them, Severn's phone didn't stop ringing.

In 1969, adidas decided to upgrade the Supergrip. While its name had served it well, against competition like the All Star and the Royal, it didn't sound as glamorous, so the new model was re-named 'Superstar'. Picking up where the Supergrip had left off, by 1973 the Superstar and the Promodel dominated basketball, with 85 per cent of all professional players in the NBA and ABA wearing them and numerous college teams making them their shoes of choice. Converse, whose All Star had been the preferred shoe since the 1920s, were in shock. This was in an era that preceded big salaries for professionals and college players, but times were changing and Converse fought back by paying players to get back into their 'Chucks'. In response, Chris Severn convinced Horst Dassler that adidas needed a superstar to go with the Superstar. The obvious choice was Kareem Abdul-Jabbar. The biggest star in basketball, he had already once signed with the company in 1971 to endorse his signature 'Jabbar' shoe. Since then he had won the NBA title four times with the

Milwaukee Bucks and two Most Valuable Player Awards, making re-signing him a no-brainer. In 1976, Horst agreed to pay a record $25,000 a year deal for Abdul-Jabbar to endorse the shoe.

Horst's success in basketball was proving to be an engine for his ambitions. The sport was now responsible for over 10 per cent of the adidas group's sales, all of which were being made by adidas France. Business was so good that Horst had to hide from his parents the fact that exports from adidas France were growing much faster than those of adidas Germany.

Despite the popularity of the Superstar, adidas were keen to innovate and expand their range of basketball shoes. With the help of Severn and, in particular, the input of NBA superstar Rick Barry, the 'Top Ten' shoe was added to the line. While newer models would have been the end of the game for most shoes, as it turned out it was only the beginning for the Superstar. Its on-court success had cemented its status as a shoe for serious street players, especially in New York, where its high cost and rarity added to its desirability. Having a pair indicated that you knew the right people. But even when it became more widely available, it lost none of its allure, and soon became part of the uniform of New York's youth and more importantly, of the new hip hop phenomenon.

In 1985, Angelo Anastasio, Horst's US entertainment promotions man, walked out of a concert and saw three young black men breakdancing on the street to a big audience. Noticing that they were wearing adidas tracksuits, he introduced himself. They explained that they wore them because the slippery material was perfect for breakdancing. Seeing that there was something cool about them, Anastasio kept in touch and when, three years later, they became Run

DMC, Anastasio ensured they had as much adidas gear as they wanted. They dressed on stage as they did on the street and the Superstar, often unlaced, prison-style, (so called because suicide watch prisoners had their laces removed) became a key part of their image. As they conquered the charts and toured the country, everywhere they went their legions of fans turned out in Superstars.

Not everyone was happy. Many, like Dr Gerald Deas, an affluent and influential black New Yorker, took exception to seeing the city's young people wearing what he called 'felon shoes', believing they were only worn by criminals and had no place on the feet of responsible young citizens. When Dr Deas released a song attacking the new sneaker culture, Run DMC responded as only they could with their own song, 'My adidas'. Topping the charts, it gave the company exposure it could not have dreamed of.

Despite having brought them a whole new audience, adidas weren't paying Run DMC a cent for their 'endorsement'. Feeling hard done by, the band invited company executives to a show at Madison Square Garden in New York City. After performing 'My adidas', the band invited anyone in the audience wearing adidas to hold them up. As Angelo Anastasio looked out at the crowd, he saw an incredible sight: an ocean of Superstars. He excitedly called Horst and convinced him that he had to see the band's next show in Munich. Horst had never even heard of hip hop, let alone Run DMC, but at the show he completely understood their power. Signing them to a $1 million endorsement deal, over the next four years Run DMC generated an estimated $100 million for adidas. Once the king of the court, the Superstar was now the king of sneaker culture and, following his father's death in 1978, Horst Dassler had become the king of adidas.

Left adidas Superstar, signed by Run DMC's Joseph Simmons, Darryl McDaniels and Jam-Master Jay (adidas Archive).

THE SPIRIT OF THE SWOOSH
1969 STEVE PREFONTAINE JOINS THE 'MEN OF OREGON'

NIKE PRE MONTREAL RACER

Once described as 'an athletic Beatle', Steve Prefontaine was America's first superstar athlete. Possessing a fighting spirit that was to captivate America and inspire generations of athletes, he remains revered today and when he became the very essence of a fledgling Oregon sports shoe company, he was to leave a legacy that resides on the feet of millions.

Born in January 1951, Steve 'Pre' Prefontaine grew up in the coastal logging town of Coos Bay in Oregon. After being benched once too often by his junior high school American football and basketball teams for being too small, he decided to try running. He discovered that he was quick, especially at cross-country, and began to completely dedicate himself to the sport. He set his first national record aged just 15 in the two-mile, won consecutive state cross-country championships and went undefeated in cross-country and track in his junior and senior years. By the time he graduated, he was an Oregon star and recruiters from 40 colleges across the state vied for his attention. While the whole world appeared to be his oyster he knew that the best distance runners in the state went to the University of Oregon, but was perplexed, even annoyed, that the college's track and field coach hadn't tried to recruit him.

The coach in question was the legendary Bill Bowerman. A principled man, he believed that as a teacher, it was not for him to recruit the student, but for the student to approach him. But after persuasion from his students and the faculty, in a rare breaking of his own rule, Bowerman wrote a letter to Prefontaine saying that he was certain that he could make him the best distance runner in the world. It was all Prefontaine needed to be convinced that his future lay with Bowerman.

At first the two clashed. In one exchange Bowerman told Prefontaine he wanted him to run the two-mile. As headstrong as he was fast, Prefontaine retorted, 'I don't run the two-mile,' and turned and walked off. Bowerman replied, 'Really? So where do you think you'll be running next week?' Prefontaine stopped and looked at Bowerman for a second. 'I'll run the two mile but I won't like it', he said. Doing as he was told, not only did he run the two-mile, but he also broke the school record.

Prefontaine's relationships with his teammates were also initially strained. They weren't used to having someone with such huge self-confidence and such a cocksure attitude on the team but the fact he could outperform them all quickly turned their animosity into admiration. Rivals from other colleges were also in awe by him, many

claiming he had an aura of invincibility about him that they found intimidating, and making Prefontaine's home track of Hayward Field, Eugene, a place they feared to compete.

While his competitors may have preferred to stay away, the crowds certainly didn't. They adored him and at Hayward Field they chanted his name during his races, 'Pre, Pre, Pre'. He seemed to feed off their energy and developed a connection with them like no one else, more like a rock star than a runner. It was a role he revelled in, once saying, 'I don't go out there and run. I like to give people watching something exciting.' Even rival fans admired him and wore 'Stop Pre' T-shirts. At a time when running was still seen as a 'geek sport', Pre's popularity helped to transform the sport's audience and participation. He made running cool.

Under the guidance of Bowerman and Bill Dellinger, Pre was unstoppable. He never lost a single collegiate race at 3 miles, 5,000m, 6 miles, or 10,000m and won seven NCAA titles and two US National Championships. In his 'backyard' at Hayward Field between 1970 and 1975 he achieved an incredible 35 out of 38 victories. During one stretch he won 21 meets in a row and broke the US 3,000m and 5,000m records. After winning the 5,000m and setting

a new US record at the 1972 Olympic Trials, he was headed
for the Munich Olympic Games.

In Munich, Pre was bullish. Some of his competitors had
criticized him for not running in Europe before, but he felt
that by staying away he kept them in the dark about his
form. However, his confidence was rocked by the terrible
events that occurred midway through the Games when 11
Israeli athletes were taken hostage by terrorists and killed.
The tragedy made him question the morality of continuing
but after much soul-searching, he and many other athletes
decided they wouldn't allow the terrorists to win and
resolved to compete.

Reaching the final of the 5,000m he found himself up
against a line-up of superstars, most notably Lasse Virén,
who had just won the 10,000m in a world record time. Pre
aimed for what he called a 'pure guts race', believing that
no one had more guts than him, and vowed to win gold
by running the final mile in under four minutes. After an
almost pedestrian first two miles, with four laps remaining,
Pre began to put his plan into action and took the lead,
dramatically upping the pace. He ran the next three laps
in 62.8, 61.0 and 60.4, dropping everybody but Virén and
defending champion, Gammoudi. Virén took the lead on the
bell and held Gammoudi off to win easily. Pre, however, had

nothing left in the tank and was passed at the last minute by Ian Stewart for the bronze medal, with Pre finishing in fourth. Pre was devastated. He had been running for gold and nothing else would do.

Returning home to Oregon, Pre was despondent. He had been so near, yet so far from reaching his goal. While he saw himself as a failure, his popularity hadn't waned, in fact the city of Eugene announced its plan to name a street after him. Pre quipped that it would probably be called 'Fourth Street'. While many told him that there was nothing shameful in coming fourth in an Olympic final aged 21, it was only when Bill Bowerman reminded him that 'the real challenge is in the losing' that he realized that he still had plenty to achieve and focused his sights on the 1976 Olympics in Montreal.

At Oregon, Pre was rarely seen in anything other than adidas, despite the fact that Bowerman was a founder of Blue Ribbon Sports (BRS), the forerunner of Nike. But he never forced his shoes on to his runners. His mantra was 'Be true to your feet' and if his runners felt faster in adidas or Puma, he would prefer they ran in them. However, in the summer of 1973, Bowerman offered Pre a $5,000 yearly allowance to help with training expenses and to relieve him of his bartending job. He began a role as BRS's 'National Director of Public Affairs', a title that led people to ask CEO Phil Knight what it actually meant. He would reply, 'It means he can run fast.' His new role meant that when he was not training he put in time at the BRS store or travelled around the Pacific Northwest speaking at schools or performing clinics introducing runners to Nike shoes. He used his personal approach to connect with athletes all over the world and introduced many to Nike products,

sending them shoes, along with personal messages. One of his conversions was Bill Rodgers, who went on to win the Boston Marathon in a pair of Nikes that Pre had sent him. He would also encourage his growing legion of fans to try Nike products and at track meets Nike T-shirts hand-printed by Phil Knight's wife Penny became hot property. He constantly pushed Bowerman and his team to keep improving their shoes, often acting as a product tester and the first to try their latest developments. He was fast becoming the heart and soul of Nike.

Pre had always been a vocal critic of the American Athletes Union (AAU), the body that controlled US track and field. But his anger grew as he saw that his fellow athletes were finding it hard to train properly while also needing to earn a living. Olympic hopefuls were required to remain amateurs, yet the AAU took the largest share of the appearance fees that were supposed to go to the athletes. Pre saw this as unfair, because it was the athletes who drew large crowds that generated millions of dollars in revenue, yet they were forced to pay all their own expenses. When he was forced to pass up an offer of $200,000 to go pro in order to remain eligible for Montreal in 1976, he made his feelings about the AAU clear and led calls for the organization to be reformed.

In May 1975 Pre helped to organize a meeting at Hayward Field against the Finnish national team in the hope of a rematch against Lasse Virén. When Virén was unable to come, Pre was disappointed but asked Frank Shorter to replace him as a headliner in the 5,000m. In the first two miles Pre trailed him but with three laps to go kicked to a 63-second pace and won in front of 7,000 of his adoring fans. That evening he celebrated at a farewell party for

the Finns but after leaving at midnight to give Shorter and his girlfriend Nancy Alleman a lift, while driving home in his prized butterscotch MG he tragically lost his life in an accident, aged just 24. The circumstances of the crash remain a mystery, although one local resident alleges that it was probably caused by another driver, who he saw driving away at speed. At the time, it was reported by the Eugene Police Department that his blood alcohol content was 0.16. However, the accuracy of the reported value and even the existence of the blood sample has always been disputed.

The day after his funeral in Coos Bay, a memorial service at Hayward Field drew thousands. At the time of his death Pre held every US outdoor track record between 2,000m and 10,000m. America was stunned by his death. The loss of such a phenomenal runner at such a young age had robbed the nation of one of its greatest athletes. For his friends and colleagues at Nike it was the loss of a brother and someone who embodied and inspired the spirit of the company. 'Pre was a rebel from a working-class background, a guy full of cockiness and guts,' said Nike co-founder Phil Knight. 'Pre's spirit is the cornerstone of this company's soul.' Pre left an enormous legacy. His belief in training hard and going all out for the win in competition continues to inspire athletes across many sports and his calls to reform the AAU were finally heard when the US Congress abolished the body in 1978. He was also chief among those who inspired millions of Americans to take up running in the 1970s. The Pre Montreal Racer, designed for him by Nike for the Games at which he believed he could win gold, continues to be popular with runners decades after his loss. The site of his death remains a place of pilgrimage for his fans to this day.

WHEN PELÉ CROWNED THE KING
1970 MEXICO WORLD CUP

PUMA KING

With a name like the King, Puma's famed football boots were always destined for greatness. Originally debuting on the feet of Portuguese star Eusebio in 1968, it was another great player who would give them legendary status and, as a consequence, re-ignite a family feud.

The 1960s had been a period of open warfare between adidas and Puma. The two companies, founded by rival brothers Adi and Rudi Dassler had, along with their sons Horst and Armin, turned world sport into their battleground. Athletes began to realize that they could take advantage of this rivalry to earn more from endorsements and other payments and, at the 1968 Mexico Olympic Games, some were literally running back and forth between the two cousins, encouraging them to outbid each other. But the Dasslers soon realized what was happening and feared that the escalating payments would eventually spiral out of control.

Wanting to avoid a repeat of the Olympic fiasco at the forthcoming 1970 World Cup, also to be held in Mexico, the two companies agreed an informal truce in the hope of avoiding further bidding wars. Horst and Armin also

Left Pelé scores against Peru in the 1970 Mexico World Cup wearing Puma Kings.

realized that there was one player neither should sign. That player was Edson Arantes do Nascimento, better known to the world as Pelé. Both knew that if either signed him, it would trigger an explosion in payment demands from other players that neither could afford. And so it was jointly agreed by the two rival cousins that he was to be completely out of bounds. Their agreement became known as the 'Pelé Pact'.

In the build-up to the 1970 World Cup, all eyes were on Pelé. He had been the star of the two previous World Cups and was certain to light up this one too. However, by the terms of the pact that had been agreed, for adidas and Puma, he simply didn't exist.

Of course, that didn't apply to the other Brazilian players, some of whom were almost as popular as Pelé. To get close to them, Puma decided to work with Hans Henningsen, a German journalist who had reported on Brazilian football for years and knew many of the players. He was encouraged to use his friendships with them to sign them up to Puma but was told in no uncertain terms not to go anywhere near Pelé. This was very awkward for him. He knew Pelé well and to make matters worse, the player was acutely aware that many of his teammates had Puma deals and wanted to know why he wasn't being offered one.

Henningsen wouldn't say, but Pelé hassled him to make an offer. The situation became too much for Henningsen and so, in defiance of the pact, he offered Pelé $25,000 for the Mexico World Cup, $100,000 for the next four years and 10 per cent royalties on sales of Pelé branded products.

Henningsen presented the deal to Puma. For Armin Dassler, the prospect of signing the world's best player was just too tempting to pass up, despite knowing full well what the repercussions would be. He delivered the cash to Pelé personally and the deal was done. However, far from trying to keep the breaking of the pact a secret, Henningsen and Pelé cooked up an idea that would show the whole world that Puma and Pelé were now together. Just before kick-off in the final between Italy and Brazil, one of the most eagerly anticipated matches in recent years, Pelé asked the referee to hold on for a moment so that he could tie his shoelaces, knowing that millions around the globe would be watching on television and that his boots would be the focus of the world for several seconds, giving Puma huge exposure.

Over at adidas, Horst Dassler was livid. He showed his obvious displeasure by squaring up to his cousin while accompanied by three of his aides. They had a far from warm and friendly chat. The short-lived peace between adidas and Puma was over and once again the gloves were off in the family feud.

With Brazil winning the cup and Pelé named Player of the Tournament, sales of the Puma King rocketed. Such was its popularity it remained the boot of choice for top players for decades, being worn by legends such as Diego Maradona, Johan Cruyff, Mario Kempes, Lothar Matthaus, Kenny Dalglish and Paul Gascoigne.

The King has gone through many evolutions during its life, the current version being much lighter and benefitting from the latest synthetic materials to keep it a contender. While no longer the first choice of big names today, the King remains one of the most popular and recognizable football boots ever. Like Pelé, the King is celebrated to this day and, despite the fact 2018 will be its 50th birthday, it shows no signs of abdicating any time soon.

Left Puma King, signed by Pelé
(Puma Archive).

THESE BOOTS WERE MADE FOR DANCING
1970 ALI VS BONAVENA

ADIDAS BOXING BOOT

Muhammad Ali was never the most loyal of athletes when it came to his boxing boots. He swapped brands a number of times during his career, but among those most remembered are the custom-made tasselled boots he first wore for his fight against the Argentinian Oscar Bonavena at Madison Square Garden in New York City.

Before Bonavena, Ali had fought in adidas boots a number of times. They had been handmade for him by Adi Dassler himself, something that was increasingly rare given Dassler's advancing years but reflected how highly Dassler regarded the famous boxer. However, for the Bonavena fight Ali decided he would fight in plain black unbranded boots. He was increasingly exploring his black heritage at the time and wanted his boxingwear to reflect this. Naturally, this set alarm bells ringing at adidas.

Perturbed by Ali's decision, Adi Dassler sent one of his right-hand men to sort out the problem. But Ali was resolute and refused; he said would be wearing black boots and that was the end of it. Enter John Bragg, long-time friend of former athlete and adidas ambassador Mike Larrabee, who had suggested he work with him on an informal basis as an adidas agent. Keen to impress Larrabee and his boss Horst Dassler, Bragg decided to see if he could persuade Ali to change his mind and

managed to get an audience with the great man at his hotel. Appealing to Ali's well-known vanity, he flattered him, saying that Adi Dassler was trying to design the best boxing boot the world had ever seen and that he could only do so with the counsel of the world's greatest boxer.

Ali thought about it for a while and then, in what seemed to Bragg like a complete non sequitur, began talking about a club he had been to the previous night. He described having seen dancers there that wore wonderful short skirts with tassels, which swayed elegantly, almost hypnotically, as they moved. Ali declared that for his fight against Bonavena, he would only wear adidas boots if they had tassels on them.

With only 24 hours to go before the fight, Bragg set about trying to work out how on earth he was going to create the tasselled boots and frantically searched the backstreets of New York to find some tassels and a sewing machine so that he could attach them.

When Bragg presented them to Ali he was over the moon. Swearing Bragg to secrecy, he instructed him to tell no one about them and at the weigh-in for the fight, he refused to

Right Tassels flying, Muhammad Ali knocks Oscar Bonavena down for the third and final time.

answer questions from the media. The only thing he spoke about was a new 'secret weapon' that adidas had made especially for him. He pointed Bragg out to the assembled journalists, telling them he had flown in all the way from Germany to deliver the secret weapon that would win him the fight. The newspapers lapped it up, all wondering what Ali had up his sleeves. All was revealed when Ali entered the ring wearing his tasselled boots in which, of course, he danced to victory.

ISN'T STAN SMITH A SHOE?

1971 ADIDAS SIGN STAN SMITH

ADIDAS STAN SMITH

It's rare that a sports shoe becomes more famous than the person it was named after, but when Stan Smith first joined forces with adidas to endorse a tennis shoe, he unwittingly became the name of a shoe that was to become a global cultural icon.

In the 1960s, times and tennis were changing. For a hundred years tennis was almost exclusively the sport of upper-crust lady and gentlemen amateurs in country clubs. But as the game became more popular and accessible, a new breed of players was emerging, who were ditching the principles of amateurism and embracing the professional game. With more and more brands attaching themselves to the sport, players were beginning to throw off their amateur status and started to accept payments from brands to endorse their products. Not only were professional players becoming the norm, the audience too was changing as star players began to draw both crowds and headlines.

Horst Dassler of adidas had seen this change happening and realized that tennis would be the perfect foundation for him to grow his adidas France empire away from the gaze of his parents, who were still unwilling to hand over the reins of the company to him. He decided that if they wouldn't give him control of adidas, he would take control himself by competing directly with them.

At the time, tennis shoes were still largely based on plimsolls, and although shoes like Dunlop's Green Flash had evolved the design, they were still based around a rubber sole with a canvas upper. Believing that something new was needed, Dassler set his designers to work creating a new, all-leather tennis shoe. He was keen for the new shoe to be endorsed by a top tennis player and approached his friend, the French No. 1 tennis player Robert Haillet, not only to endorse the new shoe but also to be involved in its creation.

The result was a shoe with a leather upper, a terry insole and a rubber cup-sole with a herringbone pattern. With most tennis tournaments at the time having all white dress codes forbidding any branding, the design was completely white and the traditional three stripes were left off but in their place were three rows of perforations for ventilation. It had a classic tennis aesthetic, but was a leap forward in performance, providing greater support than a canvas shoe and reducing the likelihood of ankle and slip injuries.

Launched in 1965 the 'Robert Haillet' was acclaimed as

Right When he won the Wimbledon Men's Singles Final against Ilie Nastase in 1972, Stan Smith became one of the select few tennis players to win a Grand Slam in shoes that bore their own name.

the best tennis shoe on the market, but its sales were not exactly stellar. As Haillet approached the end of his playing career, Dassler decided he needed a new player to endorse the shoe, someone who could generate more publicity and also get the shoe and adidas greater presence in the United States. Donald Dell, a former player and one of the first 'super agents', suggested one of his clients, Stan Smith. Being the top American player and world No. 1, he fitted the bill perfectly.

The historic first meeting between Dassler and Smith took place at midnight at the Elle et Lui, an infamous female transvestite strip club in Paris. They agreed that Smith's name would appear on the shoe and that he would receive a small royalty for every shoe sold.

With Smith's endorsement, sales of the shoe skyrocketed. As the 'Haillet', its sales had been OK, but adding Smith's name took it to a whole new level, especially after he won Wimbledon in 1972. It became so popular that even other tennis players wore it, something that Smith found very annoying when they beat him.

For a time both Haillet's and Smith's names appeared on the shoe, but in 1978 Haillet's name was removed and the shoe was renamed the 'Stan Smith'. Despite the name change, the shoe remained largely the same, the only improvements being more padding, a higher heel tab in green bearing the 'Stan Smith' name and adidas trefoil, and at Smith's request, a lace-through tongue to stop it moving around.

The iconic image of Smith that still appears on the shoe's tongue is of a moustache-less Smith taken during the only period in his career when he didn't wear one. Over 40 years later this was put right on a range of Stan Smith skateboard shoes, where Stan's moustache was there in its rightful place.

While the shoe was certainly a success on the tennis court, the Stan Smith's time really came in the 1970s when it began to be cool to wear sports apparel. At a time when wearing sports shoes off the pitch or court was deemed almost deviant, young people began wearing their All Stars, Clydes and Stan Smiths at school and on the street as a mark of distinction. It also helped that stars like Mick Jagger, John Lennon, Bob Marley and David Bowie were often seen sporting them, sometimes even immortalized on their album covers. From the university campuses of America to the football terraces of England, where it was first adopted by the Liverpool Casuals and Manchester Perry Boys, Stan Smiths had become the shoe of choice for the youth of the day.

While many shoes have come in and out of fashion, the Stan Smith has remained perennially fashionable – both ubiquitous and a cult at the same time. Much of that can be explained by its simplicity, which allows it to be elegantly simple enough to wear with anything, but also a blank canvas for a multitude of colourways, special editions, exclusives, adaptations, tie-ups and celebrity collaborations. All of which has kept the shoe in such demand that adidas have sold over 45 million pairs.

The fact that millions see Stan Smith's face on a daily basis as they lace up their shoes but have no idea who he is or that he was once a Wimbledon champion is the ultimate testamony to the shoe's perpetuity. As Smith once said, even his own children weren't sure if Stan Smith was a person or a shoe. His eight-year-old son once enquired of him, 'Dad, did they name the shoe after you, or you after the shoe?'

Right adidas 'Haillet' Stan Smith (adidas Archive).

ADIDAS STAN SMITH // 1971_79

MR BOWERMAN'S WAFFLES
1972 BIRTH OF THE WAFFLE SOLE

NIKE WAFFLE SOLE

Great ideas are often born in unusual places and one of the most significant in Nike's history didn't occur on a running track but at a kitchen table. While Bill Bowerman and his wife Barbara were making breakfast one Sunday morning in 1971, as usual, sports shoes were never far from his mind. As he watched his wife pour batter into a waffle iron, the answer to a problem he had been thinking about for a long time suddenly sprang into his head.

Like most other running tracks at the time, Oregon's Hayward Field was being converted from cinder ash to an artificial surface, and Bowerman was looking for a way to create a spikeless running sole that would provide excellent traction on any surface. He had been thinking about what shapes would make the best pattern to provide grip, even experimenting with Barbara's jewellery to see what indentations various shapes would make. As he watched his wife taking a waffle out of the iron he was struck by the shape and pattern of the nobbly spikes that were used to create the dimples. In a eureka moment, he grabbed the waffle iron and took it into his garage, where he had a vat of urethane that had been left over after the installation of a urethane-covered track at Hayward Field. He poured the urethane into the waffle iron and waited while it cooked.

While the first result wasn't great (and the waffle iron was ruined), it showed promise. Heading to the store, he bought six new irons and retreated to his basement. He continued to experiment with different materials and, after numerous attempts, finally hit upon the sole he wanted – light, flexible, durable and, most importantly, with a waffle pattern of nobbly spikes on it. After gluing it on to the heel of a running shoe he gave it to his colleague and former student Geoff Hollister to test. Hollister reported that it provided fantastic grip whatever surface the shoes were used on, whether it was track, road, grass or mud, and provided great cushioning for the heel, too. The next step was to remove the spikes and cover the entire sole with the waffle material. When the Oregon track team wore them to win the 1971 NCAA Cross-Country title no one needed convincing about the waffle shoe's effectiveness.

By then nicknamed the 'Moon Shoe' because the impression the sole made reminded him of the footprints left on the moon by Neil Armstrong and Buzz Aldrin, Bowerman and Hollister produced 10 pairs to hand out to athletes competing in the 1972 Olympic Track and Field Trials in Eugene. It was a critical event for Blue Ribbon as it was

Right Bill Bowerman working at Nike workshop in Eugene, Oregon c.1980.

where they would introduce the new Nike line to the world. While none of the Moon Shoe runners qualified for the Munich Games, the shoe was still a big hit and won Nike many fans that day. Though some runners were still sceptical that spikeless shoes could be as fast as spiked shoes, runners like Ken Moore started putting in times that came very close.

Continuing to evolve the shoe, Bowerman and Hollister's next version was the Oregon Waffle, which was the first version of the shoe made available to the public. The shoe was released in 1973 just when the running boom, partly sparked by Bowerman's promotion of jogging as exercise

in the 1960s, was happening across America. Jogging had become America's favourite pastime and people who previously rarely even run for a bus were suddenly hitting the streets and parks in running gear. With its light weight and impact-absorbing sole, the waffle-treaded shoes became popular with casual runners as well as medal contenders. The third iteration of the shoe, the Waffle Trainer, was released in 1974 and appealed even more to the weekend warrior by offering increased comfort with a sponge midsole and a roomier toe-box. It flew off the shelves faster than Blue Ribbon could restock it. Demand for the Waffle Trainer grew

so quickly that Blue Ribbon wasn't able to produce enough of the shoes to meet the orders that were flooding in, forcing Phil Knight to take out a loan in order to meet the demand.

Riding the crest of the fitness wave, during the latter half of the 1970s sales grew from $10 million to $270 million. While Nike couldn't claim sole responsibility for the running revolution, its high-quality but reasonably priced running shoes had helped 'democratize' exercise and by the end of the decade an estimated one third of the entire US population owned a pair of running shoes. An incredible half of those were Nikes.

Left Nike protoype waffe soles (Nike, inc.)

CLYDE STYLE
1972 PUMA SIGN WALT FRAZIER

PUMA CLYDE

Before the 1970s, style and fashion were almost alien concepts to basketball players, but when Walt 'Clyde' Frazier led the New York Knicks to their first NBA championship, he became the first player to bring those two things to the game. With a sense of style that was as sharp as his game, he grabbed as much attention away from the court as he did on it and became the definition of New York cool. With adidas having broken Converse's near monopoly on basketball in the late 1960s, Puma wanted in on the action too and when Karl Wallach, a manager at Puma's US distributors Beconta, heard that Walt Frazier was open to signing an endorsement deal, Puma leapt at the chance to be associated with him.

Born in March 1945 in Atlanta, Georgia, Frazier was the eldest of nine siblings. From childhood he was a great all-round sportsman, starring in his high school's American football and baseball teams. He was also an exceptional basketball player and although he didn't receive any coaching at school, learned to play on a dirt court near his home. When it came to choosing a college, despite having been offered a number of football scholarships, as there were no professional black quarterbacks but a number of black guards, he believed he would go further if he opted for basketball, and joined Southern Illinois University. It was a

wise choice, although not immediately. Due to poor grades he was initially ineligible to play basketball but worked hard and was allowed to return to the basketball court the following season. When he led Southern Illinois to win the National Invitation Tournament, he was voted one of the best in college players in the country, earning him a place on the All-American team and leading to him becoming the New York Knicks' first pick in the 1967 NBA Draft.

Averaging only nine points at the start of his rookie year, he was far from stellar, but when William 'Red' Holzman took over as coach he emphasized an aggressive defence that suited Frazier's style perfectly. As his time on court grew, so too did his confidence and his coach, teammates and even rivals were soon lavishing him with praise, describing him as 'faster than a lizard's tongue' and 'the only player I've ever seen I would describe as an artist'. He sealed his place in Knicks' history when during the 1969/70 season NBA finals, he put in a performance hailed as one of the best ever in a Finals Game 7: scoring 36 points, 19 assists and five steals and helping the Knicks to win the Championship

Right Walt 'Clyde' Frazier, playing in Puma Clydes against the Seattle Supersonics, is screened by future Chicago Bulls and LA Lakers coach Phil Jackson.

decider 113-99, and their first NBA title.

With a Knicks' title under his belt, Frazier had become a hero in New York and the fans and press fell in love with him. His cool temperament and unflappable nature were much admired, as was the fact he very rarely got into arguments with rival players or officials. Sports writers waxed lyrical about him and one even romantically compared his movement on court to Fred Astaire's on the dance floor.

Frazier soon became as well-known for his elegance and style off the court as he was on it. Players at the time wore dress suits off-court and Frazier enjoyed trying to find ways to look sharper than his teammates. On a shopping trip in Baltimore he spotted what would become his trademark, a wide-brimmed Borsalino hat. When he first bought the hat his teammates made fun of him, but two weeks later the film *Bonnie and Clyde* was released and his hat became the hottest thing in town. It also earned him the nickname 'Clyde' after the infamous robber Clyde Barrow. The hat was often part of an outfit that included a fur coat, a pair of fine dress shoes from his huge collection, a cane and sometimes a 'Bonnie' or two on his arm. One of the first basketball players to own a Rolls-Royce, he was described by Beconta's Jim Woolner as 'the epitome of cool', making him just the player they wanted to endorse Puma.

When Frazier and his agent met with the Beconta execs, they didn't even try to up the first offer they received: $25,000 per year and a ¢25 royalty on every pair of Frazier's signature shoes sold. Called the 'Clyde', it would be the first basketball shoe to be named after a player. Reports differ on its origins. While some recall it as simply a rebadged version of the Suede, according to Frazier it was based on Puma's first basketball shoe, the Basket, but borrowed the Suede's upper. According to Frazier, when he first saw it he felt it was too 'clunky', and keen to keep him happy, Puma offered to customize it to make it exactly the way he wanted. To reduce weight, some padding was removed; it was made slightly narrower and the thickness of the midsole was reduced.

The shoe was an instant hit, and when Frazier won a second NBA title with the Knicks in 1973 the fans just had to have them. Just as Frazier did as part of his flamboyant outfits, they wore them as fashion shoes on the streets as well as sports shoes on the ball courts, making them one of the first to make the crossover from sportswear to streetwear. Puma sold over a million pairs of Clydes by the time he retired in 1980, and like Frazier's outfits they came in a huge range of colours.

Frazier's retirement from the game didn't dampen enthusiasm for the shoe at all and in the 1980s it gained popularity for a completely different type of performance, B-boying. Better known as breakdancing, its popularity in New York led the Clyde to become the shoe of choice for B-boys like the New York City Breakers and the Rock Steady Crew. In the 1990s Clydes enjoyed an unexpected resurgence in popularity and played a role in Puma's comeback when the Beastie Boys wore them during a concert, causing Puma to ramp up production to cope with the resultant increase in demand.

Now well into its fourth decade of production, like adidas's Stan Smith, many of its present-day fans aren't even aware of the man it was named after or its origins as a basketball shoe. Despite that, the Clyde remains one of Puma's best-sellers. Its simple, clean design is as fresh today as it was in the 1970s and, as the frequent subject of numerous collaborations and special editions, still looks great, just like Walt Frazier, who now brings his style to the airwaves as a commentator. Indeed, many Knicks fans still consider him the most dapper man in New York.

Below Puma Clyde, signed by Walt 'Clyde' Frazier (Puma Archive).

LE COQ SPORTIF ARTHUR ASHE

Born in Richmond, Virginia, the former capital city of the Confederacy, in July 1943, Arthur Ashe was also born into segregation. Raised alone by their father after the death of their mother, Ashe and his brother lived in the grounds of Brookfield Park, Richmond's largest black-only public park and where their father was the caretaker. Living in sight of the park's tennis courts, Ashe began playing tennis aged seven and it wasn't long before his talent was spotted by tennis instructor Ron Charity. Charity saw he had potential and encouraged him to enter tournaments. But with Richmond still very resistant to integration, Ashe often found himself turned away. This infuriated him and despite his youth, set his resolve to do something that would help to end segregation and inspire black Americans to overcome the barriers they faced.

As he walked out on to Centre Court for the final of the 1975 Wimbledon Championships against Jimmy Connors, Ashe could have looked back to the moment he decided his life's mission and justifiably felt satisfaction about what he had achieved. After graduating with a degree in Business Administration from UCLA he had won both the United States Amateur Championships and the US Open in the same year, two Davis Cups and the Australian Open. He was also president of the players union, the Association of Tennis Professionals (ATP). Yet despite all these achievements, Ashe was far from satisfied, knowing that there was still so much to do in the fight to achieve equality. But he knew that winning Wimbledon would be another step on the road to achieving it.

One man who saw beyond the colour of Ashe's skin and was praying for his victory was Horst Dassler of adidas. Ashe oozed class, grace, composure and good sportsmanship, exactly the qualities he wanted to be reflected in his newly acquired sportswear brand, Le Coq Sportif. As with many things in which Horst Dassler was involved, his acquisition of the renowned French sportswear brand was not without a little drama and chicanery.

Founded by Émile Camuset in 1882, Le Coq Sportif was originally a manufacturer of woollen textiles but first found success when it moved into making sportswear, supplying team strips and tracksuits to French rugby and football teams. But it wasn't until the company was appointed to make the yellow jersey for the Tour de France in 1951 that Le Coq Sportif earned its place as a symbol of French sporting pride.

In the 1960s, Horst Dassler had realized that sportswear was a potentially huge market. But, as was often the case, his father Adi Dassler didn't agree. He had reluctantly agreed to have tracksuits made for some German football teams but felt that even those were a step too far. However, with help from his mother, Horst managed to convince his father to extend the adidas name to sportswear. He believed that allying adidas with a textile manufacturer was the best way to enter the market, as it would allow them to offer teams a combined clothing and footwear deal. He approached Le Coq Sportif, now the largest French sports brand, and the two companies agreed a deal that allowed the Camusets to produce adidas branded sports clothing in France. All was well until they started making Le Coq Sportif branded clothing that also bore adidas's three stripes. Despite repeated pleas from Horst for them to stop, the Camusets ignored him, saying that as they held the French rights to use the three stripes, they could do what they wanted with them. The Dasslers were beyond furious. How could anyone dare to use their famous three stripes without their approval? They attempted to sue, but the French court ruled in favour of Le Coq Sportif. It meant war.

Opposite Arthur Ashe at the 1975 Wimbledon Championships wearing adidas Matchplays, one the models that would later influence the design of his Le Coq Sportif signature shoes..

adidas began flooding the French market with sportswear and fielded a crack team of salesmen to push its products across France. Horst also used his relationship with the French football federation to end the national team's strip deal with Le Coq Sportif. Attempting to counter-attack, the Camusets tried to increase production by buying a new plant and building another, but the increased debt and mountains of unsold stock only led to them being thrown off the board of their own company and a buyer being sought for it. adidas had won, but realizing that the three stripes could still fall into other hands, the Dasslers now attempted to buy Le Coq Sportif. The company's shares were split between the founder's children, Mireille Gouserry-Camuset, who held 51 per cent, and her brother, Roland Camuset, who held the remaining 49 per cent. While Roland was happy to sell, Mireille, who had been in the French Resistance during the war, abhorred the idea that Le Coq Sportif would fall into German hands and refused to sell. But with the company nearing liquidation, the French government stepped in to calm the trade unions and put forward their preferred buyer, French entrepreneur André Guelfi, to whom she sold her shares.

One of Guelfi's first acts as majority shareholder was to tell Horst Dassler he would not allow adidas to take back the three stripes. However, when the two met, Horst completely disarmed Guelfi with his charm and the two became good friends, especially when Guelfi realized that Horst was probably the best man to run Le Coq Sportif. The two new friends came to a secret agreement. Guelfi gave 2 per cent of his shares to Horst, along with an option to buy the rest at any point. Critically, the deal was made with Horst, not

adidas, giving him control of Le Coq Sportif rather than his parents. With Guelfi appearing to hold control of the company, they wouldn't suspect a thing. Horst swore his employees at adidas France to secrecy and many found themselves working for Le Coq Sportif. Horst's paranoia was such that they even had to use false identities when going to meetings and used different business cards depending on which company they were representing.

Fearing his parents would wonder why he was spending so much time on Le Coq Sportif, Horst entrusted the brand's global redevelopment to his most trusted partners around the world. In the United States, Donald Dell, the former Davis Cup captain who brought Stan Smith to adidas, became responsible for the brand and turned it into a more premium sports fashion label. Horst felt that Arthur Ashe would be the perfect player to endorse the brand and encouraged Dell to persuade him to wear Le Coq Sportif. Ashe was given his own Le Coq Sportif signature shoe, but initially played in adidas Matchplays until a bespoke branded line could be created for him. As the brand had never made shoes before, the eventual Le Coq Sportif signature model incorporated design cues from the existing family of adidas tennis shoes such as the Matchplay and Stan Smith and still bears a resemblance to its adidas cousins of the time.

Ashe's final against Connors had the extra edge of being a grudge match. Connors was suing the ATP, of which Ashe was president, for alleged restraint of trade after he had been barred from playing in the 1974 French Open due to his membership of World Team Tennis. Two days before the final Connors announced that he was suing Ashe for

$5 million as a result of comments he made in a letter to ATP members criticizing Connors' boycott of the Davis Cup and his demand that team captain Dennis Ralston be fired for dropping him for a match against the West Indies in 1972. As a riposte to what he saw as Connors' 'unpatriotic' stance, Ashe wore his US Davis Cup jacket on to Centre Court and wore red, white and blue wristbands too. Connors was the overwhelming favourite. He was the defending champion and the underdog Ashe had never beaten him in any previous matches. However, Ashe started the match by taking the first set 6-1, surprising both Connors and the watching crowd with his tactical game. He continued to dominate in the second, winning it 6-1 again. In the third Connors fought back bravely to recover from 3-1 down to lead 6-5 then won his serve to take the set. It was grace versus guts. But in the fourth set Ashe broke Connors' serve in the ninth game and went on to win the set 6-4 and the match by 3 sets to 1. Grace had won.

Ashe's victory was one of the first and finest examples of a player winning with his mind. He had varied his game throughout the match, frustrating and riling Connors, who just didn't know how to play him and could not find an opening no matter what he tried. At one point when a member of the crowd shouted, 'Come on, Connors,' he retorted, 'I'm trying, for Chrissake!' Proudly accepting the winner's trophy in his US Davis Cup jacket, Ashe was as characteristically calm and serene as he had been throughout the game. The perfect example of a gentleman player, he was perhaps one of the most fitting Wimbledon champions of all time. Horst Dassler had most certainly chosen the right man.

A NEW ERA
1976 VANS CREATE THE STYLE #95

VANS STYLE #95 ERA

The story of Vans begins at a Boston horse racing track in the mid-1940s, where a young Paul Van Doren, having dropped out of school aged 14, spent most of his days giving punters the odds on horses for a dollar a time. Unimpressed with his chosen career, his mother hauled him over to Randy's, the shoe factory where she worked, and managed to get him a job making shoes and sweeping up. Twenty years later he was executive vice president and Randy's was the third largest shoe manufacturer in the United States. When one of their factories was underperforming Van Doren was sent, along with his brother James and friend Gordon Lee, to get it working properly again. They did such a great job it was soon outperforming the Boston factory.

The experience made Van Doren think about setting up his own shoe manufacturing company. At Randy's he realized that the people who made the most money in the shoe business were the retailers. His idea was to start a company that not only made shoes but had its own retail outlets so that it could sell direct to the public without the

Left Tony 'Mad Dog' Alva wearing Vans Style #95s during a skate demo at a school in Toronto in the late 1970s.

middleman. Between himself, Gordon Lee and his friend Serge D'Elia, an investor based in Japan, he believed that they had the experience and skills to set up on their own. In 1966 the three men moved to California and founded the Van Doren Rubber Company. In the first year they constructed a new purpose-built factory along with a 400-square-foot retail store in Anaheim, and were also joined by Van Doren's younger brother, James. The company was split between the four of them, with Paul Van Doren and D'Elia each owning 40 per cent of the firm and James and Gordon 10 per cent each.

On 16 March 1966, they opened their store. But there was a problem: they had no stock, just display models and empty boxes. Despite this, they still served 12 customers, who chose the style and colour they wanted and were asked to come back in the afternoon to pick up their shoes. This allowed Paul and Gordon to rush back to the factory to make the shoes and have them ready by the time the customers came back to pick them up. There was just one more problem, though. They had forgotten to get any cash to give as change. Not wanting to annoy their very first customers, they allowed them to take the shoes away as long as they returned the next day to pay for them. Thankfully, all of them came back.

Below Vans Style #95 Era (The Other Side of the Pillow Collection).

The company was soon opening a store a week and within a year and a half of opening the first, the 50th was opened. They earned a reputation for making bespoke shoes with material that customers brought in. This came about after customers began asking for all sorts of colours but, as it was impossible to stock so many varieties, Paul Van Doren told them to find a piece of fabric in the colour they wanted and he would make an upper out of it for them. Customers wanting their own specific colours and patterns for schoolchildren and cheerleaders wanting shoes that matched their uniforms were happy to pay more for their own custom-made Vans.

In the early 1970s, Vans started to attract a new group of customers who would become devoted to the company's shoes and define its brand: skateboarders. Skateboarding was huge, especially in California, where it had developed out of the surfing culture, and because of its sticky waffle style soles, bulletproof construction and reasonable price, Vans' Style #44 (later named the Authentic) became the skaters' favourite shoe. Another reason for their devotion was that Vans stores sold single shoes. Early boards were very narrow, meaning one foot was used for control and steering and the other as a brake. That meant that one shoe often wore out a lot faster than the other. Unlike other retailers, Vans stores had no problem selling one at a time.

The Z-Boys (short for Zephyr), an influential competition skateboarding team in Santa Monica whose members included future legends Tony Alva and Stacy Peralta, were among the most ardent of Vans' fans and Alva and Peralta were to play a huge role in shaping not just Vans shoes but also the company's culture. They often saw the Van Dorens in Vans stores and developed a great relationship with them

because they were always happy to listen to their ideas on how they could make their shoes better. Their suggestions included padding in the collar to make the shoe more comfortable, a heel counter for more protection and thicker canvas for greater durability.

Vans' first response was an evolution of the #44 that incorporated many of Alva and Peralta's requests. It was called the Style #95, but was to become better known as the Era. The shoe also marked the first time Vans added the 'Off the Wall' tab to the back to denote that it was a skate-specific shoe. The inspiration behind the phrase came from Tony Alva, who was skating in an empty swimming pool and while still gripping his skateboard, he and his board went airborne over the edge of the pool. Amazed, Skip Engblom, founder of the Z-Boys competition team, said, 'Man, you just went off the wall!'

As skateboarding grew even more popular, Vans managers began regularly attending contests and organizing demonstrations all over California. Realizing that kids were buying the gear that they saw their heroes wearing in skate magazines, Paul Van Doren paid Stacy Peralta $300 to wear Vans shoes for a year as he travelled the globe, going to skating competitions. Vans stores across the country also began giving shoes away to local skate stars who had a following in their neighbourhoods.

As the skateboarding craze swept across America, Vans went with it and a pair became as much an essential part of a skater's gear as the board was. Today, even though Vans make shoes for many sports, its association with skateboarding is as strong as ever and the Style #95 Era has become a rare example of a sports shoe that 40 years after its debut is still widely used in the sport for which it was made and earned a place as an icon of fashion.

DOUBLE JEOPARDY
1976 MONTREAL OLYMPIC GAMES

ONITSUKA TIGER (ASICS) RUNSPARK

The 1972 Munich Olympic Games were a triumph for Lasse Virén. The Finnish police officer and long-distance runner had won gold in both the 5,000m and, despite a fall, in the 10,000m, making him only the fourth person in Olympic history to do the double. At the next Olympics in Montreal he looked set to repeat the feat and become the first athlete to win both long-distance races in consecutive Games. Yet his dreams of a 'double double' came crashing down, all thanks to a controversy over a pair of Onitsuka Tiger Runsparks.

Often said to be the father of modern athletics, Finn Lasse Virén was the prototype long-distance runner. He was a staunch believer in the Finnish code of 'Sisu', the ability to endure and overcome any pain or barriers through self-reliance, fortitude and mental strength, traits that are key to the success of an endurance athlete. Long before his rivals, he understood that mental fitness was just as important as physical fitness.

In the years after Munich, several poor results and the fact he was recovering from surgery to remedy pain he was suffering in his legs made a second double look doubtful. But, by applying 'Sisu' and a regimented approach to training, Virén arrived at the Stade Olympique in Montreal for the 10,000m looking like a contender. Initially, no one appeared ready to stake their claim on the race, with the lead changing several times until, on lap eight (of 25), Carlos Lopes took the front. He pushed the pace, lap after grinding lap, and began pulling away. Virén, however, had a plan and was able to stay with him. Comfortable with the pace, he shadowed Lopes like a hawk, ready to pounce when the right time came. That came 600 metres from the finishing line. Glancing over his shoulder, he saw Brendan Foster was a distant third and the rest of the field even further behind. It was time to attack. Virén overtook Lopes easily and accelerated away to the finish, crossing the line 20 metres ahead of the Portuguese runner. The double double was on. But not for long. As the elated Virén began his lap of honour he took off his Onitsuka Tiger Runspark spikes and waved them aloft in victory. Little did he realize that this gesture was to put his hopes in jeopardy.

Shortly after the race, to his shock Virén was informed by the International Olympic Committee that the waving of his Runsparks to the crowd was deemed illegal. With the amateur code still prevalent in athletics, brand

Right Following his win in the 10,000m at the 1976 Montreal Olympic Games, Lasse Virén controversially holds his Onitsuka Tiger Runsparks aloft on his victory lap.

endorsement was forbidden and any act of promotion was punishable by suspension from the rest of the Games. The double double now looked impossible.

In despair Virén appealed, explaining that he had only removed his spikes because he had developed a blister in the race. Few thought the decision would be reversed but to Virén's amazement, just two hours before the 5,000m was to start, the suspension was overturned. Few would have the mental resolve to prepare for a race in such a short time, but not Lasse Virén. In what is often described as the greatest distance race of all time, Virén took gold and completed the double double.

THE MESSENGER

ADIDAS ORION

For many people, losing a leg to cancer would only result in despair but for Terry Fox it inspired him to attempt the biggest challenge of his life. Determined to overcome his disability and spread a message of hope, he decided to run across the entire length of his home country of Canada.

Born in 1958 in Winnipeg, Manitoba, Terry Fox was an active sports-mad teenager playing everything from soccer to rugby and baseball to basketball. But aged just 18 he was diagnosed with osteosarcoma, a cancer that had started near his knee, and received the devastating news that his leg would have to be amputated and that he would require chemotherapy. Refusing to let his disability disable him, he was walking with the aid of a prosthetic leg just three weeks later.

During 16 months of chemotherapy Fox was deeply affected by the suffering that his fellow patients, many of them children, had to endure. He resolved to do something about it. Having benefited from advances in cancer treatment, Fox pledged his life to advancing research into a cure. Inspired by Dick Traum, the first amputee to complete the New York Marathon, he decided to run across Canada, running a marathon a day. It would be a 'Marathon of Hope', raising awareness and money for research, with the goal of raising $25 million, a dollar from every Canadian.

Preparing for the marathon, Fox wrote an impassioned letter to adidas appealing for the donation of running shoes. They responded by contributing 26 pairs of Orion shoes. Light and flexible but durable and with good shock absorption, they were well suited to the rigours that Fox would put them through.

On 12 April 1980, near St John's in Newfoundland, Fox filled two bottles with water from the Atlantic Ocean: one to keep, the other to pour into the Pacific at the end of his journey. To mark the beginning of the Marathon of Hope he dipped his right leg in the Atlantic and started his 5,300-mile journey. While initially struggling to attract attention, as his quest began to receive media coverage, enthusiasm mounted. When he arrived in Port aux Basques, Newfoundland, the town presented him with a donation of over $10,000 and by the time he arrived in Montreal on 22 June, one third of the way, he had raised over $200,000.

However, Fox was disappointed, he hoped to have raised more money by this time, until hotelier Isadore Sharp, who had lost a son to cancer, persuaded almost 1,000

Right Terry Fox wearing one of the many pairs of adidas Orions he wore during the Marathon of Hope.

corporations to sponsor him, giving Fox renewed purpose. As attention grew, he made public appearances at which thousands of people turned out to donate. While the diversions lengthened his journey, it showed the marathon was working and Fox was frequently moved by the reception he received. Empowered by their support, despite the physical toll a marathon a day was having on his body, Fox refused to take days off despite suffering from tendonitis, an inflamed knee, shin splints and cysts on his stump. However, on 1 September he suffered an intense coughing fit and chest pains, but continued running. A few

miles further, breathless and still in pain, he asked to be taken to hospital. The next day, Fox held a tearful press conference and revealed that his cancer had returned and spread to his lungs. After 143 days, 5,373km and having raised $1.7 million, he was forced to end his run.

Typically selfless, Fox realized that with the nation about to see the consequences of cancer he might raise more money and a week after his run ended, a nationwide telethon raised $10.5 million. Despite multiple treatments, the cancer continued to spread. After falling into a coma, Terry Fox died on 28 June 1981 with his family at his

side. Flags across Canada were lowered to half-mast and communities throughout the nation held memorial services. His funeral was broadcast on TV and Canadians across the country overwhelmed the Cancer Society with donations.

Terry Fox's message of hope has led to over $650 million being raised for cancer research and cure rates for osteosarcoma are now at almost 80 per cent. His courage and spirit changed attitudes to cancer and disability. He remains a national hero to Canada and an inspiration to the world.

Below adidas Orion, worn by Terry Fox (Bata Shoe Museum Collection).

TEEN ANGEL VS SUPERBRAT
1980 WIMBLEDON CHAMPIONSHIPS FINAL

DIADORA BJÖRN BORG

The 1980 Wimbledon Men's Singles Final had all the elements of a Hollywood script. A cool, gentlemanly, Swedish blonde and four-time defending champion versus the brash young rebel American making his first ever appearance in a Wimbledon final. It was ice versus fire or, as the British press would have you believe, 'Teen Angel vs Superbrat', and was to go down in sporting history as one of the greatest finals in the history of tennis.

As the two men walked out on to Centre Court, both heard the very rare sound of booing from the seats. Even before the match had started, the usually respectful crowd were making their feelings clear to John McEnroe about his fiery confrontations with officials during his semi-final clash with Jimmy Connors. While the game had certainly modernized since it had gone professional, the fans still largely had old-fashioned sensibilities. McEnroe's path to Wimbledon's scorn had begun three years earlier when he made his first appearance in SW19. For McEnroe the tournament officials appeared to be just as much the enemy as his opponents, something that didn't endear him to the fans at all. But one person who was attracted by this behaviour was Nike's Phil Knight. He liked the young New Yorker's rebel spirit, a spirit that Nike shared and which persuaded Knight to sign him up in 1978.

While in terms of temperament he belonged to the gentlemen players of a previous age, Björn Borg had also been born into the new era of the professional game that had ended the hypocrisy of 'shamateurism'. As early as the age of 15 he had signed with super-agent Mark McCormack's IMG, who had quickly made him one of the richest players in tennis. He was endorsing everything from breakfast cereals to beers and rackets to tennis shoes and when it came to his shoes his chosen brand was Diadora, who had given him his own signature shoes.

Although the Italian brand was a relative newcomer to tennis, it had a history that dated back to 1948. It was founded by Marcelo Danieli in the Trevigiani Hills of Veneto as a mountain climbing boot manufacturer supplying footwear to the Italian army. The company's name came from the Greek dia-dorea which meant 'to share gifts and honours'. It was in the 1950s that Diadora started to gain a nationwide reputation for the quality of its products and it put them in a good place when Italy's economy began to grow in the 1960s. Italians started to enjoy sport and recreation as a regular pastime and when skiing became popular, Diadora began manufacturing ski boots and the first après-ski boots. However, due to his dedication to handcrafting, when plastic ski boots became popular,

rather than change to plastic production Danieli stopped producing them altogether. Instead he introduced walking shoes and soon after tennis shoes, which allowed him to continue Diadora's tradition of handcrafted production in Italy.

With Diadora's finest on his feet, Borg started the match slowly. He had always been a slow starter but in the opening set he looked uncharacteristically lost at times. Much to the crowd's surprise it was McEnroe who was playing with the confidence of a four-time champion and he dominated the first set to win 6-1. The second set was a different story. Now looking like he knew where he was, Borg used his signature stinging serve and two-handed backhand to take control and win it 7-5. In the third he hit his usual superhuman stride to win 6-3. Borg coasted through the fourth set and was suddenly serving at Championship point, but McEnroe refused to go down and produced a series of brilliant shots to break back and set up a tiebreak.

As the tiebreak unravelled, both players refused to

Opposite In his custom-made Diadoras, Björn Borg stretches for the ball during his classic 1980 Wimbledon Men's Singles Final against John McEnroe.

Below Diadora Björn Borg, worn by Björn Borg (Wimbledon Museum).

succumb and match and set points were played on almost every other point. The tiebreak seemed to go on for ever. McEnroe finally got his first set point at 8-7, but Borg sent a forehand return down the line for which McEnroe dived in vain. A series of match and set points followed. As the tension of the tiebreak continued, McEnroe at times looked on the verge of tears. On it went until on his seventh set point, McEnroe finally took it 18-16. Having taken 22 minutes, it had only been five minutes shorter than the entire first set and had been an awesome display of tennis. Borg later described losing it as one of the worst points of his entire career. And there was still another set to be played.

The momentum of the match now seemed to be with McEnroe. Incredibly, he had even won over the previously hostile crowd, who having started 100 per cent for Borg, now appeared 50:50. When Borg lost the first two points on his serve it looked like they had started to back the right man. But they had forgotten that this was Björn Borg. Seemingly from nowhere, he didn't lose a point on his serve until the 10th game of the set, a 19-point stretch.

In the second game McEnroe fought to hold serve from 0-40 and did the same to get to 4-all. The strain was beginning to show, but he managed to battle Borg point for point until the cooler and more experienced Borg began to pull ahead. Like the fourth, the fifth set went to 6-6, but with no tiebreaker in the final set, the title would be won

by the first man to go two games ahead. With McEnroe clearly exhausted, Borg took advantage and won the 13th and 14th games to take the Wimbledon title for the fifth straight year, sinking to his knees as he did so. Borg would later recall it as, 'Mentally, the best set of tennis I ever played.' McEnroe looked distraught as Borg held the Wimbledon trophy but the New Yorker had rattled the Swede and as Borg later admitted, for the first time in his career he had feared losing.

It had been an extraordinary match, the sheer thrill of which wouldn't be rivalled until the 2008 Nadal/Federer Wimbledon final classic, and over 30 years later the Borg/McEnroe match-up continues to be hailed as not just the greatest final in tennis, but one of the greatest finals in sport. It was also to mark the moment when Björn Borg set himself on the path to retirement. The two men would meet again in the 1981 Wimbledon and US Open Finals but it was McEnroe who was the victor in both. The 1980 Final seemed to have convinced Borg that despite being only 25, his time was over. His heart just wasn't in the game any more and while many say it was a fear of a new generation of players, like McEnroe, it was just as much due to the strains of being one of the most famous people in the world. He would win one more Grand Slam title at the French Open in 1981, but in 1983, despite McEnroe trying to persuade him not to, he retired gracefully, aged 26.

FEEL THE FORCE
1982 LAUNCH OF AIR FORCE 1

NIKE AIR FORCE 1

In the history of sports shoes very few have received as much love as Nike's Air Force 1. Treasured by millions and the pride of many collectors, it started life as a professional basketball shoe but became a symbol of the culture that was inspired by and developed around the game. More than 30 years after its launch it remains one of Nike's biggest sellers and a testament to the fans who wouldn't let it fade away.

Designed by Bruce Kilgore in 1982, and just like the aircraft it was named after, the Air Force 1 featured innovations that weren't immediately obvious. It was the first basketball shoe to feature Nike's Air cushioning technology and although the Air system had made its debut on the Tailwind running shoe four years earlier, the demands of running being so different to basketball meant it had to be completely redesigned for the Air Force 1. It brought a whole new level of comfort to a basketball shoe. But as well as being comfortable, Kilgore designed it to have tank-like durability and gave it a cup-sole, providing more foot and ankle support because the foot rested 'in' the sole, instead of on top of it. The outsole featured a circular pattern that provided better grip when pivoting the feet. Initially featuring mesh on the upper, an all-leather construction was used on later versions to improve

durability and justify its higher price point. It was also one of the first basketball shoes to feature an ankle strap on the hi-top to increase support and stability.

During testing, the Air Force 1 was said to be so comfortable that many testers didn't want to give them back. One of those testers was the now legendary designer Tinker Hatfield, who was Nike's corporate architect. After trying the shoes in a career-defining moment, he decided he wanted to design shoes, not buildings. The first Air Force 1s made were given to a select group of defensive specialists: Moses Malone and Bobby Jones of the Philadelphia 76ers, Calvin Natt and Mychal Thompson of the Portland Trail Blazers and Michael Cooper and Jamal Wilkes of the LA Lakers. When Malone led the 76ers to the 1982/83 title the Air Force 1 was immortalized in the affections of Philadelphians.

As was usual practice at the time, Nike only intended the Air Force 1 to have a short life and in 1984, just two years after its launch, it was retired. What Nike didn't realize was that the shoe had already begun a second life. Its combination of unrivalled durability and comfort, along with

Right Moses Malone of the Philadelphia 76ers wearing Air Force 1s on court.

its availability in hi-top, mid- and low- versions, had won it many fans, especially among streetballers of New York, Philadelphia and Baltimore. As hip hop and basketball were becoming increasingly interwoven, the Air Force 1 became a symbol of the growing culture. Their popularity on the streets of Harlem and The Bronx even led to them de-crowning the Pro-Keds 69er of their honorary nickname 'uptowns'. So when their favourite sneakers began to disappear from the stores, the fans began to demand their return.

With so much demand for the now-cancelled shoe, distributors began to ask Nike about bringing them back, something that was almost unheard of. From Nike's point of view it just didn't make sense to start making an 'old' shoe again. As a company they only looked forward, not back. But when a group of independent stores in Baltimore approached them with enough orders to justify re-starting the line, Nike reluctantly agreed and what began as the re-issuing of just two styles then became a new one each month and eventually, in 1986, a full return to Nike's line-up. Fan power had resurrected the Air Force 1.

Over 30 years and 2,000 designs and colourways later, the Air Force 1 is one of the best-selling sports shoes of all time. The fans' continuing love affair means it has become the canvas for a multitude of designs expressing affection and dedication. And yet it has always remained unmistakably the Air Force 1.

Below Nike Air Force 1
(Nike Archive).

GIRL POWERED
1982 THE AEROBICS REVOLUTION

REEBOK FREESTYLE

The Reebok story really begins with the ending of another: J.W. Foster & Sons, whose shoes had dominated British athletics tracks since the late 1800s, was under attack. In the 1950s the Bolton-based company had failed to keep up with competition from adidas and Puma, who were making less expensive but more advanced shoes. At the time the company was run by James and William Foster, sons of its founder Joseph. Following the family tradition, their sons Joseph and Jeffrey, the third generation of shoemaking Fosters, also joined the business. But soon frustrated by their fathers' lack of innovation and vision, the two cousins decided to leave in 1958 to set up their own business. Without their ideas and drive, the original company began to flounder, and by 1970 was no more.

Having departed the family business, Joe and Jeff set up Mercury Sports, but in 1960 renamed it Reebok, an anglicized version of 'Rhebok', the Afrikaans name for a type of antelope. Although now in competition with their fathers, Joe and Jeff ensured Reebok lived up to their grandfather's legacy, manufacturing high-quality sports

footwear and ensuring it remained a family firm, with their wives, younger brother and children working alongside them in the business.

While the running boom was sweeping America in the 1970s, Joe began looking for a distributor in the United States and at a Chicago trade fair met a 35-year-old entrepreneur by the name of Paul Fireman. More experienced at distributing fishing and camping goods, Fireman saw potential in Reebok's offerings and negotiated a deal to licence and distribute the Reebok brand in the United States in return for a 3.5 per cent royalty on net sales. The division was called Reebok USA and began by offering three styles of Reebok running shoes. At $60 a pair, they were among the most expensive shoes on the US market, but their quality was such that customers felt they were worth the price. Despite this the new company struggled at first. Facing bankruptcy at one point, Fireman was forced to sell 55 per cent of Reebok USA to Stephen Rubin of Pentland Industries (previously known as the Liverpool Shoe Company, inventors of the plimsoll) in return for financing and production staff, but its fortunes were soon to turn around, thanks in part to a fortunate mistake.

Fireman had noticed that Nike were increasingly competing on technology rather than comfort and had ignored the

rapidly growing niche in the women's market that was being fuelled by the popularity of aerobics. The benefits of aerobics had first been embraced by famed doctor Kenneth Cooper in the 1960s but, as women were living increasingly busy lives, its popularity was booming. Aerobics gave working women and time-pressed homemakers a convenient and flexible workout that could be done at home or in a gym with friends. Reebok's answer was the Freestyle. Whereas most of their competitors followed the 'pink 'em and shrink 'em' approach to making women's shoes, the Freestyle was an athletic shoe designed with women specifically in mind and also the world's first aerobics shoe. It had a simple, elegant design that made feet look petite and was made of very soft and light leather that had only been used due to a serendipitous manufacturing error. When the first samples of the shoes were sent to the US by Reebok's Korean manufacturing partner, they had accidentally been made using a soft grade usually only used for gloves. They were accompanied by a letter from the factory owner apologizing for wrinkles in the toe and explaining that they would be ironed out in the final production run. But Reebok loved the wrinkles because they gave the shoes a ballet slipper-like appearance, so they told the factory to keep using the same leather and to keep the wrinkles in.

Left Reebok Freestyle (Reebok Archive).

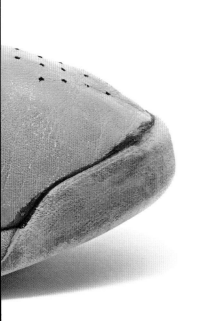

The Freestyle was an immediate hit. It was light, didn't need breaking in and came in simple colours, unlike Nike and adidas's increasingly garish shoes. And best of all from Reebok's point of view, they were the only company who made a shoe specifically for aerobics. From sales of $300,000 in 1980, by 1983 sales reached $12.8 million. With a limited budget for advertising Fireman and his managers used a door-to-door approach to sales and gave away shoes to aerobics instructors, who were in a position to influence the increasingly large classes they were teaching. When Fireman approached retailers he was interested to find that not only were they happy to have a product that perfectly met the increasing demand for aerobics shoes, but that many of them were growing dissatisfied at the arrogant way Nike had begun to treat them. He was also interested to hear that Nike didn't even have an aerobics product in the works.

Just as adidas had dismissed jogging as not being a proper sport, Nike appeared to have done the same with aerobics. Nike's marketing chief Rob Strasser was said to have called it, 'nothing more than a bunch of fat ladies dancing to music', and when Nike's R&D people first saw the Freestyle, they laughed at it. When reality started to hit and orders for Nike women's products began to drop, rather than producing an aerobics shoe the company decided to move into the women's casual market, in effect abandoning the idea that Nike only made products for sports. A range of women's casual shoes were made, launched with a fashion show and sold in department stores, almost alien territory for Nike, where it had no experience and struggled to compete with established brands who had been making women's wear for a lot longer. Unsurprisingly, the line flopped.

Fireman's recognition of the power of the women's market had been the making of Reebok and by 1984 the company's revenues had soared to $66 million. The following year it was Reeboks, not Nikes, that were the shoe to be seen in and when Reebok's sales hit $307 million in 1985, for the first time in their history, Nike were the ones watching their backs. As Rob Strasser reportedly said to himself when he saw someone wearing Reebok shoes as he walked through an airport, 'We're f****d. They're hot and we're not.'

LIKE BUTTER ON STUDS
1982 SPAIN WORLD CUP

ADIDAS COPA MUNDIAL

If you were to close your eyes and think of a football boot, the first one to come into your mind's eye would probably look exactly like the adidas Copa Mundial. While by no means the oldest football boot in the game, its acclaim and longevity have made it the most archetypal one. Launched in 1979 to coincide with the qualifying rounds for the 1982 World Cup in Spain, it was the last shoe to be created by adidas founder Adi Dassler and changed the way football boots were made.

Like many of adidas's products from the 1970s, the 'Copa' as its fans call it, still remains highly popular and has continued to grace football pitches all over the world for more than 35 years. Selling 10 million pairs since 1979, it has retained almost exactly the same design since the day it was launched.

One of the secrets of the Copa's success was its kangaroo leather construction, which was buttery soft and smooth, but very strong. While the Copa wasn't the first football boot to use kangaroo leather, it's the one that has used its properties to the best effect. Kangaroo leather, or k-leather as it is more often referred to, is far more durable than traditional cowhide because it is much more fibrous, giving it 10 times the tensile strength. This allows it to be worked much thinner while still retaining its strength and durability. All of this

added up to make it a players' favourite. It needed little breaking-in due to the softness of the leather but could last for season after season. It was so soft, in fact, that many players found that wearing a size down from their actual size gave them a boot that fitted like a glove, providing them with ball control that was exactly the same no matter what part of the foot was used.

The global stage of the 1982 World Cup was perfect for the Copa to make its debut and, worn by tournament stars like Franz Beckenbauer, Karl-Heinz Rummenigge, Michel Platini, Trevor Francis and Falcão, it netted many goals. In its very first World Cup Final it played a key role on the feet of Marco Tardelli, who scored Italy's second goal in their 3-1 victory over West Germany.

For the first 34 years of its life the Copa was only available in black but in 2013 adidas released a white version with black stripes and, later that year, the 'Samba' pack featuring the Copa in purple, red, blue, orange and green.

Weighing in at 11.7oz, at the time of launch the Copa was one of the lightest boots on the market and although in comparison to modern boots it is a lot heavier, its weight

Right Marco Tardelli playing for Italy in Copa Mundials at the 1982 World Cup.

seems to have had little impact on its sales. Although it lacked the technology of the Predator (see pages 142–145) the Copa sold alongside its younger brother with very respectable sales. The fact it continues to be sold by adidas while the Predator has now been retired speaks volumes for the status and affection footballers, and even rugby players, still hold for the shoe. Despite its age, with a fan base that has already run through several generations, it may well be seen on pitches for many more years to come.

....

Left adidas Copa Mundial Original and 25th Anniversary models (adidas Archive).

DRINK BEER AND TRAIN LIKE AN ANIMAL
1983 NEW YORK MARATHON

SAUCONY DXN

Rod Dixon is arguably the most versatile runner of all time. Born in Nelson, New Zealand, in July 1950 he was inspired to run and trained by his brother John. In the 1970s Dixon was part of a group of Kiwi runners who trained according to the Lydiard method, a high-mileage training programme that focuses on building endurance. During the 1970s and 1980s he set world records in various distances, from the 1,500m to the marathon, won two bronze medals in the World Cross-Country Championships and was among the most successful athletes on the American road racing circuit. But all of that was just training for the race that would define his entire career.

As he lined up at the start of the 1983 New York Marathon, Dixon knew that he was in his prime. He believed in training hard while also making time to enjoy life, but for the marathon he had trained like he had never done before; six months of the most intensive training he had ever undertaken. No distractions, no breaks and in complete

Left Saucony DXN (Saucony).

Opposite Rod Dixon wins the 1983 New York Marathon in Saucony shoes of his own design.

isolation. He was so confident in his training regime that if he wasn't going to win, it could be only because another man had trained even harder.

His preparation even extended to his shoes. Approaching Saucony, a brand with a small but incredibly loyal following often called 'the runner's best kept secret', he had an idea how they could modify their shoes to make them even better for the marathon. The company was the result of a merger that took place in 1963. One of the companies had been founded in 1898 in Saucony Creek (pronounced 'sock-a-knee'), Kurtztown, Pennsylvania, while the other began in Cambridge, Massachusetts, in 1890 when Russian immigrant Abraham Hyde started A.R. Hyde & Sons, which started making slippers from carpet remnants. On the way to making running shoes that won awards for their quality, Saucony also made boots for the US army and navy that won the only award for excellence given by the forces to a shoe manufacturer due to their sturdiness. Their military pedigree led to a contract producing footwear for NASA and consequently they made the boots used for the first space walk. Keen to ensure Dixon's shoes were exactly the way he wanted them, Saucony's engineers listened to his ideas and worked alongside him. Dixon was keen for them to be made of kangaroo leather, but as it was illegal to import it into the US, he personally smuggled some in for Saucony to use. The end result was his perfect marathon shoe.

After five miles Dixon had settled into the race. His approach was to be patient and methodical and to run to his own plan and no one else's. At 10 miles, the leaders were getting away from him, but he remained unperturbed. If he stuck to his plan, he'd be fine. At 15 miles he had a good rhythm going but the leaders were now well ahead. To the rest of the world, the race was starting to look over for him, but Dixon knew if he stuck to his plan he was on track to run the best time of his life. At 20 miles he was still two and half minutes behind the leaders and knew the last six miles were critical. He began catching the leader, British runner Geoff Smith, but realized that based on his split times, he was going to 'run out of real estate' before he caught him. At the 23rd mile, Smith was now in sight but as he couldn't run any faster, Dixon knew he had to do something special. If he couldn't run faster, he would run smarter. Noticing that Smith was running in the middle of the road, Dixon realized that if he ran the apex of each turn he would be able to catch Smith by saving a few yards each time, in effect running a shorter race.

The plan worked. As Dixon later described, 'I was the hunter, he was the hunted,' and at 26 miles, Dixon made his move. Smith was visibly distraught as Dixon passed him and despite trying to fight back he was simply unable to summon the strength. Seeing the finish line, Dixon powered on to take the win by nine seconds. Crossing the line, he raised his hands to the sky while behind him Smith collapsed in exhaustion. It was one of the most dramatic finishes of all time and a masterclass in how to win a marathon.

Speaking years later, Dixon reflected that as he watched the stream of runners crossing the finish line after him he realized that he was just one of thousands of champions that day, 'Everybody who took the challenge to cross the finish line was a winner.' Still an active runner today, he set up the Rod Dixon's Kid's Marathon Foundation with the aim of inspiring children to take up that challenge too. While one of the few victories that escaped him was an Olympic one, he believes getting kids active is a far better reward than the gold medal that eluded him. Still often called 'the runner's runner', his famous quote, 'All I want to do is drink beer and train like an animal' is a mantra for millions of runners who, like Dixon, believe in playing hard but training even harder.

BATTLEFIELD LA
1984 LOS ANGELES OLYMPIC GAMES

NIKE ZOOM RUNNING SPIKES

Following the death of his father Adi Dassler in 1978 and mother Käthe in 1984, Horst Dassler was the undisputed king of the adidas Group. He had coveted control of the company for many years and now he finally had it. From his new throne, the future looked bright. Business had never been better and his connections and influence throughout sport's governing bodies had made him the 'Godfather' of world sport. But from his lofty position at the top of fortress adidas, he wasn't even aware that they were under attack.

When his US distributors first mentioned the growing threat from Nike, Dassler took no notice. His focus was firmly on building his new sports marketing empire and besides, he still believed the real battle was with his cousins at Puma, not the upstarts from Oregon. When the Americans had brought pairs of Nikes to show him and his father, they believed that their waffle shoes were poorly designed biomechanically, were far too soft and were also badly made, clearly just further evidence they had nothing to worry about. And with demand so great that adidas could barely keep up with orders, especially in the US, Dassler appeared to be right. However, it was exactly adidas's inability to meet that demand that Nike was exploiting.

With their focus mainly on Europe, the Germans had been slow to react to the running boom in America, believing that jogging was just a passing fad and not really a sport anyway. Yet Americans were buying running shoes in their millions and with adidas shoes in short supply, retailers were facing the nightmare of unprecedented demand and little to sell, so increasingly began to look to Nike as an alternative. It also didn't help that adidas's attitude meant that they didn't even have a product that suited jogging. Nike, however, with its range of Air shoes, gave joggers numerous options to suit their needs. Without realizing it, adidas's short-sightedness was providing fule for Nike's growth.

From day one, beating adidas had been Nike's number one goal and CEO Phil Knight and his team knew that the upcoming Los Angeles Olympics in 1984 would be a great chance to deliver adidas a blow that they wouldn't even see coming. It was the first Olympics in Nike's lifetime for which the company was in a strong position to exploit, having been either too small or forbidden by the Moscow boycott. Although Converse was the official sponsor of the Olympics, Nike's intention was to ambush the Games and make it theirs.

For adidas, the Olympic Games were familiar territory and with all of the company's heads present, the Los Angeles Hilton became the company's unofficial headquarters for the duration. Horst Dassler and his men were in their element,

wining and dining athletes, officials, the great and the good. With a budget of $15 million for the Games, much of that set aside for athlete 'incentives', they were well prepared. Although the communist boycott meant that many national teams who wore adidas wouldn't be present, its products would still be overwhelmingly well represented.

Nike's approach was completely different. While the adidas execs were most likely to be found at champagne receptions in five-star hotel penthouses, the Steve Prefontaine spirit that still coursed through Nike meant they loathed the suited establishment types they felt were corrupting world sport. Rather than a luxury hotel, Nike rented a frat house and you were far more likely to find their execs at a beach party with buckets of beer, dancing with athletes and Hollywood stars.

In the battle against adidas for the Games, Nike had two aces up their sleeves. While they knew they couldn't match the Germans in the number of athletes representing them, they were sure they could match them in sheer quality. With Mary Decker, Joan Benoit, Alberto Salazar, Al Joyner,

Opposite Carl Lewis on his way to victory in the 100m final at the 1984 Los Angeles Olympic Games wearing Nike Zoom spikes (Olympic Multimedia Library).

Sebastian Coe, Steve Ovett and most notably Carl Lewis all running in Nike, they felt sure that Nike would be in the headlines. Giving Nike a reason to be proud was the fact that many of them had come through from Athletics West, a running club that Nike had started in Eugene, Oregon, that provided athletes with subsidies, a coach, training facilities, medical supervision and tuition or part-time jobs.

The second ace was an inspired advertising campaign. Across Los Angeles the sides of skyscrapers featured huge images of Nike athletes in action, including Carl Lewis in flight over a sand pit, Joan Benoit crossing a finish line and a rebellious-looking John McEnroe in a leather coat. Along with the skyline-dominating billboards, before and during the Games, a commercial was aired featuring Lewis and Decker set to the music of Randy Newman's song, 'I Love LA'. The ambush campaign proved so effective that most who saw it believed that Nike was the official sponsor of the Games rather than Converse, who were nowhere. The *Los Angeles Times* went so far as to describe it as 'art'. It was a style of advertising unlike anything seen before in sport and made adidas and many other official sponsors' efforts look outdated in comparison.

Nike's headline athletes didn't deliver the performances expected of them, however. With Salazar failing to medal, Decker tripping up and Ovett collapsing from respiratory problems, it was left to Carl Lewis to be Nike's headline athlete. Competing in the 100m, 200m, 4×100m relay and the long jump, Lewis was aiming to equal Jesse Owens' record of four gold medals in a single Games. However, his relationship with Nike, his fellow athletes and the American public was strained at best. In the press he was presented

as an egotist, more concerned with his public image and preparing for a stellar career after athletics than in winning medals. His teammates described him as remote and singular and his reluctance to give much of his time didn't endear him to Nike. When his manager Joe Douglas predicted that Lewis's fame would rival Michael Jackson's, it just seemed to confirm everyone's suspicions that Lewis was self-obsessed, and his popularity plummeted.

Consequently, after winning his first gold medal Lewis was criticized for his celebration, and after winning his second he was booed for not exerting himself or attempting to break Bob Beamon's world record in the long jump. All in all, despite equalling Owens' record, one of the greatest performances in Olympic history, Lewis was hugely under-celebrated. To make things worse, Coca-Cola withdrew their sponsorship offer and Nike too, fully aware of the American public's disinclination towards Lewis and having had their own strained relationship with him, ended their association with him soon after the Games had finished.

In the eyes of Horst Dassler, Nike had put on an expensive but ultimately short-lived show. But in the eyes of the public, Nike had stolen the Games. While predictably through sheer numbers of athletes adidas had taken the lion's share of medals (259 to Nike's 63), including all but three of the medals in track and field, the Games' centrepiece events had been won by Nike athletes and when Nike sales in California increased by 30 per cent, it was clear who had won the battle of Los Angeles. Summing up the battle between adidas and Nike, Horst Dassler later conceded that, 'It's not only what we didn't do, but what someone else did well. Nike just did a better job.'

THE LEGEND BEGINS
1984 NIKE SIGN MICHAEL JORDAN

NIKE AIR JORDAN I

Sometimes when an athlete and a brand come together the stars align perfectly and a partnership is created that becomes legendary. The courtship and marriage of Michael Jordan and Nike is undoubtedly the greatest of these. What began as a love triangle and a tale of unrequited love would eventually result in an inseparable partnership that would change Nike's destiny and forever change the relationship between athletes and brands.

By the early 1980s, Nike had gone from selling Onitsuka Tigers out of a car boot to becoming America's number one sports shoe manufacturer, with revenue growing from $28.7 million in 1973 to $867 million by 1983. But in February 1984, the company made its first loss. The LA Games had been great for Nike but the company's top execs realized they weren't going to build an empire on track and field alone, and so Phil Knight and Rob Strasser turned their focus to the fastest-growing sport in the country, basketball. The company had already made an impact, with almost half of the NBA wearing Nike, but to tighten their grip, Nike felt they needed to sign fresh blood. Enter Sonny Vaccaro. Vaccaro ran the Dapper Dan Roundball Classic, a basketball tournament featuring All-Star players from Pennsylvania against those from the rest of the United States. With its great media coverage and fan following, the tournament was an important recruiting event for college coaches and scouts.

Nike and Vaccaro first met when he pitched an idea for a basketball sandal that could be used outdoors in the summer. They turned it down, but began to discuss how he could help Nike make inroads into college basketball. Vaccaro advised that the best way in was to pay college coaches to endorse Nike shoes and encourage their players to wear them. Initially, the Nike executives worried about the legality of it, but there was nothing in the rules to say it was illegal. From the point of view of the coaches and colleges, it was a way of incentivising top-level coaches to stay at the collegiate level, allowing them to create 'nurseries' of talent to feed into the pro game. It also had the benefit of creating a pool of players loyal to Nike even before they hit the draft.

Nike's plan was to sign three of the 1983 draft's most promising picks: Akeem Olajuwon, Charles Barkley and John Stockton. But being aware of the real talent in college basketball, Vaccaro pushed Nike to instead put all of their money on just one player: Michael Jordan. Having seen him play in a North Carolina vs Georgetown game, he had fallen in love. Something told him that Jordan was the man for Nike. There was a problem, though. Jordan's head was filled only with dreams of three stripes and trefoils. A self-professed adidas 'nut', he had never even worn Nike.

Such was his allegiance that despite his North Carolina team being sponsored by Converse, he insisted on training in adidas. And having already received a $100,000 offer from adidas, which seemed fair, being the same amount they paid the legendary Kareem Abdul-Jabbar, Jordan was delighted at the prospect of joining adidas.

Vaccaro made it his mission to convert Jordan to the Church of Nike. He approached his friend George Raveling to make an introduction. Raveling was assistant coach when Jordan was part of the 1984 US Olympic team and had become close to him. Jordan was reluctant to meet him but Raveling convinced him to hear Vaccaro out. After the two met, he remained unconvinced and said to Raveling, 'I told you, I'm an adidas guy.' But Vaccaro refused to take no for an answer and decided the only way to win Jordan over would be to get him to come to Nike's HQ in Beaverton, Oregon. When the invitation came, Jordan made his feelings clear. 'I have no interest in going there,' he told his agent David Falk, 'Just do what you need to do to get me with adidas.' But feeling that Nike were hungrier and more market savvy, as well as having a great relationship with Nike's Rob Strasser, Falk was determined to get Jordan in front of Nike and so enlisted the help of his parents. The night before they were due to fly to Beaverton, the obstinate Jordan told his mother

he wasn't going. 'You will be on that plane, Michael,' said Deloris Jordan. Although his father was a military man, there was no disobeying the real general in the family, his mother, and Jordan was indeed on the plane the next day.

The red carpet was rolled out when the Jordans arrived. During a presentation attended by Vaccaro and Nike's top brass, Jordan was shown a highlight tape of himself that ran with the Pointer Sisters' track 'Jump' and creative director Peter Moore unveiled a red and black design concept for Jordan's signature shoe. His first reaction was said to be: 'I can't wear that shoe, those are devil colours.' But this was no ordinary signature shoe. The idea was that Jordan would become a brand in its own right, still under the Nike umbrella but with its own identity. When Jordan mentioned that one of the reasons he liked adidas was because they were lower to the ground, Moore said he would happily tailor Jordan's shoe to his exact liking. At a time when signature shoes were often rebadged versions of existing lines, this made it clear just how much Nike wanted him. However, Jordan remained almost emotionless throughout the pitch and the Nike men were completely unable to gauge his thinking. That night Falk asked Jordan what he thought. He replied, 'I don't want to go to another meeting.' To Falk's disappointment, he was still clearly besotted with adidas.

Undaunted, Vaccaro decided the way to break Jordan's affinity for adidas was with cold hard cash. Nike offered $500,000 a year in cash for five years, with stock options and bonuses that would earn Jordan $7 million over that period, an unheard-of figure at the time. In addition, he would earn royalties not just on every pair of Air Jordan's sold, but also on all Nike Air shoes sold exceeding the 400,000 pairs sold

Left Recently signed to Nike, Michael Jordan appears in his very first photoshoot for his signature Air Jordan shoes (Nike Collection).

the previous year. It was an astounding offer but Jordan still wanted to give adidas a chance to match it.

'I was very loyal, I went back to my adidas contact and said, "This is the Nike contract, if you come anywhere close, I'll sign with you guys."' But adidas declined to increase their $100,000 offer. With Horst Dassler's focus fixed on building his sports marketing empire, Jordan's potential just hadn't registered on his usually prescient radar. Nike weren't alone in having seen it however, and Converse and Spot-Bilt, Saucony's basketball brand, also had offers on the table. But Converse didn't have enough ideas or hunger to impress the Jordans, and while if it was down to pure money Spot-Bilt would have won the deal, the $1 million Nike had pledged to spend on marketing put them ahead. With adidas out, and having been impressed by how much Nike wanted him, Jordan finally told Falk to make the deal happen.

Despite his previous reluctance, Jordan wore the black and red Nikes that were to become the icon of an entire industry for the first time at a pre-season game in September 1984 at Madison Square Garden. Being in the colours of his new team, Jordan couldn't protest too much, but that didn't stop the NBA. The Chicago Bulls were warned that the shoes were in breach of the 'uniformity of uniforms' rule that stated players had to wear shoes that not only matched his team's uniform, but also had to match the shoes worn by their teammates. If Jordan wore them, the Bulls would be fined $1,000, and if he wore them a second time the fine would increase to $5,000. A third time would lead to the team forfeiting the game. When Bulls' manager Rod Thorn expressed his concern to Rob Strasser; his reply was 'Wear 'em. We'll cover you.' But when the season opened, not wanting to put Jordan or his team in a difficult position in his first game, he wore Nike's Air Ship model, effectively a prototype of the signature Jordan shoe Peter Moore was

busy designing. However, just one game later, Jordan wore a black and red version and the Bulls were fined $1,000. Strasser wasn't worried though. He knew it was a tiny price to pay when the fans and press began talking about them. The excitement they created prompted the *Chicago Journal* to write that, 'Michael Jordan is not the most incredible, the most colourful, the most amazing, the most flashy, or the most mind-boggling thing in the NBA. His shoes are.'

Although some in the press criticized Nike for the price they had paid for Jordan, they were soon eating their words. Jordan's first season couldn't have gone much better. Averaging 28.2 points per game he became a favourite with fans, even those of opposing teams, and led to him being voted in as an All-Star in only his rookie season and, just a month into his career, he was on the front cover of *Sports Illustrated*, with the headline 'A Star is Born'. The attention he received soon led to jealousy among other players and during the All-Star game he was 'frozen out' by his teammate who wouldn't pass him the ball. Jordan's refusal to let it affect him only drew more praise. Despite finishing the season 38-44, and losing in the first round of the play-offs in four games to the Milwaukee Bucks, attendances at Chicago Stadium had doubled and the year ended on a high for Jordan when he was voted Rookie of the Year.

The Jordan effect wasn't just making waves in the NBA; it also had a profound effect on Nike. As a company Nike had gotten used to slow linear processes, but to get the Air Jordan out in time Rob Strasser knew he would have to shake things up and get his departments working simultaneously to meet the tight deadline. Forming the 'Launch Group', he created a whole new way of developing a product that bypassed previously lengthy processes and resulted in a new shoe that, although it wasn't particularly advanced, would reach the market on time. Initially Nike's sales people

questioned it. With their focus on beating Reebok, what they wanted was an answer to the Freestyle, not a basketball shoe. There were also concerns that having the smallest Air capsule to go into a Nike shoe yet, it barely merited the 'Air' name, but as Peter Moore had designed it to be lower to the ground as Jordan had requested, it was the only solution.

When the Air Jordan I was released in April 1985 it was sold only in speciality sporting goods stores in seven cities for the unheard-of price of $65 a pair. But the price clearly didn't put anyone off. People lined up to buy them and many even bought sizes that didn't fit them just to own a pair. Some sold theirs minutes after buying them for double the retail price. By May, Nike had sold $70 million worth of Jordan shoes and by the end of the year the Air Jordan brand alone had made over $100 million in sales. The previous year's sales for the entire Nike company had been $150 million, meaning the Air Jordan line alone had made a staggering two-thirds of the main brand's revenue. It had been the most successful athlete endorsement in history.

With adidas now fast disappearing from the basketball courts, they could only reflect on the chance they had let slip through their fingers. Most experts feel that even if the Germans had signed Jordan, it would not have been the fairytale partnership that he continues to enjoy with Nike. However, there is little doubt that adidas's passing on Jordan was the critical point at which Nike began to dominate the sports business.

Such is the impact of Jordan and Nike on sport and culture that in 2014 Jordan brand sales had risen by 12.5 per cent on the previous year to $2.6 billion, eight times those of the number two best-selling shoes of LeBron James. Considering that Jordan hadn't played in the NBA for over 10 years and that many buyers never saw him play, the power of the Jordan and Nike relationship remains as potent as ever.

Left Nike Air Jordan I (Northampton Museum Collection).

WIMBLEDON GOES BOOM BOOM
1985 WIMBLEDON CHAMPIONSHIPS

PUMA BORIS BECKER

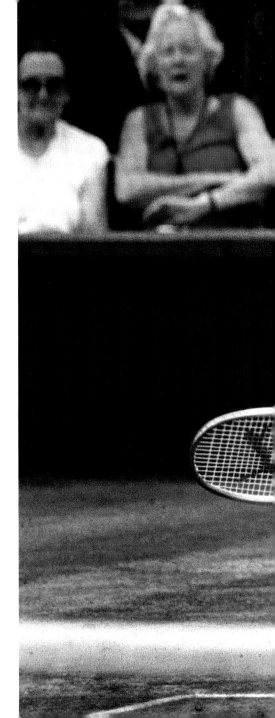

After his defeat at the hands of a 17-year-old German boy in the 1985 pre-Wimbledon Queen's Club tournament, few took South African Johan Kriek seriously when he said, 'If he plays like that, he'll win Wimbledon.' In an era when Wimbledon champions were usually closer in age to 30 than 20, the very idea of such a young champion seemed laughable. But, as the world was about to find out, Boris 'Boom Boom' Becker was certainly no child.

In 1984, Armin Dassler of Puma made a decision. Puma would make tennis rackets. Tennis was booming and besides, his cousins at adidas across the river in Herzogenaurach were already making tennis rackets, so why not? But with Guillermo Villas, Puma's headline male player, now in the twilight of his career, he needed a new player to go with the new rackets. Ion Tiriac, the Romanian former tennis player, mentioned that he was managing a young German prodigy by the name of Boris Becker, who in training at Monte Carlo had wiped the floor with Villas. Intrigued, Armin asked to meet him.

However, as Becker was already playing with adidas rackets and shoes, Tiriac's first meeting in Herzogenaurch was not with Armin but with his cousin, Horst. Tiriac is said to have demanded 400,000 marks (approximately $200,000) per season, an incredible amount for an unknown player ranked 750th in the world. Naturally, Horst refused. Besides, as far as he was concerned, with Stefan Edberg wearing three stripes they already had the world's best player. Tiriac headed over the river to Puma and, knowing of the enmity between Armin and Horst, goaded Armin, saying, 'Go on, take on Boris, that'll really make your cousin mad.' Despite the high price, the chance to get one over his cousin was too good to miss and Armin agreed to the fee.

Boris Becker now likes to call 7 July his second birthday, but as he walked out on to Wimbledon's Centre Court and headed for his 'lucky chair' that day in 1985, any thoughts of victory were probably far behind the hope that the final wouldn't be as dramatic as his journey to it. In the third round his opponent, Joakim Nystrom, had twice served for the match but Becker managed to take it to a fifth set, which he won 9-7. In the fourth round, facing Tim Mayotte, he was ready to concede the match after badly twisting his ankle but was persuaded by Tiriac to take a rest break, tape up his ankle and continue. He did so and won the

Right Always attempting to cover every inch of the court, Boris Becker became well-known for his tumbles, which here show off his signature Pumas.

match 6-3, 4-6, 6-7, 7-6, 6-2. After a less strenuous win over Henri Leconte in the quarter-finals, he faced Anders Jarryd in the semis and, after being a set and a break down, came through to win the rain-delayed match 6-3, 6-7, 7-6, 6-4.

His opponent in the final was the South African Kevin Curren. On his route to the final Curren had taken the scalps of two former Wimbledon champions, John McEnroe and Jimmy Connors, in straight sets, and the winner of the Australian Open, Stefan Edberg, making the 8th seed favourite in the minds of most. The fact the 27-year-old had 10 years on 'the boy' also served to make him the obvious choice.

Curren too appeared to believe he was favourite – rather than resting the night before he had been to a Bruce Springsteen concert. But all thoughts of his evening off were soon gone when Becker broke his serve in the very first game. He was not alone in being surprised when the 17-year-old won the first set comfortably, 6-3. Becker had immediately settled into the game and Curren quickly realized this would be no walkover against an inexperienced foe and that he would need to step up his game. He did, and took the second set 7-6 after winning the tiebreak. In the third Curren was a break up and starting to think that Becker would now begin to crumble. But nothing could be further from the truth as he discovered that Becker was also able to step up his

game. Becker took the set in a tiebreak that showcased his soon-to-be trademark style, with the German diving and stretching for balls that most players would have given up.

Becker opened the fourth set by breaking Curren again, playing every bit like a man of much greater years. His lack of experience only appeared to show when serving for the title in the fourth set. He began with a double fault, won the next three points with his huge serve, but then served up another double fault. There was now only one Championship point remaining. As Becker said afterwards, 'I just started looking up, and I started praying: "God, give me a first serve, because I don't know what I'm going to do with that second serve."' His prayers were obviously answered because he took the victory with a final thunderbolt.

Armin Dassler's decision to sign Becker turned out to be a prescient one. In the week after his win Puma sold 10,000 tennis rackets, despite the fact they were actually Villas' signature rackets. When Becker signature rackets were hastily launched, along with Becker signature shoes, they sold another 300,000.

While many thought that Becker's win at such a young age might open the floodgates to other young Wimbledon champions, it wasn't the case. Making his achievement even more remarkable is the fact that players of the calibre of Andre Agassi, Pete Sampras and Roger Federer never made it past the first round aged 17. To date he remains the youngest-ever male Wimbledon Champion.

Below Puma Boris Becker Ace, worn by
Boris Becker (Wimbledon Museum).

McENROE GETS CROSS
1986 VOLVO INVITATIONAL

NIKE AIR TRAINER 1

John McEnroe was completely burned out. Between 1979 and 1985 he had won a total of 14 Grand Slam singles and doubles titles but the gruelling pressures of life on the tour had finally got the better of him. He had also recently had a son with the American actress Tatum O'Neal and was keen to spend time with his new family. So, in 1986, he decided to take a sabbatical from tennis.

Six months later, newly married and feeling refreshed, McEnroe was ready to get back on court after his break and began preparing for his comeback tournament (and honeymoon) at the Volvo International at the Stratton Mountain Resort in Vermont. As he prepared for his return, McEnroe was sent the Nike Air Trainer 1, a new kind of sports shoe called a 'Cross Trainer'. McEnroe had been one of the company's highest profile stars since 1978, and they were keen to get his opinion on their new prototype shoe.

It had been designed by Nike's architect-turned-designer, Tinker Hatfield, after he noticed that his fellow gym members were performing a number of different activities in shoes that were only suitable for one of them. Running

Left John McEnroe wearing Air Trainer 1s, which he described as the best tennis shoes Nike ever made.

shoes were obviously perfect for running-based activities but didn't provide the kind of support needed when lifting weights, for example. He was also increasingly fed up with having to bring four different pairs of shoes to the gym: one for running, one for weights, one for basketball and another for tennis. After giving it some thought he realized that the answer lay in a single shoe that could be worn for a number of activities, a 'cross' trainer.

Despite his bosses being unconvinced by the idea, Hatfield set about designing his cross trainer from the ground up. Basketball shoes at the time were fairly flat, with an 8mm heel lift, while running shoes had a higher lift, of 12 to 15mm, so Hatfield designed the new shoe to be in the sweet spot between the two, with enough heel lift for running but also low enough to provide great stability. With a mid-top's height it provided great support but also allowed plenty of ankle dexterity. It also featured a Velcro strap for increased forefoot support and external midsole supports to provide lateral support and stability. Like most Nike models at the time the Air Trainer 1 also featured the brand's Air capsule technology. It was like nothing that Nike had previously made before, looking like a cross between a tennis shoe and a basketball shoe.

The colourway of the prototype was also inspired by

Below Nike Air Trainer 1 'Chlorophyll', signed by John McEnroe (Nike Archive).

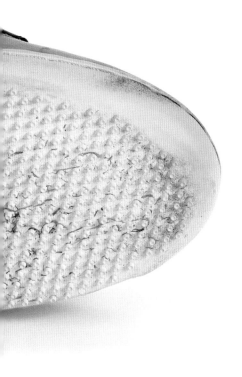

Hatfield's gym trips. He had noticed that gym equipment at the time tended to be black and white with green text. Made from black premium leather, grey suede and with green accents, the 'Chlorophyll' design as it came to be known, fitted right in. The end result was a shoe that combined three, perhaps even four shoes in one, and could be used in the gym, on court, for weight lifting and for running. No wonder the Nike execs remained unconvinced.

However, unbeknownst to them, the running boom that had started in the 1970s which had left a legacy of runners well into the 1980s, was now coming to an end. With time becoming even more precious, the idea of spending hours running in parks or on the streets began to seem frivolous. Appealing to time-poor people, health clubs and leisure centres began opening up in which people could do a wide range of exercises, efficiently planned out for them by personal trainers. Being a health club member was part of the desirable 'yuppie' lifestyle and dressing in the right sportswear when there was essential, meaning a new demographic of people were emerging, who were turning the whole pursuit of health and fitness into a fashion show.

Although McEnroe understood that the Air Trainer 1 was just a prototype and wasn't even a tennis-specific shoe, as soon as he tried it on, it immediately felt right for him. Feeling that basketball style high-tops were too high, but low-tops were outdated and too small, he loved the mid-top cut-off, as it was the best of both worlds. He also loved the mid-foot strap because he preferred his shoes to be tight and the strap allowed him to easily adjust them. The cherry on the cake was the shoe's comfort. Admitting that he was 'starting to get a bit older and could use some more of that support and cushion', the Air Trainer 1 fitted the bill perfectly.

Even though he had been told that the development prototype shoes were not to be worn in competition McEnroe, being McEnroe, decided he was going to wear them in his upcoming tournament. When Hatfield saw on television that McEnroe was wearing them he couldn't believe it. 'It was a jaw-dropping experience for me because I didn't know he was going to wear them. Nobody did,' he remembers. 'He wasn't supposed to. He just did it.' When McEnroe was asked to return the shoes he was his usual defiant self and protested, saying, 'These are the best tennis shoes you ass-holes have ever made!' With that kind of endorsement it was difficult for the top brass at Nike not to put them into production, especially as McEnroe had won the doubles trophy in them. Thanks to his endorsement, the Air Trainer 1 was released for public consumption in 1987, creating the cross-trainer market, a whole new category of sports shoe that dominated the floors of gyms and health clubs throughout the 1990s.

AS GOOD AS GOLD
1988 STEFFI GRAF'S GOLDEN SLAM

ADIDAS GRAND SLAM

It's often said that records are made to be broken but there are some achievements that look like they may never be surpassed. One of those is Steffi Graf's 1988 season, when she became the only woman to date to achieve a Golden Slam by winning all four majors and Olympic Gold in one calendar year.

Her first taste of tennis came at the age of three when she began practising with her father at home using a racket with the end sawn off. They used the couch as a net, and if Steffi was able to rally for 25 shots she was rewarded with an ice cream – but when the living-room furniture started to suffer, her father had to take her to a real tennis court. By the age of five, she was already winning tournaments, and from there her progression was almost unprecedented. At the age of 13 she became a pro, beat Martina Navratilova and Chris Evert aged 16, won her first major at 17 and was ranked world No. 1 by the age of 18.

In 1985 it was clear to adidas's Horst Dassler that Graf was something special. Having passed up the chance to sign Boris Becker, he wanted to be sure he signed Germany's new tennis prodigy and she was duly equipped with one of adidas's latest innovations, the peg system. Her custom-made Grand Slam shoes featured a midsole with three lateral holes that could be filled with pegs made

of materials of different densities that allowed the wearer to change the level of cushioning and support. This made them ideal when playing on a variety of different surfaces, and Graf quickly fell in love with the shoes.

Before the 1988 season, Graf had led the younger challengers in the generational battle against the older established players such as Navratilova and Evert. Between them they had completely dominated women's tennis from the mid-1970s and throughout the 1980s. Despite increasingly coming under fire from the new generation, no one had been able to consistently and convincingly force them to cede their crowns. But 1988 was to be the year when Steffi Graf would finally knock them off their perches.

Given her nationality, many liked to compare Graf's abilities to those of a certain luxury car: powerful, precise, balanced and agile. But, as she was about to demonstrate, she was more like a force of nature, a tornado that would destroy anything that stood in her way. She began her path of destruction at the Australian Open at the newly opened Flinders Park. It's new and bouncy surface suited Graf's powerful forehand and reaching the final she took down the first of the old guard, Chris Evert, not losing a single set during the entire tournament.

At the French Open Graf was mighty once again, repeating her Australian Open feat by not dropping a set as she marched relentlessly to the final. In the final, she devastated Natasha Zvereva, tossing her aside in just 32 minutes in a 6-0, 6-0 humiliation, the first ever 'double bagel' in French Open final history. As she accepted her trophy Graf apologized to the crowd, 'I'm very sorry it was so fast'.

Graf's victories and her popularity made her a dream athlete for adidas's marketing people. The Steffi Graf clothing collection they had introduced as far back as 1987 continued to be one of the company's most popular tennis ranges and she remained involved in its design and development throughout her career. The same was also true of her shoes and, unbeknownst to most, her love affair with the Grand Slam shoe had secretly continued even after it had been replaced with a new design. So keen was Graf on the comfort of the Grand Slam that for her own playing shoes she insisted that adidas keep the peg system midsole of the Grand Slam but mate it with

Opposite Steffi Graf serving in adidas Grand Slams during her gold medal-winning performance at the 1988 Seoul Olympic Games.

the upper of its replacement model, so that it appeared to be adidas's latest model. This kept the marketing people happy and allowed Graf to retain the feel and comfort of the shoes she had got so used to winning in.

Despite having won the last two majors, many were sure that in the final at Wimbledon against Martina Navratilova Graf wouldn't have it so easy. Having won six consecutive women's singles there, the hallowed lawns almost seemed like Martina's own backyard. After the first set, it looked like the reign of the 'Queen of the Green' wouldn't be ending anytime soon when Graf lost the first set, the first she had lost in a major that year. But in the second set, with Navratilova serving at 2-0 up, Steffi broke back. The Graf tornado began to spin and she proceeded to win nine games in a row. Her speed on the court and ability to reach balls most would miss made Navratilova look a little ponderous. After Graf took her first Wimbledon title, 5-7, 6-2, 6-1, Navratilova later reflected, 'It was like trying to stop a runaway train.'

Having dethroned the two queens of tennis, it was fitting that at the US Open Graf met one of her own generation in the final, Gabriela Sabatini. What would make this final different was that Sabatini was a friend, as well as Graf's doubles partner. However, with the prospect of becoming only the third woman to win a calendar grand slam foremost on her mind, any sentiment was cast aside and she defeated Sabatini 6-3, 3-6, 6-1. Only six years after

her debut, she had achieved the holy grail of tennis.

While in most years the US Open marked the end of the majors season, in 1988 tennis became an Olympic sport once again after a 64-year absence, meaning there was one more prize in Graf's sights, a gold medal. Making her imperious way to the final in Seoul, South Korea, Graf found herself up against Sabatini once again. In New York she had given her friend a glimmer of hope when she lost the second set, but this time Sabatini had almost no hope and Graf defeated her 6-3, 6-3 to win the gold medal and achieve the Golden Slam.

Sadly, Horst Dassler wasn't to witness Graf's golden year, having passed away from cancer in 1987, aged only 51. In the days before his death, despite being very ill and in hospital, as usual the future of adidas was foremost on his mind. Keen to re-sign Graf but also to get a good deal, he had initially instructed Thomas Bach (the future IOC president) to draw out the negotiations with her father but when he realized his time was running out, he told Bach to finalize the deal as quickly as possible in order to ensure that the company retained her services. No doubt he would have been overjoyed at her success and the fact that she remained an adidas ambassador long after her retirement. Despite a stellar career that still sees her hailed as the greatest female tennis player of all time, Graf says she rarely has the time to look back on her playing career, she is far too busy being a full-time mother.

PUMP UP AND AIR OUT
1991 NBA SLAM DUNK CONTEST

REEBOK THE PUMP

In the second half of the 1980s the unthinkable happened. Just as Nike had knocked adidas off top spot powered by the success of the Freestyle, Reebok had replaced Nike as the number one sports shoe maker in the world. But Nike wasn't taking it lying down and by 1989 the success of the Air Jordan range and its new Air Max 1 and Air Trainer 1 ranges was propelling the Oregonians back in Reebok's direction.

Reebok's CEO Paul Fireman was only too aware that Nike were hot on their heels and knew he couldn't count on the Freestyle to keep them on top. Having seen how Nike's Air technology was getting attention with its fusion of science and comfort, he felt that Reebok needed its own unique technology. Inspired by a prototype of a combination ski boot and shoe that Ellesse USA (which Reebok had acquired) were working on, based around an inflatable air splint, Fireman briefed Paul Litchfield, an engineer in the company's R&D department, to look into developing a customizable shoe with an adjustable air bladder.

Working together with design firm Design Continuum,

Litchfield found the biggest problem was how to keep air stable but flexible in a sealed pouch. Drawing on medical technology, Litchfield and his designers used a blood pressure cuff's air bladder to create a shoe whose fit was customizable depending on how much air was pumped into it. Not only did it improve comfort, it was a solution to the foot and ankle problems common in basketball.

Litchfield created two prototypes: one inflated manually and the other inflated as the wearer walked. He preferred the automatic version because it gave the impression the shoe was 'intelligent', but when local basketball teams tested the prototypes, they overwhelmingly preferred the manual version because it allowed the wearer to fine-tune the amount of inflation they wanted. It also made a cool hissing sound when deflated. The prototypes were far from pretty, however, and Litchfield worked with Paul Brown, Reebok's vice-president of design, to make them more visually appealing. One of Brown's ideas was to make the pump mechanism look like a basketball, which product testers loved.

When the shoe was launched at a trade show in 1989 Paul Fireman hailed it as 'the Freestyle of the 1990s' and it immediately caught the interest of the sports shoe trade. But at the same show Nike launched a very similar

customizable air pocket product they called 'Air Pressure'. Fireman and Litchfield were worried that they had been beaten to the punch but were reassured when they realized that Nike's system had a literal Achilles heel; with no on-board pumping mechanism it needed an external inflator to inflate it. Knowing that it wouldn't take long for Nike to realize their mistake Fireman wasted no time and instructed Litchfield to have The Pump ready to go into production by November that year, giving him only eight months to get it ready.

The Pump's production process was complicated. The shoes were made in Korea, but the air bladders were manufactured by a medical supplies company in Massachusetts. This meant Litchfield would get a shipment of bladders, test them twice, then send them to Korea to be sewn into the shoes. The Korean manufacturer would test them again before sewing them in, and then again after the shoe had been assembled to check that the air bladders hadn't been punctured during the sewing process. The first batch of 7,000 shoes ordered by Footlocker arrived in Boston on time but when they were given their final pre-delivery test it was discovered they had a fundamental problem: they wouldn't inflate. Litchfield received a panicked phone call from the warehouse and immediately headed over. After he inspected a few pairs the reason became clear. The shoe factory had decided to use a sewing machine (without the needle, of course) to test the pump but in the process had damaged it by kinking the plastic mould. Litchfield and a team of six had to remove the stitches, take out the damaged pumps, replace them with new ones and sew them back up, for all 7,000 pairs. Incredibly, they still managed to deliver on time.

The Pump's launch in November 1989 was immediately controversial. Not because of its technology, but because it was priced at $170, an incredible price for a sports shoe at the time. While the high price was in part due to Reebok needing to recoup its development costs, it was also due to the fact that sports shoes had become an aspirational status symbol, a sign of difference on the streets. So much so that people were even being mugged for their shoes. Reebok knew that if The Pump became the number one must-have shoe, people would be willing to pay the price for them.

The Pump quickly won the battle with Nike's Air Pressure. Nike's shoe didn't look anywhere near as good as The Pump and was a flop as soon as it launched. While many thought that The Pump was just a gimmick, Reebok rolled out an ad campaign based around the idea that no two feet were the same and that The Pump allowed wearers to custom-fit their shoes to suit their feet and requirements. The advertising described how a right foot might need 21 'pumps' while the left foot might only need 16. Another campaign specifically targeted Nike's Air technology and

Michael Jordan and featured Reebok's star basketball player Dominique Wilkins goading his rival by saying, 'Michael, my man, if you want to fly first class, pump up and air out!' Another featured tennis star Michael Chang taunting his Nike-sponsored rival Andre Agassi by saying, 'If you want to beat those rock 'n' roll tennis guys, pump up and air out!' Nike attempted to downplay the Air Pressure's almost immediate death and explained it away as having been intended only for players with ankle problems, hence the small production run of only 35,000 pairs. Reebok lapped it up, however, and featured the Air Pressure in a TV commercial that depicted a bungee-jumping Air Pressure wearer plummeting to his presumed death, while The Pump wearer stayed safely in his shoes. The advert was soon banned, only adding to The Pump's perceived coolness. By the end of 1990, Nike had orders totalling only $10 million for the Air Pressure. The Pump in comparison had $500 million.

The moment that really crowned The Pump as the winner in the inflatable wars happened in February 1991 at the NBA Slam Dunk Contest held in Charlotte, North Carolina, close to Michael Jordan's alma mater. Dee Brown, a relatively unknown rookie guard with the Boston Celtics, had been called up at the last moment when another player had to drop out. Being the contest's underdog, he wanted to get the crowd behind him, so as he prepared for his jumps, to the crowd's amusement he began pumping up his Reebok Omni Zone IIs before going on to perform the contest's most spectacular dunks. The crowd and

the watching TV audience loved it and the underdog and his shoes sealed his stealing of the show when having already won the title on points, he unleashed his soon-to-be legendary 'no-look' dunk with his forearm across his eyes. Brown and The Pump were a sensation. Without any prompting from Reebok he had made the shoes part of the show and had visibly demonstrated them in front of a global audience.

The impact of what he had done hadn't gone unnoticed by the biggest name in the game. Back at his hotel during the after-party, Brown later recalled meeting one of his heroes, Michael Jordan, who congratulated him but also had a warning for him, saying, 'You did a great job out there, young fella, but you know you started a shoe war. And as much as I want to crush you on the court, I'm gonna have to crush you off the court.'

Despite the warning, by the end of 1991 Reebok's sales had increased by 26 per cent to $2.7 billion and it was estimated that if The Pump was a brand on its own it would be number four in the industry. Pump technology was incorporated across many of Reebok's lines, finding its way into shoes for tennis, running, golf and aerobics, which was still Reebok's cornerstone. It remains one of the standout technologies of the 1980s that characterized one of the most fiercely competitive times in the sports shoe industry when brands battled each other using creativity and technology rather than nostalgia. While its popularity has waxed and waned over time, more than 20 years later The Pump still remains a part of Reebok's product line-up.

Left Reebok The Pump
(Reebok Archive).

NO HALF MEASURES
1992 VANS FANS CREATE THE HALF CAB

VANS HALF CAB

From the day it first opened its doors the Vans shoe company has listened to its customers. From custom-made Style #44 Authentics to the development of the Style #95 Era skateboarding shoe, the Van Doren brothers have always tried to create products that were a direct response to what their customers wanted and after Vans skater Steve Caballero noticed that skaters were modifying his signature Vans Caballero high-top, Vans gave the fans exactly what they wanted once again in the form of the legendary Half Cab.

When Steve Caballero first caught former Z-Boy Stacy Peralta's attention at a national skateboarding competition it wasn't because he had won. Finishing in fifth place, he hadn't even come close, but what impressed Peralta was his 'fire'. He was the smallest skater that he had ever seen yet as Peralta describes, 'He was doing things he shouldn't have been able to do.' Born in November 1964, Caballero had started off riding BMX after being inspired by Evel Knievel but began skating aged 12, just as skate parks started appearing all over California. It was while skating for the Campbell Skate Park team that Peralta first spotted him.

Peralta had recently co-founded the skateboard maker Powell Peralta and was looking to create a competition team. But instead of established pros he wanted unknown amateurs that he could help develop and Caballero was exactly the kind of skater he was looking for. Peralta's new team was named the Bones Brigade and although he didn't know it at the time, they would go on to become legends in the sport. The first members included Caballero, Tommy Guerrero, Tony Hawk, Mike McGill, Lance Mountain and Rodney Mullen, six kids who between them would dominate the sport. Peralta drove the team all over California to compete in competitions and they were soon winning trophies and became a constant presence in skate magazines, becoming heroes and an inspiration to thousands of American skaters.

Despite being a close unit, the excellence of each member of the team drove all of them to improve and they constantly created new tricks and manoeuvres like the McTwist, the Flatground Ollie and the 360 Flip. Caballero's contribution was the Caballerial. Feeling he had reached a point where he knew every trick in the book, Caballero decided to try something different by taking a half-pipe ollie (a leap where the rider 'pops' the tail of the board to cause it to jump) and performing a 360-degree spin in the air. The move was described as a game changer because it was done without hands and showed other skaters that they could perform aerial tricks without needing to grab on to the board.

As the Bones Brigade began to make names for themselves in the sport and develop a following, Peralta started to think about ways to market and advertise them, and with his interest in film-making decided to make a video. Titled *The Bones Brigade Video Show* it was popular enough to spawn a series of films that became cult classics in the skating community, heightening the fame of the Brigade members and making them stars.

Towards the end of the 1980s skating as a sport began to die. Skate parks across America were being ripped up, in part due to bad design and also because of rocketing insurance prices. Many pro-skaters suddenly found themselves jobless and companies like Vans, who had a huge following in the skate community, began to suffer. But a new era started when skaters began to build half-pipes in their own backyards and gardens and the sport started growing again. Needing to rein in its spending, it was around this time that Vans stopped giving shoes away to popular skaters. A flood of competitors who were selling cheaper imitations and knock-offs of the brand's designs forced the

Opposite Still skating in his fifties, Steve Caballero's Half Cab shoes remain one of Vans' most popular lines.

company to drop its prices, meaning every pair of shoes sold was generating a loss. But as skating began to recover and the US authorities shut down several counterfeit shoe operations, the company began to recover too.

Having got through their problems and knowing the power of endorsement, Vans were keen to reconnect with the skating community and in 1988 they approached the now-legendary Caballero with the offer of a sponsorship deal. Having worn their shoes since 1977, it was an easy decision for him to sign. A few months later they approached him again, this time with the idea of creating a Caballero signature model, about which he was delighted. But when he looked through his contract he realized that it was structured in such a way that the more Caballero shoes they sold, the lower his percentage of royalties became. Having earned $1 per board from Powell Peralta, this just didn't make sense to Caballero. Although keen on the sponsorship deal, he was unsure about the royalties, as he didn't want to feel he was being ripped off. However, Vans were insistent and when Caballero spoke to his friend, fellow Bones Brigade rider Lance Mountain, he suggested that he either, 'not get ripped off and make no money, or get ripped off and make a lot of money'. And so Caballero signed.

When working on the design of his signature model Caballero was inspired by hi-top shoes like the Vans Style #138 and Nike's Air Jordan that he and many other skaters had been wearing. He was keen to create a shoe that had a similar hi-top basketball-style silhouette but with the traits of the traditional Vans-models he had grown up with. Vans were keen to include a nod to the dragon that had been Caballero's board symbol (he was born in the Year of the Dragon) and so part of the upper was made from a textured material that looked like 'dragon skin'.

Launched in 1989, the Caballero became popular with skaters but came at a time where the sport was changing and street skating was becoming more popular than the original vertical style. Caballero began to see a trend where street skaters were cutting off the hi-top part of their shoes and duct-taping it to make it a mid-top, giving them more dexterity and mobility. Caballero himself began doing this but after his third pair became fed up with it and got in touch with Vans to suggest they started making a new 'half' version of the Caballero. A lower-cut version of the shoe was clearly what skaters wanted and Vans were keen to give it to them. In coming up with a new logo for the shoe depicting him doing his signature Half Cab trick, Caballero also ended up naming the new shoe.

When it was launched in 1992 the Half Cab was a hit and played a big role in resurrecting the fortunes of Vans. Over the years it has been made available in hundreds of different colourways and collaborations. For its 20th anniversary in 2012 Vans released limited edition specials every month for a year, including 20 that were hand-cut and duct-taped by Steve Caballero himself and sold exclusively by Supreme. More than 20 years later the Half Cab is still a favourite with skaters and Steve Caballero is still riding with Vans.

THE DISC GAMBLE
1993 IAAF WORLD CHAMPIONSHIPS

PUMA DISC

As he prepared for the final of 110m hurdles at the 1993 World Championships in Stuttgart, Colin Jackson had an important decision to make. Should he wear Puma's latest Disc shoes or not? Reviews had described them as a 'love 'em or hate 'em' shoe, echoing the thoughts of other athletes and even some of the public. Jackson's Great Britain teammate Linford Christie had refused to try them, seeing them at best as a gimmick and at worst a liability. With a gold medal at stake, Jackson's decision was critical.

In the late 1980s Puma had been in dire straits. Mounting debts and poor sales had led to the company being put in the hands of Deutsche Bank. Armin Dassler and his sons had been forced out of the company their father and grandfather had founded. The company had then changed hands a number of times before being bought by Swedish investment company Proventus. Puma's problem was that it was now deemed a 'cheap' brand. Half of all sales came from shoes in lower price ranges that only generated minimal profits. To achieve success once again, Puma needed to break back into the premium markets that it had once dominated alongside its neighbour adidas, but were now the domain of Nike and Reebok.

In the spring of 1992 Puma's senior management presented the technology that they hoped would help take

them back to where they once belonged: the Puma 'Disc', the world's first laceless sports shoe. Using a system of internal wires it allowed the wearer to fine-tune the fit of the shoe using a disc 'dial' mechanism and, as Puma put it, 'making you and shoe become one'. The system had originally been created as a ski-boot locking system and Puma had bought the technology from its Swiss patent holder. With a sole made from a new material called Hypalon, it also boasted being lighter, stronger and offering better cushioning and impact absorption than traditional neoprene-based soles.

It was pitched to dealers as a high-tech product that would compete with the likes of Reebok's Pump and Nike's Air Pressure technologies and, backed by an expensive launch campaign, was a hit as soon as it hit the shelves, despite its high price tag of 120 marks (approximately $75/£50).

Puma signed German athlete Heike Drechsler in time for the 1992 Olympic Games in Barcelona and she was fascinated by the new Disc system. When the company decided to introduce it on a running spike she was keen

Right Colin Jackson's gamble pays off, as he wins the 110m hurdles final at the 1993 World Championships in Puma Discs.

to be the first to try it. Wearing the Disc, she took the gold medal in the long jump with a length of 7.14m. The Disc had won its first gold.

While Drechsler's victory had been great PR for the Disc and it had initially sold well, it had a fundamental problem: it didn't work properly. Having been rushed to market, despite extensive testing many of the first batch of mass-market shoes were jamming and customers were angrily returning them to the stores. Puma's latest technology appeared to be a failure. Who could blame Linford Christie for not wanting to try them?

It was in the face of this scepticism that Colin Jackson needed to make his decision. As a hurdler his shoes were arguably even more critical to his performance than they were in other running disciplines. His performances in the previous two years hadn't been great but he now had a good shot at winning the title. Dare he risk gambling a gold medal on the Disc? He made the decision to give it a try. Jackson hurdled his way to the biggest achievement of his career, taking the gold medal and also breaking the world record that had stood since 1972 with a time of 12.91. On the world stage Jackson and the Disc had proved the doubters wrong.

As history shows, the Disc wasn't to be the wonder technology that saved Puma nor did it go on to replace laces. However, it did establish itself as a popular and ultimately reliable technology in Puma's running and lifestyle ranges, and over 20 years after its launch its latest incarnation was worn by Puma athletes at the 2016 Rio Olympic Games.

Right Puma Disc, worn by Colin Jackson. (Puma Archive)

SKIPPY'S NEW BOOTS
1994 CRAIG JOHNSTON INVENTS THE PREDATOR

ADIDAS PREDATOR

'You are the worst footballer I have ever seen in my life,' was the feedback that Jack Charlton had for the 15-year-old Australian Craig Johnston after a trial at Middlesborough in 1975. Harsh, but it was to be the beginning of a career that saw Johnston play for one of the world's greatest football clubs and along the way reinvent the football boot.

Johnston was undeterred by Charlton's comments and spent all his spare time practising his ball skills in Middlesbrough's Ayresome Park car park. But things changed when John Neal took over. He was impressed by Johnston's dedication and skill and put him straight into the first team. Aged just 17, he became the club's youngest ever player. After four years at Middlesbrough Johnston was bought by Bob Paisley, manager of the First Division champions Liverpool, on the recommendation of Graeme Souness.

At a time when foreign players were still a novelty he was considered 'exotic' by his new teammates, but his talent and hard work quickly led to him becoming a favourite with

players and supporters, who soon nicknamed him 'Skippy'. During his time with the club he won five First Division Championships, three League Cups and the European Cup. He also became the first Australian to score in the FA Cup final at Wembley in 1986, when Liverpool beat Everton 3-1.

Just days before the 1988 FA Cup final against Wimbledon, Johnston shocked his team by announcing his retirement. His manager Kenny Dalglish was incensed but on discovering the reason for his decision gave him his blessing. Earlier that year Johnston's sister had became seriously ill and had fallen into a coma after an accident in Morocco. He wanted to return home to support his family and help provide round-the-clock care for his sister.

Back in Australia, Johnston began coaching a group of children who had asked him to train them. During his sessions he instructed them to try and swerve the ball by 'brushing' it like a table tennis player did with their bat. But when they complained that swerving the ball with leather boots wasn't very effective, Johnston had a eureka moment. Rushing home, he took the rubber off a table tennis bat and glued it to his boots. He discovered that when he kicked the ball, the rubber engaged with the surface of the ball and gave him a new level of control. He spent the next three years and over £250,000 on prototypes

and a patent, before perfecting his boot, which featured rubber ridges that he had designed himself to provide the grip that allowed players to swerve the ball. He was now ready to present his revolutionary new boots to the world.

Johnston went to adidas, Puma, Nike and Reebok with the boots, but none of them showed much interest. Disappointed but undaunted, he decided that he needed to demonstrate the boot to them so that they could see for themselves why it was such a leap forward. Interrupting a boardroom meeting at Bayern Munich, he managed to convince Franz Beckenbauer, Karl-Heinz Rummenigge and Paul Breitner to try his boots. Bringing a video camera with him, Johnston filmed them as they tried them in the snow. They quickly understood the potential and demonstrated on camera the improved control and swerve the boots gave them.

Of all the brands that had rejected him, Johnston felt that only adidas had showed any understanding of the boot. In some respects this was hardly surprising because as far back as the 1960s, adidas had experimented with prototype football boots that featured rubber spikes and even sharkskin on the forefoot to create more swerve and precision. Feeling sure that the Germans could still be persuaded, Johnston headed back to adidas and

Opposite Scotland's John Collins (left), the first person to score a goal in adidas Predators, tackles England's David Beckham (right), who helped develop them and played in them for much of his career.

interrupted yet another board meeting. Persuading them to view the video, when it was over, the entire room is said to have stood up and applauded. He was offered a deal on the spot.

What Johnston hadn't realized was that at the time adidas was only just getting back on its feet after the most difficult period in its history. The passing of Horst Dassler in 1987 at the age of only 51 following a battle with cancer had left the company paralysed. Without leadership, under attack from Nike and Reebok and losing money, adidas had been plagued by family infighting and a disastrous spell under French entrepreneur Bernard Tapie had left the company insolvent. The answer to the company's problems ironically lay in two men who were partly responsible for putting adidas in its ailing position in the first place.

As Nike's marketing and creative directors, Rob Strasser and Peter Moore had been part of the team that had helped Nike grow from selling running shoes out of the back of a car to the No. 1 sports brand in the world. After becoming disillusioned with life at Nike they had started their own business but soon found themselves joining their former competitor and spearheading its revival. They introduced two lines that were literally to save adidas: Equipment and Originals. More a philosophy than a range, Equipment was a range of products that took adidas back to what it knew best, making pure sports products with genuine advantages and no gimmicks. If Equipment was a new philosophy, then Originals was a return to an old one. Particularly in America and Japan, young people were clamouring for vintage-style sportswear and shoes like adidas's Gazelle and Superstar

became sought-after again. Seeing a potential whole new market for its most popular ranges from the past, the Originals line was created to breathe life into classics for a new generation of adidas fans.

Alongside the Equipment ranges it was felt that what adidas needed was a 'wow' product that could restore their reputation for innovation and, when Johnston presented his invention to the board, they knew they had found it. The new boot was tested in a converted swimming pool in a school in adidas's home town of Herzogenaurach and the results were said to be revolutionary. Together with input from David Beckham, Johnston's prototype was further refined to make it lighter.

Naming the new boot 'Predator', adidas launched it in 1994 with a great fanfare. It was hailed by players and the media alike, as a leap in football boot design and the unprecedented level of control quickly made the boots a players' favourite, winning honours on the feet of numerous great players as well as awards for innovation and design. John Collins of Celtic took the honour of becoming the first ever player to score a goal with them in a match against Rangers in April 1994. However, it was six years later on the feet of David Beckham and Zinedine Zidane during Euro 2000 that the Predator caught the world's imagination when it was used to score one in every four goals during the tournament. After 20 years and numerous evolutions the Predator was finally retired in 2014 but remains a special boot to millions of football players and especially to adidas for its role in the company's revival.

Below adidas Predator, worn by Alexi Lalas (adidas Archive).

FILA GRANT HILL

Grant Hill grew up with great expectations. Born in October 1972, his father Calvin Hill was a Yale graduate and NFL running back, and his mother Janet worked at the Pentagon for the secretary of the army. When he showed an aptitude for basketball at South Lakes High School in Reston, Virginia, his coach was so impressed that he wanted to put him straight into the varsity team despite only being in his first year.

When it was time to decide on a college, Hill's mother wanted him to go to Georgetown, while his father preferred North Carolina, but keen to make his own decision he chose Duke University. Having grown up as an only child, as part of the Duke team he found a family who appreciated his personality and found it was reflected in his play, inspiring and smart but modest and unselfish. Duke had never won a national title but with Hill they stunned everyone to win back-to-back titles in 1991 and 1992. By the time he graduated, Hill was the first player in college history to collect over 1,900 points, 700 rebounds, 400 assists, 200 steals and 100 blocked shots and, in recognition, Duke retired his number 33 jersey.

In the 1994 NBA Draft, Hill was third pick and was drafted by the Detroit Pistons. With Michael Jordan having retired to play baseball, many touted Hill as his natural

Below Fila Grant Hill Olympic (Fondazione Fila Museum).

successor and the antithesis of a new crop of players who looked and played like streetballers rather than college graduates. His clean-cut image and upper-middle-class background appealed not just to the fans and media but also to Italian sportswear brand Fila. After years of relative anonymity in the United States, Fila were making a niche for themselves as a sports fashion label and saw Hill as a way to boost their presence in basketball and overcome their reputation for style at the expense of performance. After signing with Fila, when Hill was voted an All Star and shared the honour of being named Rookie of the Year, his signature shoe began flying off the shelves. It sold 1.5 million pairs, becoming Fila's most successful shoe and the fastest-selling basketball shoe since the Air Jordan I. After leading the All Star voting again in only his second season, helping to take the Pistons to the 1996 play-offs and winning a gold medal with the US Olympic team, Hill was on top of the world. In his third season he was already an icon of the NBA and his second signature model Filas were best-sellers. Even Tupac was wearing them. However, the very qualities that endeared him to Fila and his fans were not so beloved by some of his rivals and Hill was frequently targeted and fouled on court. When the Pistons failed to reach the play-offs in his fourth season, Hill began to receive criticism for lacking toughness and a killer instinct. But with his signature line making in the region of $100 million a year, this didn't dissuade Fila from signing him to an $80 million seven-year deal, second only in size to

Left Grant Hill's style on court was surpassed only by his signature Filas.

Michael Jordan. In an industry experiencing a slowdown in sales across all brands, Fila hoped that by strengthening its relationship with Hill, they would ride out the downturn.

To silence his critics Hill worked harder in the off-season than ever before and helped turn the Pistons around. By spring of 1999 the team were in the play-offs again and Hill was averaging over 25 points per game and drawing compliments from NBA legends. His future never looked brighter. But as the 2000 play-offs approached he began to experience pain in his ankle. Thinking it was just a bone bruise, he played through it but against Miami in the middle of Game 2 he was in such pain that he pulled out of the game in the third quarter. After the game, when he had his ankle X-rayed, his trainer was shocked at what he saw. He had completely broken it. His year was immediately over and so was his contract with the Pistons. As a free agent he moved to the Orlando Magic but was plagued with further ankle injuries that never allowed him to return to his full strength. After an operation that required breaking a bone in his heel to correct the alignment of his legs, he contracted MRSA in hospital and endured a debilitating six-month recovery. Sadly, Hill was never able to reach the level he had before his injury and his time with Orlando and spells with the Phoenix Suns and LA Clippers, while showing promise, were also punctuated with further injuries and health problems.

Looking back on the impact of his early career it's clear the NBA was robbed of one of its most promising talents since Michael Jordan. However, the times he graced the courts with his Filas are still greatly celebrated by sneakerheads for the style and performance they brought to the game.

MESMERIZING
1995/96 NBA CHAMPIONSHIP

REEBOK SHAQNOSIS

It used to be said in the sports shoe trade that, 'big men don't sell sneakers'. It also used to be the case that centres were among the last to get attention from the big sports shoe brands but when Shaquille O'Neal first hit the NBA draft in 1992 as the No. 1 pick, he became the first exception to the rule.

Courted by both Reebok and Nike, O'Neal immediately felt an affinity for Reebok when he visited their HQ in Boston for the first time and was greeted by Reebok staff wearing T-shirts declaring 'WE WANT SHAQ'. He and his manager, Leonard Armato, spent a day talking to CEO Paul Fireman about Reebok's plans for him and while O'Neal was ready to sign there and then, his manager insisted they consider Nike's offer. When O'Neal, his father and Armato visited Nike's headquarters in Oregon, O'Neal already knew who he wanted to sign with and made it clear by wearing a Reebok jacket during the visit, much to the displeasure of both his manager and Nike's Phil Knight but to the great amusement of Paul Fireman, who was said to have been so happy he upped his offer to O'Neal after hearing about it.

Despite their keenness, O'Neal's signing was a gamble for Reebok. At the time the company had no big names in basketball and were staking their future in the sport on a player who was still unproven in the NBA. Their gamble paid off though when O'Neal quickly became the most marketable player in the game and his signature model, the 'Shaq Attaq', became one of Reebok's biggest sellers in 1992.

After four successful Shaq Attaq models, for the 1995/96 NBA season Reebok wanted to try something new. One of Reebok's designers, Jonathan Morris, was working on a design for a shoe that incorporated a new style of cushioning in the footbed. He wanted to create a look for the shoe that emphasized this and created a design based around concentric circles that appeared to be pulsing away from the cushioning with the pattern rippling into the midsole and the upper. He coloured the circles black and white, immediately giving the shoe a bold, striking, almost hypnotic look. When Paul Fireman saw the design he immediately loved it and decided on the spot that it should be Shaquille O'Neal's new signature model instead of a design that was currently in development.

O'Neal was famed for being hands-on with anything that related to the marketing of his name and had even directed one of Reebok's commercials for the Shaq Attaq. He was equally involved with the design of his new shoe, which was just as well considering that his dimensions, 7ft 1in frame, 325 pound weight and size 22 feet, were extreme, even in the NBA. This meant the shoes on his feet had to work

extra hard and making them durable and stable enough was a challenge. This led to the design team incorporating Reebok's InstaPump technology into the shoe, although it wasn't incorporated into the first versions released to the public. Pitched at professional athletes, InstaPump was an evolution of Reebok's Pump line that used an external canister to inflate the shoes from carbon dioxide cartridges.

Another challenge came from the pulsing concentric circle pattern, which proved difficult to manufacture, as the circles had to match up perfectly with the pattern on the midsole. Naming the new model was one of the few things about the shoe that wasn't a challenge and its name, Shaqnosis, came easily to O'Neal, 'Look at that shit long enough and you'll be hypnotized'.

The shoe featured the return of O'Neal's knees-up dunk logo on the tongue and heel, which had originally been inspired by Michael Jordan's 'Jumpman' which had been popular when O'Neal was in college. Brand minded from an early age, O'Neal had been learning about trademarks in his business class and decided to go to the local Baton Rouge

---

Opposite Shaq in his truly hypnotic Reebok Shaqnosis during the 1996 NBA All-Star game.

trademark office to trademark his own logo, meaning he owned the rights to it rather than Reebok.

Reebok knew the Shaqnosis design would make it a 'love it or hate it' shoe with the public but this was completely in line with Reebok's new creative direction, which aimed to evoke passionate responses, whether positive or negative. It was purposely only released in one colourway, black and white, to ensure its design remained iconic. In later re-issues Reebok did experiment with more colourways but none were as hypnotic as the original.

The Shaqnosis was about far more than its looks, however, and O'Neal wore it in the 1995/96 season, his landmark final year with the Orlando Magic. Despite being injured for 28 games, wearing the Shaqnosis, he still averaged 26.6 points, 11 rebounds and 2 blocks per game and played in his fourth All-Star game. O'Neal helped the Magic finish with a regular season record of 60-22, the team's best ever win-loss record.

The design of the Shaqnosis inspired a whole range of dazzling black-and-white Reebok shoes, including the Big Hurt, the Blast and the Kamikaze II. Although Reebok and O'Neal were to split in 1998 after O'Neal's contract ended and Reebok began to look at signing new players, the Shaqnosis is still hailed as one of Reebok's greatest shoes and remains both O'Neal's and many of his fans' favourite Shaq shoe.

Left Reebok Shaqnosis (Reebok Archive).

THE ANSWER'S QUESTION
1996 NBA DRAFT

REEBOK THE QUESTION

Allen Iverson is without doubt one of the greatest players to have graced the NBA but also unquestionably the most controversial. Since its inception NBA players had always been fierce competitors on court, but gentlemanly and demure off it. Iverson, however, was the first player to proudly immerse himself in the hip-hop culture that had developed around the game, and the first one to bring its defiant attitude and style on to the court.

Born in June 1975 in Hampton, Virginia, Iverson's life was tough from the start. Born to Ann Iverson when she was only 15, his father left while he was only a few years old. Growing up in a rough neighbourhood, Iverson saw his first murder aged only eight and witnessed the death of many of his close friends and acquaintances. His only escape from his violent surroundings was sport and he was determined to become a professional athlete one day. Athletic from an early age, he excelled in both basketball and American football and was key to helping his high school, Bethel, win the state championships in both sports.

With a promising athletic career ahead of him, Iverson's

future was suddenly derailed in 1993 when he was accused of involvement in a racially motivated brawl. The fight resulted in two white people being knocked unconscious and Iverson was accused of hitting a woman over the head with a chair. Despite video evidence that appeared to show him leaving the scene as soon as the fight started, he and four others were convicted of maiming by mob, a statute ironically first instituted to stop the lynching of black Virginians. Iverson was given a 15-year prison sentence with 10 years suspended, but after serving four months was granted clemency by the Governor of Virginia, Douglas Wilder. In 1995, the Court of Appeals also overturned his conviction due to inconsistent evidence, however, the ruling came too late to prevent him being expelled from Bethel and he was forced to complete his diploma at a school for at-risk students. The feeling that he had been wronged had a profound affect on him and he was determined never to be knocked down by anyone in authority ever again.

Believing her son needed a strong father figure and determined to get him back on track to playing professional basketball, Ann Iverson pleaded with John Thompson, head coach of Georgetown University, to take Allen under his wing and offer him a basketball scholarship. Thompson agreed, guiding him so well that he was twice named Big

East Defensive Player of the Year and earned All-American status when he averaged 25 points. When his young sister began suffering from seizures, Iverson felt he needed to do something about it and decided the only way he could help was by leaving Georgetown early and entering the next NBA draft to raise funds.

At this stage Iverson was already on the radar of both the NBA teams and Reebok. Determined to sign a player they felt came once in a lifetime, Reebok had designed a version of Allen's first signature shoe even before he had left college. He was a blood, sweat and tears player who could change a game single-handed and Reebok saw an opportunity to craft a relationship between a player and a shoe that would help catapult the company over Nike's Jordan brand. When Iverson announced his draft entry, Reebok immediately moved to sign him to a 10-year contract. The shoe they had developed was designed to excel on court while simultaneously making a noise in street fashion. It was named 'The Question', a counterpart to Iverson's nickname, 'The Answer', which had been given to him by a close friend, who believed he was going to be the 'answer to all of the NBA's woes'. In hindsight, 'The Problem' might have been a better choice.

In the 1996 draft Iverson was the number one pick and

at 'only' 6ft was the shortest first overall pick in NBA history. Selected by the Philadelphia 76ers, who had finished the previous season with a win-loss record of 18-64, he brought new hope to a city craving success. In his first season Iverson averaged 23.5 points per game and broke Wilt Chamberlain's rookie season record of three consecutive games, scoring at least 40 points, and doing so in five straight games, including a 50-pointer against the Cavaliers. Iverson was named the NBA Rookie of the Year. However, Philadelphia still lost 60 games and began to look for a new coach.

The man they chose was Larry Brown, a strait-laced 60-year-old Jewish white man, the absolute polar opposite of Iverson. The two clashed immediately when Brown disapproved of his on-court behaviour. Iverson had an aggressive style of play and seemed to model himself on a gangster rapper, covered in tattoos, braiding his hair in cornrows (a popular prison hairstyle), and wearing a bandana. Brown wasn't alone in his disapproval. When Iverson appeared on the cover of the NBA's magazine his tattoos were airbrushed out and older players like Charles Barkley and Michael Jordan made it clear they felt he had no respect for the game and wasn't setting the right example. When Iverson was arrested for possession of marijuana and a concealed weapon, it only served to show their concerns were justified.

Despite this, there was no denying Iverson was hugely talented and he led the 76ers to vastly improved performances over the next two seasons, reaching the play-offs in both and finishing with more wins than losses. He continued to butt heads with his coach, however, regularly failing to turn up or arriving late for practice, and whenever Brown took him off the court he would mutter curses under his breath. At times their relationship was so

strained that the two couldn't bear to be in the same room together. Things came to a head when Brown stated that unless Iverson was traded, he would leave. With Iverson sharing the same sentiment a trade was negotiated to the Detroit Pistons but fell through, as did another to the Los Angeles Clippers, leading Iverson to begin thinking about repairing his relationship with Brown.

Having patched things up, Iverson led the 76ers to open the 2000/01 season with 10 wins in a row and finish with the best win-loss record in the Eastern Conference. The 76ers also reached the finals for the first time in 18 years and Iverson earned himself the Most Valuable Player title. During the season he began using a compression sleeve to aide his recovery from bursitis in his right elbow. Such was his influence on both the game and its fans that other players, including Kobe Bryant, began wearing them too, as did his fans, who wore the sleeve along with his replica 76ers shirt, at the time the best-selling shirt in the NBA. It didn't end there. When other players adopted the 'gangsta' look off-court, the NBA became so concerned about the sport's image that they instituted a players' dress code, requiring them to wear businesslike attire when off-court and forbidding chains, medallions, headbands, sneakers, sunglasses indoors and headphones when in public. Naturally, Iverson failed to conform. With The Question flying off the shelves and a key part of his look, Reebok were probably relieved.

After two early play-off exits in the 2001/02 and 2002/03 seasons, Larry Brown left for Detroit. Despite having improved their relationship, it deteriorated again and resulted in an argument with Brown, which was followed by an infamous press conference. During the conference a still riled and allegedly drunk Iverson began arguing with reporters when they questioned him more about his

not showing up for practice than about the game. His infamous quote, 'we talkin' about practice, man, not a game', is still parodied today. Brown was replaced by a series of coaches under whom Iverson's behaviour began to spiral out of control. Interim head coach Chris Ford's disciplinarian approach led to Iverson being suspended for missing practice, fined for failing to inform him he would miss a game due to illness and refusing to play because Ford wanted him to start from the bench. Iverson was also starting to make more headlines off the court than on it after he was involved in a domestic disturbance involving his wife that led to him threatening two men, one of them his cousin, with a gun, attracting blanket media coverage. While he was only sentenced to community service, his real punishment came via criticism by the media, who labelled him a thug and lambasted him for failing to understand the responsibility that came with his stardom.

Although the 76ers bounced back in the 2004/05 season and Iverson averaged a career high of 33 points per game, they missed the play-offs for the second time in three years. A bad end to the season was compounded when Iverson and teammate Chris Webber turned up late for the fans appreciation night, incensing manager Billy King, who railed at Iverson and King in a profanity-filled rant. The following year, Iverson demanded a trade and was told that as a result he would no longer play any games, effectively ending a 10-year career with the 76ers. Traded to the Denver Nuggets, he was again involved in controversy when he was fined $25,000 for criticizing referee Steve Javie, alleging that he had a personal grudge against him. After two years at the Nuggets and bench-warming spells at the Detroit Pistons and Memphis Grizzlies, in November 2009 he returned to Philadelphia and received a standing ovation from the fans.

After having to leave the 76ers due to his daughter's health issues and a short spell playing in Turkey, on 30 October 2013 Iverson officially announced his retirement from basketball in a tear-filled press conference in which he said, 'with the mistakes that I made in my life I created a picture of me that is not me. I did a lot of things when I was young that I'm not proud of but I think those things helped me be the man that I am now'. Iverson's legacy remains questionable. While his performances were among the greatest ever in NBA history, he is largely remembered for the controversies that clouded his career. In 2016 Reebok marked the 20th anniversary of the Question with a special re-issue version celebrating Iverson's career that was covered in newspaper headlines from his time in the NBA. They named it 'Bad News'.

Below Reebok Question, Golden State All-Star Game, Unworn PE (Reebok Archive).

THE LAST VAULT
1996 ATLANTA OLYMPIC GAMES

ASICS GYM ULTRA

Ask any American what their memories are of the 1996 Atlanta Olympic Games and most will tell you it was Kerri Strug's last vault. It is an event that has gone down in Olympic history as a moment of true courage and elevated the 19-year-old from Tuscon, Arizona, to the status of American hero. It was also an event that inadvertently brought a lot of attention to her humble ASICS gymnastics shoes.

Traditionally, gymnastics had been an event dominated by Russia, but on their home turf, the United States felt they had a great chance to win the gold. The team was led by Béla Károlyi, the Romanian who had successfully coached Nadia Comâneci to her perfect 10s in Montreal in 1976, but who had defected to the United States after falling out with the Romanian gymnastics federation. While his training methods were later alleged to be controversial and abusive, he had a track record that appeared to guarantee the United States gymnastics team success. Dubbed 'The Magnificent Seven', the team featured the USA's strongest ever line-up, including Kerri Strug.

Strug knew as early as the age of three that she wanted to be a gymnast. Her mother described her as spending her childhood, 'upside down more than she was right side up'. Inspired by US Olympic gymnast Mary Lou Retton's perfect 10 performance at the 1984 Los Angeles Olympic Games,

she entered her first competition a year later and showed her potential immediately. By the age of 13 she had become the youngest female to win an event at the USA Gymnastic Championships when she won the vault title, and a year later, in 1992, was competing for the United States at the Olympic Games in Barcelona. Aged just 14, she was the youngest member of the team and when they won the team bronze she became one of the youngest Olympic medal winners in history.

After day one of the compulsory routines in Atlanta, the United States was in second place behind Russia, but with some of their best routines coming on the second day, they were still in with a chance. After excellent performances in the uneven parallel bars, balance beam and floor exercise, the Americans were feeling confident. Of the seven members of the team, six were selected to compete in each event with the best five scores counting, meaning that the lowest score could be discarded. With every member putting in the performance of their lives, all of them scored well, putting the US into the lead, 0.897 points ahead of the Russians.

The next event was the vault. Full of confidence and feeding off each other's energy, the Americans felt they were on the verge of securing the United States'

first women's gymnastics gold medal. But then, as the 32,000-strong and expectant crowd looked on, everything went wrong. Vault after vault, on both of their permitted attempts, the first four Americans struggled to make clean landings, stumbling slightly or taking steps and hops. With so much at stake their nerves had got the better of them and confidence had begun to turn into panic. The fifth American to try was Dominique Moceanu, one of the stars of the team, but to the shock of the watching audience she fell on both attempts and scored poorly. With Russia still completing their floor routines there was a real danger that they could pip the Americans to the post and snatch the gold medal away. It was all down to Kerri Strug.

As she prepared for her run up, Strug knew that the expectations of a whole nation were on her shoulders. She waited for the green light that told her it was her turn, ran down the runway, performed a round off on to the springboard and flipped off the horse. But to the spectators' dismay, just like her teammates, disaster struck as she under-rotated, causing her to fall as she

Opposite Coach Béla Károlyi carries Kerri Strug to the podium in her ASICS Gym Ultras. Strug's heroics while wearing them caused the shoes to become the focus of an entire nation.

Below ASICS Gym Ultra, worn by Kerri Strug (Olympic Museum Collection).

landed and injure her ankle amid cries from the shocked crowd. As she limped back to her coach, it looked like the United States was losing its grip on the gold but steadfast Béla Károlyi, unwilling to even contemplate the idea of silver, said to Strug, 'Kerri, we need you to go one more time. We need you one more time for the gold.' Telling her to forget the pain with an expression that was to be later adopted and parodied by the nation, he shouted to her, 'Shake it off, you can do it!'

This was it, the last chance. Once more, Strug accelerated down the runway, performed a round off on to the springboard and flipped off the horse as the crowd held its breath. This time she landed well, on both feet, although only for the briefest of moments before the pain caused her to hop almost instantly on to her good foot before collapsing to her knees in crushing pain. America watched in horror as she dragged herself off the crash mat with the help of her coaches. With the judges scoring her 9.712, the crowd erupted. Strug had done it! She had secured the gold medal for the United States. Fully appreciating what she had gone through in order to win it, the entire crowd stood in grateful applause.

With a third-degree lateral sprain and tendon damage, Strug was unable to walk to the medal ceremony and so Károlyi carried her to the podium to join her teammates and receive her gold medal. After Russian Roza Galieva put in a poor performance in the floor exercise, the United States' score would have been enough to win gold even if Strug hadn't performed her second vault, but as Galieva had performed after her, there was no way they could be sure and Strug became a national hero. With her feet becoming the focus of millions on television as she limped back up the runway after her first vault and injured them after her second, Strug's humble ASICS Gym Ultras inadvertently became minor stars and one of the pairs she used in Atlanta now resides in the Olympic Museum in Lausanne, Switzerland, a proud representation of the moment Kerri Strug put her nation's pride before her own pain.

GOLD AND BOLD
1996 ATLANTA OLYMPIC GAMES

NIKE GOLD RUNNING SPIKES

When Michael Johnson famously wore a pair of gold Nikes at the 1996 Atlanta Olympics many believed it to be a sign of arrogance bordering on cockiness. On the face it, who could argue with them? Gold shoes, whether they are a pair of stilettos or running spikes, are a bold statement of confidence. Even some of the world's greatest athletes probably wouldn't have had the guts to wear gold shoes for fear of not living up to the expectations that come with them. But when Johnson did, he became the ultimate example of an athlete with supreme confidence in his own ability.

Born in September 1967 in Dallas, Texas, Michael Johnson was the youngest of Ruby and Paul Johnson's five children and credits his success to his upbringing. The Johnsons taught their children from an early age the importance of having a plan for each stage of their lives, following it and being prepared for any eventuality. They also believed that as parents the best thing they could give their children was a good education. Their guidance had a profound impact on Michael Johnson and he was focused and meticulous to the point of being a perfectionist from a

young age. As an illustration of this, in high school Johnson was on both the track and field and American football teams but gave up football, feeling the aggression required to become a great player was not within him. Aggression meant being out of control, yet control was what he felt was most required to achieve his goals, so he focused on athletics, a sport far more in line with the focus and efficiency that would come to define his character.

Ironically, what would become his signature running style initially raised both eyebrows and doubts over its apparent inefficiency. A long torso and leaned-back running gait, combined with short, low strides went against all conventional wisdom. 'I'd be lying if I said I thought Michael was going to be a world-class sprinter,' said his coach Clyde Hart at Baylor College. However, much like the myth that the laws of aerodynamics prove bumblebees shouldn't be able to fly, Johnson appeared to defy physics and in his first race broke the school record for the 200m, going on to win numerous indoor and outdoor NCAA sprint and relay titles.

Despite his coach's initial misgivings, Johnson soon became world class in the 200m and 400m and began planning his path to Olympic glory. Those plans had to be put on hold, however, when a stress fracture led to him

missing the chance to qualify for the 1988 Seoul Olympics. While this would have been a huge blow to most people, Johnson had prepared for all eventualities as he had been taught and simply adapted his plans and refocused them on the 1992 Games in Barcelona. When he graduated from Baylor in 1990 he appeared on track to do so, holding the No. 1 ranking in the world in both the 200m and the 400m. However, his plans were to be foiled once again. After competing in a warm-up event two weeks before Barcelona, Johnson and his agent were heading for a meal at Burger King but decided instead to go to a Spanish restaurant they had enjoyed the night before. The burger would have been the better option as both came down with food poisoning. Even after he had recovered, Johnson found that the weight loss he experienced had affected his strength, resulting in the favourite to win the 200m gold medal being eliminated in the semi-finals. While he did win gold as part of the US 4x400m relay team, he left Spain disappointed, as it wasn't one of the medals he was targeting.

After Barcelona Johnson dominated the 200m and 400m, winning US and world titles in the 400m in 1993, and his first 200m and 400m double at the 1995 World Championships. As he lined up for the final of the 400m in Atlanta, Johnson stood out in his gold Nike running

Left Nike Gold Zytel running spikes
(Olympic Museum Collection).

spikes. The fact they were gold said many things but chief among them was that Michael Johnson had no plan other than to win. Given that Johnson had won 54 straight finals since Barcelona, gold was a more than apt choice. Two years in the making, the shoes had been developed by Nike to relaunch themselves on to the market. Nike had been falling behind their rivals in terms of quality, performance and technology. American sprinter and Olympic Champion Quincy Watts' Nike spikes had come apart as he ran in the 400m final of the 1993 World Championships. While it was an isolated incident and Johnson, the winner, had worn the same shoes, it had happened with the whole world watching and the embarrassment spurred Nike into improving their spikes.

Johnson had worn Nike since university and until 1990 wore what were essentially the same 'Zoom' spikes Nike had made since the 1984 Olympics in Los Angeles. But when they went out of production, Johnson wasn't a fan of the replacement. Keen to keep him in the Nike family, the company took all the plates of his preferred older model that they had left and kept them so that they could make bespoke shoes for him.

Then in 1995 Nike approached him about collaborating on a project to completely overhaul their sprint shoes and set out to make his perfect shoe. During the two-year development process the focus was on creating shoes that would help Johnson perform better based on his particular body mechanics and the events in which he competed. At a 200m event, Nike set up a high-speed camera that would allow them to analyse the movements of his feet and discovered that it was different on the straight than in the bend and even varied between his feet. The distance run also had an impact. The result was that Nike developed

different models for the 200m and 400m and also made slight differences between the left and right shoes.

When it came to the new model's appearance, Johnson and Nike considered everything from a clear shoe to a mirrored effect and even silver before settling on Johnson's final choice, gold. And while it was this that grabbed headlines it was their weight that was really remarkable. A milestone in minimal shoe design, they were made from Zytel, a super-light but super-strong nylon, and weighed a mere 3oz each, probably no more than Johnson's trademark gold necklace. Made from a three-piece upper, a feather-light carbon graphite spike plate with ceramic aluminium spikes and lacking a rear outsole, they were designed for one reason and one reason only: to help the wearer go as fast as he possibly could.

Johnson's gold medal seemed a foregone conclusion. His main rival, Roger Black, predicted his victory even before the race saying, 'The final is really to see who will win silver and bronze.' But even he couldn't have predicted how big his margin of victory would be. When he crossed the line Johnson was just shy of an entire second ahead, the largest winning margin in a 400m final since 1896. Taking victory in a new Olympic record time of 43.49 seconds, Johnson was characteristically calm and collected. Winning the 400m had only been part of the overall plan. To be satisfied he had to do the double and win the 200m too. It was fitting that the first people he greeted were his parents, the original architects of his life's plan, and to whom he gave his winning gold Nikes.

Unlike the 400m, Johnson's victory in the 200m was by no means certain. Frankie Fredericks of Namibia had meted out Johnson's first defeat after 21 consecutive victories just

before the Games and had won all of his heats. But losing wasn't part of Johnson's plan. On the starting blocks he was a picture of pure and unemotional concentrated focus. Both started well but on his third step Johnson stumbled. Characteristically, he cast it aside and, coming out of the curve, again looked like the winner. Powering down the straight, his lean-back style made it look easy but as he crossed the line to win he had run the final 100m in an incredible 9.2 seconds. Just as remarkable was that he had felt his hamstring tighten after taking the lead but still pulled away to set a new world record of 19.32 seconds, breaking the record he had set by more than three-tenths of a second, the largest ever improvement on a 200m world record. Having become the first man to win both the 200m and 400m in one Games, Johnson was uncharacteristically but more than justifiably elated. His plan had been accomplished.

Johnson competed at just one more Games and won the 400m gold in Sydney, but injury caused him to miss the chance to defend his 200m title. His Atlanta double remains the highlight of his career and a testament to his pursuit of perfection and the successful execution of a plan that didn't always go as envisioned, but remained his core focus and was performed with almost ruthless efficiency.

Johnson's gold shoes made him the face, and feet, of Atlanta and now reside in pride of place at his parents' home. While it's not surprising they are proud of their son's athletic achievements, they value even more highly the guidance and education that built his son's confidence in himself and still prize his bachelor's degree far more than all of his gold medals: 'We are very proud of the gold medals, yes. But that degree was the number one thing for us.'

DAVID WHO?

NIKE AIR ZOOM MIA HAMM

Move over David Beckham, the person who really put football on the map in the United States wasn't a man; it was a woman by the name of Mia Hamm. One of the pioneers of not just women's, but world soccer, she became the most recognizable and admired female player in the world and broke new ground for female athletes in soccer and beyond.

Born in Selma, Alabama, in March 1972, Mia Hamm was an unlikely athlete, having been born with a club foot for which she wore corrective shoes as a toddler. Growing up, she idolized her adopted older brother Garrett, who was a natural athlete and inspired and encouraged her to take up sports and practise hard. Her soccer talents were first spotted by Anson Dorrance while she played at the North Texas State Tryouts. Dorrance had been given the role of team coach of the US national women's soccer team and was scouting for new players. He knew as soon as he saw Hamm that she was something special, describing her as 'moving like she had been shot out of a cannon'. Aged only 15, Hamm found herself in the US national team.

Initially, she felt intimidated as one of the youngest players on the team and Dorrance was criticized for bringing her and others into the team at such a young age while rejecting some older, more experienced players.

Dorrance was undeterred, however, feeling that the drive and hard work demonstrated by the younger players was just what the team needed to become potential future champions.

With the focus of the US Soccer Federation (USSF) being on the men's team, the women's team received little funding and attention. They travelled to matches by bus and often played in front of no more than 100 people, many of whom were friends and family. They stayed in budget motels and received no pay apart from a daily allowance of $10. Despite this, the team's players bonded closely.

In 1991, Hamm and her teammates headed to China for the first FIFA Women's World Cup, a name that was only retrospectively applied to the tournament, as FIFA were unsure if it would be worthy of the title. (At the time it was named the FIFA Women's World Championship.) To everyone's surprise the hosts rose to the occasion with a fervour that most nations reserved for the men's tournament. The US women powered their way through it, wowing with their high pressure and high-scoring game, beating Sweden, Brazil and Japan in the group stages, with Hamm scoring twice. In the quarter-finals they overpowered Taipei 7-0 and in the semis defeated joint favourites Germany 5-2. Against all expectation the

US reached the final. No American team had ever played for a world championship before and yet here they were, a group of young women, largely uncelebrated at home, shaking hands with Pelé in front of 65,000 people. It was like nothing they had seen before. In the final they faced Norway, one of the best teams in the world. The Americans scored first but the Norwegians drew level shortly after. The score remained the same and the match looked to be heading for extra time before Michelle Akers struck for the second time 10 minutes before the end to put the US into the lead, a lead they kept until the final whistle. They had done it, the US were champions of the world!

But, after the elation of victory, the team returned home to a welcoming committee of three people. Despite being champions of the world, the future of women's soccer still appeared bleak. At home their victory had barely made the news and appeared to have done little to attract potential new players or fans. Not that this, however, appeared to have dampened Mia Hamm's enthusiasm for the game. While at the University of North Carolina she

Opposite Mia Hamm in action in the 1999 Women's World Cup Final between the US and China, wearing her signature Nike soccer boots.

had been key to winning the university four NCAA women's championships, and in 1993 she signed with Nike to become the brand's first female soccer player and one of the first in the US with a paid sports endorsement deal.

In 1995 the team attempted to defend their title at the World Cup in Sweden. They reached the semi-finals, but with Michelle Akers suffering from Chronic Fatigue Syndrome, having sustained concussion and a knee injury early in the tournament, the team was not at full strength and lost to arch-rivals Norway. The manner of Norway's celebrations irked the Americans and they felt determined to exact revenge. When women's soccer became an Olympic sport for the first time at the 1996 Atlanta Games, they got their chance.

The run-up to the Games wasn't smooth, however – the team coming close to going on strike, demanding parity with the US men's salaries and bonuses. Eventually a settlement was reached and fate determined that the US would face their adversaries Norway once again in the semi-final. Such was their enmity that the US women had a picture of the Norwegians, or the 'Viking Bitches' as they called them, on their dressing-room door, on which they would focus their loathing. The match was an extra-time thriller. Deadlocked at 1-1 after 90 minutes, the US scored a golden goal to take them through to the final against China, which they won 2-1 to take the gold medal.

Sadly, the game wasn't even broadcast live. Despite having been world and Olympic champions, women's football still wasn't getting the attention it deserved. Thankfully, Madison Avenue had seen its potential and especially that of Mia Hamm, who between 1994 and 1998 won five successive US Soccer Federation Female Athlete of the Year awards. She quickly became the face of US soccer and was appearing

in commercials for everything from Pert Plus shampoo to Gatorade. In one TV spot, she famously ran rings around Michael Jordan in every sport they tried. She also became one of the leading faces in Nike's line-up of female athletes and worked with the company to refine their range of women's soccer boots. The 'pink 'em and shrink 'em' approach used by most brands didn't work with soccer boots and Hamm played a key role in designing Nike's Air Zoom M9, Nike's first boots created expressly for women.

Ever modest, Hamm shied away from the attention she was getting and didn't let it go to her head, telling her teammates to ensure that they kept her grounded. Remaining a close-knit group, never did she value them more than when her brother Garrett, who had inspired her success, passed away as a result of aplastic anaemia, a bone marrow disease he had suffered since the age of 16. On winning her gold medal in Atlanta he had been the first person she hugged. After his diagnosis she doubled her efforts in order that he could fulfil some of his dreams through her. After his death, in a show of solidarity in her mourning, the entire team played in black armbands.

Scoring her 108th goal in a match against Brazil on 22 May 1999, she broke the all-time international goalscoring record and, in recognition of her remarkable achievement, Nike named its largest corporate campus building after her. It was also the year that the Women's World Cup was to be held in the United States. The organizers had planned to hold games in small stadiums but when tickets went on sale, they realized that they had underestimated the potential of the event and games were instead moved to larger venues. As the tournament began the US women were overwhelmed by the support they received, first realizing something special was happening when they saw

long queues of traffic heading to watch them at Giants Stadium in New York. America was suddenly officially in love with the US Women's team. Whole families came to give their support, with as many men attending as women. Even teenage boys had 'I Love Mia' painted on their bodies.

In the opening game Hamm scored first against Denmark in a 3-0 win and scored again in a 7-1 thrashing of Nigeria. Advancing to the quarter-finals after a 3-0 victory over North Korea, the US faced Germany and won 3-2. Beating Brazil 2-0 in the semis, they faced China once again in the final. Held in the Rose Bowl, Pasadena, in front of 90,000 fans, including President Clinton, it wasn't just the largest crowd ever for a women's sporting event but also one of the largest ever for a sports final. Having lost twice to China earlier in the year, the Americans knew it would be a difficult game. It was close. At full time the score was 0-0 and remained so after extra time. The match would go to penalties. At 3-3 Hamm stepped forward. Despite having missed all her attempts in practice, when it mattered she slotted home to make it 4-3. After China's Sun Wen made it 4-4 it was up to Hamm's teammate Brandi Chastain to take the final spot kick. Despite the Chinese goalkeeper doing her best to put her off, Chastain scored and the Americans were world champions again. This time, however, the whole nation celebrated.

It was to be Hamm's last World Cup victory before her retirement in 2005 and probably her finest hour. Not for her own achievement, but because she had played a key role in putting American women's soccer on the map. While there was and still is a long way to go, Hamm and her teammates had proved to a whole nation that with hard work and determination, barriers can be broken and World Cups can be won.

Below Nike Air Zoom Mia Hamm
(Author's Collection).

THE WARRIOR
1999 RUGBY WORLD CUP

ADIDAS EQUIPMENT RUGBY

Only very rarely does a player emerge in a sport who has such a colossal impact on it that they come to redefine what it means to be great. They tear up the history books, completely redefine superlatives and leave even established legends quaking. In rugby, that player was Jonah Lomu.

Born in Pukekohe, New Zealand, in 1975 to Tongan parents, Jonah Tali Lomu endured a difficult start in life, spending his early years in Tonga before returning to Auckland following his parents' divorce. Living with his mother in Mangere, a town plagued with violence between rival Maori, Samoan and Tongan gangs, Lomu often found himself getting into fights. After his uncle and cousin were murdered his mother sent him away to Wesley College, a Methodist boarding school, to remove him from the increasingly brutal environment.

Wesley proved to be his making and he was able to channel his resentment and anger into sports at which he soon began to excel. At 14, he made Wesley history when he came first in the 100m, 100m hurdles, 200m, 400m, discus, shot-put, javelin, long jump, high jump and triple jump at the school's athletics championships. The same year he was noticed by captain of the New Zealand Sevens team, Eric Rush. When the 6ft 5in 259lb Lomu ran Rush over during a game of touch rugby, he was so impressed that he invited him to a Singapore Sevens tournament, leaving the next day.

Despite being 10 years younger than most of his teammates he rose to the occasion and, in the opening game scored New Zealand's first try. It was while playing in the Hong Kong Sevens in 1994 that the world first took notice of Lomu. He became the youngest ever All Blacks player, aged 19 years 45 days, and was key to New Zealand winning the title. Having witnessed his impact, New Zealand coach Laurie Mains made the decision to include him in his 1995 Rugby World Cup side. Even before many of his rivals had seen him, rumours of a superhuman giant had gone round the other competing nations.

In his first appearance at the World Cup he scored two tries in a victory over Ireland, but it was against England that he announced his arrival on the world stage. The Five Nations Grand Slam winners were feeling justifiably confident before the game but Lomu quite literally knocked it out of them. Within 70 seconds he scored New Zealand's first try and then proceeded to take England apart almost single-handed. Even England's most seasoned players quickly realized that tackling just didn't work against the mountainous but lightning-fast Lomu. Mike Catt was famously trampled underfoot as Lomu steamrollered over him.

Over the course of 80 minutes and four tries, Lomu managed to reduce England, one of the leading contenders to win the World Cup, into a side that looked lucky to even be playing in the tournament. The following day his performance hit the headlines, making the front pages of many newspapers. Despite New Zealand's defeat in the final against South Africa, a new star had been born. What made Lomu's performance all the more impressive was that before the tournament he had received news that was to cloud the rest of his career, having been told by a specialist that he had nephrotic syndrome, a serious kidney disorder.

Refusing to let it affect his rugby, Lomu played on, and despite missing much of the 1997 season due to his condition, he received lucrative offers from NFL teams to play in America, but as rugby became a professional sport he pledged his future to it and signed with New Zealand Rugby Union. He was now the game's first global superstar and in 1999 he began what was to become a long association with adidas when the company became a sponsor of the New Zealand national side. For the 1999 World Cup, held in grounds across the UK and France, adidas made a special All Blacks edition of their Equipment rugby boot and all

---

Opposite Jonah Lomu powers his way through the England defence during the 1999 Rugby World Cup.

the boots were handmade in adidas's 'made to measure' manufacturing plant at Scheinfeld in Germany.

At the World Cup the world marvelled again at Lomu, but despite scoring eight tries and putting in another awe-inspiring performance against England, the almost unthinkable happened when the All Blacks were dumped out of the World Cup by France at the semi-final stage. In one of the biggest upsets in the World Cup history, though sheer guts and flair France staged a second-half comeback to beat the team that had seemed unbeatable. After the tournament, despite Lomu continuing to battle with his condition, he remained in the starting line up for New Zealand but, as his performances began to be affected, he increasingly found himself starting from the bench and his final test match for New Zealand came against Wales in November 2002.

Before his retirement Lomu had begun working with adidas as part of a collaboration with the All Blacks to develop a new rugby boot, the Nine15. Aimed at professional and serious players, it was a position-specific boot, its name inspired by the players it was designed for, the backs, the players positioned at the rear of the formation numbered between 9 and 15 and characterized by skilful passing and kicking. Lomu was able to bring his experience as a centre to the design of the boot. His key requirements were traction, lightness, stability and good kicking feel. These made kangaroo skin ideal due to its great strength, but being thin enough to provide extra feel and remain lightweight. To give extra stability the boot was given an external heel counter and to ensure it was flexible, rather than having a traditional full length midsole it was split in two parts between the forefoot and rear, leaving the central area free to flex. The boot underwent a season of testing on Lomu's differently sized 14 and 13.5 feet before being released to the public in 2002 after two years of development.

By 2003, with his kidneys now deteriorating, Lomu required dialysis three times a week. A side effect of his treatment led to severe nerve damage in his feet and legs and doctors warned that without a transplant he faced life in a wheelchair. Spending six hours a day, three times a week on a dialysis machine was debilitating, yet he remained optimistic and in July 2004, Lomu underwent a kidney transplant, donated by his friend, radio presenter Grant Kereama. With a new lease of life, he began playing rugby again with the goal of returning to the All Blacks for the 2007 Rugby World Cup but it was an injury plagued comeback and when he failed to get a Super Rugby contract, he decided it was time to retire.

Despite his health problems, adidas remained loyal to Lomu. While other sponsors had deserted him he was inducted into the adidas Hall of Fame, effectively making him an ambassador for life. While carrying out his ambassadorial roles for adidas and the New Zealand Rugby Union in 2011, his body began to reject his donated kidney and he was forced to undergo dialysis again. While still on the waiting list for a donor kidney he was again on ambassadorial duties at the 2015 Rugby World Cup in England but in November he unexpectedly died from a heart attack brought on by his nephrotic syndrome. He was only 40. The entire rugby world deeply mourned the passing of its first global superstar. Teammates and rivals were united in grief for a man who had been so powerful and dominant on the pitch, but so warm and gentlemanly off it.

Not long before his passing Lomu had revealed just how much his illness had affected his career, describing it as 'like playing with the handbrake on', making his achievements all the more extraordinary. Not once did Lomu ever use his condition as an excuse for his later drop in form and yet we are left with the spine-tingling notion of how much more dominating he would have been with full health on his side.

Below adidas Equipment Rugby
boots, worn by Jonah Lomu
(adidas Archive).

FLYING FLAGS
2000 SYDNEY OLYMPIC GAMES

NIKE 'ABORIGINAL FLAG' RUNNING SPIKES

Cathy Freeman was a dreamer as a youngster. Born in Mackay, Queensland, in February 1973 to parents of Aboriginal descent, she grew up with a head filled with dreams of Olympic glory. But growing up in a country where the indigenous population had been treated as second-class citizens for 200 years, the idea of an aboriginal woman having a successful athletics career and representing her nation sounded like a dream too far for most.

From the moment she finished her first race aged eight, Freeman was hooked on running and athletics became her passion. At primary school one of her teachers recognized her talent and raised money to buy her a pair of running shoes in which to compete at the state primary school championships. Even at this age Freeman understood that her running galvanized the support of her fellow indigenous people, giving them the rare chance to cheer on one of their own. When she was 14, Freeman told her high school careers officer that her only ambition was to become a

Opposite Wearing the colours of Australia on her 'speed suit' and the Aboriginal flag on her running spikes, Cathy Freeman took victory in the 400m at the 2000 Sydney Olympic Games and united a nation (Olympic Multimedia Library).

professional athlete and to win an Olympic medal. Having already won national titles in the 100m, 200m, 400m and high jump, it appeared she didn't need any advice on the right path to take to get there.

Freeman's abilities gained her a scholarship to Fairholme College in Toowoomba, Queensland, in 1988. Being one of the few aboriginal students at the famed boarding school, she felt very much out of place. Usually the preserve of girls from wealthy backgrounds, it was run along strict traditional Presbyterian values, rules and routines that were alien to Freeman. Her background and timid nature made her feel she didn't belong among white people and led to her underperforming academically. However, she flourished athletically, leading her to be selected to join Australia's 4x100m relay team for the 1990 Commonwealth Games in New Zealand. When the team won the gold medal, Freeman became the first Aboriginal Commonwealth Games gold medallist, and at 16, one of the youngest.

It was while travelling to athletics events that Freeman first experienced racism close up when she was shouted at for lying down on a train seat and shooed away from a shop. Later at university, she made friends with politically active Aboriginal students and became more aware of the

history of Australia's indigenous people and the effects of colonization on them. When she spent time with African-American athletes as part of an international exchange and during the 1992 Barcelona Olympics her belief that history had caused Aboriginal society to become introverted seemed to be confirmed. She was astonished by the self-confidence and ambition of the Americans, and it increased her resolve to use athletics as a way for her to act as a representative of the Aboriginal people and, more importantly, to inspire them.

In 1992, Freeman signed a sponsorship deal with Nike, the brand with which she would later become synonymous, and was employed as an assistant in a post office as part of Australia Post's Olympic Job Opportunities Program, allowing her to take on a job and earn a living while also focusing on training for the 1994 Commonwealth Games in Canada. It paid off. In Victoria, Freeman won gold in the 200m and 400m, as well as silver in the 4x100m relay. She arranged for an Aboriginal flag to be waiting for her if she won, which along with the Australian flag, she proudly waved on her victory laps, hoping that her expression of pride in her Aboriginal roots would counter negative stereotypes. At the IAAF Grand Prix final the same year she finished second in the 400m to French athlete Marie Jose

Perec, the runner who would become her greatest rival. When the two faced off again in the 1996 Athens Olympics 400m final Perec once again got the better of her, although Freeman did set a new Australian record of 48.63 seconds in taking silver.

In 1997, Freeman was named Young Australian of the Year in recognition of her achievements. She won the 400m at the World Championships in Athens and her only loss in the distance that year was in Oslo, where she injured her foot. This led her to her taking a year away from the track in 1998 to recover. Taking up where she left off, in the run-up to the 2000 Sydney Olympic Games she didn't lose a single race in the 400m, setting up a thrilling showdown with her rival Perec.

Perhaps for the first time the Games were more than a celebration of sport, they were a symbol of the reconciliation and greater understanding that was beginning to take place between Australia's white and indigenous population. The Olympic torch relay and opening ceremony had included indigenous torch bearers and other elements and it was kept a tightly guarded secret that Freeman would be given the honour of taking the Olympic flame on the final part of its journey to the cauldron. Ahead of the Games she had been encouraged by sections of the Aboriginal community to boycott them, but she felt strongly that she could better represent Australia's indigenous people by being there. Wearing a silver Lycra body suit, she appeared to float above water as she lit a ring of flame that rose above her and was then carried into position (after a four-minute delay caused by a technical hitch) above the stadium.

Freeman would be wearing another type of body suit later in the Games. Two years prior to the Sydney Olympics Nike had begun work on a new technology they believed could make track and field athletes faster. Called 'Project Swift', it was an all-over body suit with a hood that covered an athlete's body from head to toe. Made from a textured material that reduced drag, Nike claimed that it could shave tenths of a second off a runner's time by making them more aerodynamically efficient. While tenths sound very little, they can be the difference between gold and silver or even a world record. Although athletes rarely exceed 28mph, a speed too low for aerodynamics to make a big difference, their lower legs can move in excess of 45mph, a speed at which they can. When Freeman first tried the body suit after its unveiling in 1999 she felt odd, but as she got more used to it, she said she felt lighter and faster in it as though she was 'cutting through the air'. But she also felt self-conscious in it and decided to wear it only for a special occasion.

That came when Freeman lined up for the start of the 400m final. The suit immediately grabbed attention. Many thought it little more than a Nike PR stunt and others later criticized Freeman because it hid the very thing she was trying to highlight: the colour of her skin. With the suit in Australian green and gold, along with her Nike spikes, which were in the colours of the Aboriginal flag, black, red and yellow, Freeman was representing the entire nation.

As the athletes prepared for the race in front of a crowd of 112,000 people there was one notable absence. Marie Jose Perec had pulled out of the Games, claiming she had been insulted and threatened and that the Australian media had been harassing her and trying to sabotage her chances. Being rivals, the two had never been close friends, but there was great mutual respect between them and while Freeman was saddened by her departure, it was no surprise that the Australian public was not.

As the athletes settled into their blocks almost every pair of eyeballs in Australia, either on television or in the stadium, was fixed on Cathy Freeman. Even officials and judges from other events stopped to watch. As the race began the entire stadium roared. As she rounded the bend she was in cruise control and telling herself to relax, but as she approached the 200m mark, began to increase her pace. Entering the final bend, she held her speed in check, ready for the final kick. Exiting the bend, she was third, but on the final straight knew she had plenty of speed on tap. As she began her kick with 80 metres to go she realized that her rivals didn't have the strength to stay with her and, with a five-metre lead, crossed the finish line to take gold as all of Australia erupted in delight. Exhausted and overawed by the reception, Freeman removed her hood and spikes and sat down on the track, seemingly unable to take in the enormity what she had just done.

As she began her victory lap she went to the crowd and got them to throw Australian and Aboriginal flags to her. Conscious that she didn't want to be appear to prefer one flag over the other, she allowed them to fall to the track and then picked up two flags together as one, tied them together and draped them around her neck. She had done it! The little Aboriginal girl from Mackay with a head full of dreams had won an Olympic gold medal and united her country in celebration.

KOBE'S KICKS MIX
2002 NBA CHAMPIONSHIP

NIKE/REEBOK/CONVERSE/VARIOUS MODELS

The 2002/03 NBA season was an extraordinary one for Kobe Bryant. Not just because he set a single game record for three-pointers and averaged 30 points per game, but because of what was on his feet. Or rather what wasn't.

Bryant began what was to be one of the greatest careers in basketball in 1996, becoming the first guard in the NBA to be drafted straight from high school and, aged 18 years 2 months and 11 days, also the youngest. At Lower Merion High School in Pennsylvania, he was rated the top high school basketball player in the United States and even before entering the NBA draft he was signed by adidas to an incredible $48 million, six-year deal. Having taken a back seat to Nike and Reebok in basketball during the 1980s and 1990s, adidas hoped that the 18-year-old would help propel them back to number one.

He began his time with adidas wearing the EQT Elevation but as Bryant wasn't always a starter in his rookie year, they had minimal court time. They became popular with fans after he chose to wear a special edition in Lakers team colours when he won the 1997 dunk-contest. His first signature shoe, the KB8, came in time for the 1997/98 season and is still hailed one of the greatest ever basketball shoes adidas ever produced. It featured 'Feet You Wear' technology, a design that adidas licensed

from American inventor Frampton Ellis that had a sole which, rather than being flat, had contact patches based on those of the human foot, the idea being to improve stability and provide as natural a fitting shoe as possible. It was influential enough that Nike's Air Jordan XIII featured a similar pod-based sole and the technology continued to feature on Bryant's shoes until the KB III, his third signature model. But when a licensing dispute developed between adidas and Frampton Ellis's Anatomic Research company, adidas ceased to incorporate the 'Feet You Wear' design into its shoes, leading to a whole new design direction that proved to be a major factor in souring Bryant's relationship with the company.

For the 2000/01 season adidas produced 'The Kobe', a shoe that remains hugely polarizing among Bryant's fans and sneakerheads alike. Designed in collaboration with Audi, Bryant's favourite car brand, it was like nothing ever seen before. Featuring a moulded upper inspired by Audi's design language, its appearance was characterized by continuous body lines, flat sides, a bullet-nosed front and a metallic finish. It was also adidas's response to Nike's Foamposite technology.

Since the nineteenth century sports shoes had traditionally mostly been made of either canvas or leather

stitched together. Foamposite was an entirely new way of making shoes. The upper was made from polyurethane foam that was heated until liquid and then poured into moulds in which it cooled and became solid. Providing a glove-like fit, the foam shaped itself to the form of the foot, making it very comfortable to wear. While the Kobe was certainly unique, its boxy looks made it a shoe you either loved or hated, and most seemed to hate it, even though Bryant won his first NBA championship with the Lakers while wearing a pair.

While Bryant wore the Kobe throughout the NBA season he disliked its successor the Kobe II so much that he reverted back to the Kobe I at numerous matches during the 2001/02 season. Intended to be a refined evolution on the I, the II had a simplified design, an Audi-inspired shell-toe and a 'hood' that covered the laces. While the Kobe was clearly influenced by car design, the II simply looked like a van, and a very ugly one at that. Unhappy with their comfort and even more disillusioned with adidas's design direction, Bryant decided to do the almost unthinkable and

....

Opposite The unusual sight of Kobe Bryant in Reebok Questions during his 'free' year in 2002, as he drives against the Hornets' George Lynch at Staples Center in Los Angeles.

Below Nike Zoom Kobe 1, signed by Kobe Bryant (3PEAT LA LLC).

bought out his contract with the company in mid-2002 for a reported $8 million. adidas's director of basketball Sonny Vaccaro (having parted ways with Nike) said, 'We had two different views on what we should do. Kobe is Kobe and adidas basketball is adidas basketball and we just felt we couldn't answer each other's questions anymore.'

As part of his severance agreement, Bryant was unable to sign with another brand for a full calendar year, leaving one of the NBA's top players without a shoe endorsement, something almost unimaginable in the modern era of sports where even journeyman players had lucrative shoe contracts. It did, however, mean that he had that rare thing among top athletes, a year of being a free agent who could wear whatever he wanted. Of course, he was courted by adidas's rivals, and speculation over what Bryant would be wearing from game to game was a treat for sneakerheads hoping for rare player editions of popular shoes.

The first non-adidas shoes Bryant wore were a pair of Nike Air Force 1s during a game at the legendary Rucker Park streetball court in Harlem, New York. His 'Uptowns' were a popular choice, having been taken to the hearts of New York street players since the early 1980s. At the beginning of the 2002/03 season Air Force 1s remained on his feet in a specially made player's edition in white and Lakers gold. During the pre-season Bryant also wore retro Nike Air Jordan XIs. Originally released in 1995, they were Michael Jordan's 11th signature shoes and came with an upper trimmed in patent leather. Early in the season he also wore Nike Air Max

Elites and Zoom Turbines, which fans began to interpret as a clear sign that Nike was Bryant's intended destination once the season was over. When he wore Converse Weapons for a few games, they appeared to be more a tribute to his Lakers' predecessor, Magic Johnson, rather than a sign he was also being courted by Converse, and showed Bryant was having fun with his free agent status. Experiments with AND1's Game Time and Desire models during a few games made it clear he was enjoying the freedom to try shoes by the smaller brands too.

When he began to wear player edition Reebok Questions and Answer IVs, Allen Iverson's signature shoes, the logo that would appear on Bryant's shoes the following season seemed unclear. Wearing them in a range of colourways during the season, speculation rose that Reebok were in with a shout of securing his endorsement. Bryant had visited Reebok's headquarters in Canton, Massachusetts, and had been impressed by their plans and the fact they had gone so far as to create a prototype signature shoe for him dubbed 'The Assassin'. But despite setting the record for most three-pointers in a game in Reeboks, the two sides couldn't come to an agreement, with Bryant saying he wasn't happy with Reebok's negotiating tactics and Reebok saying they didn't think they could justify the costs – believing they could exceed the benefits.

Nike took a different view, however, and given that Bryant had mainly worn Nike or Jordan brand models during the season, it wasn't a real surprise when he signed a five-year

deal with the Swoosh for the 2002/03 season for a reported $45 million. That same year Bryant was involved in alleged sexual assault and while the brand stood by him, rather than creating a signature line off the bat, Nike put him in Air Zoom Huarache 2K4s, which in effect became his unofficial signature shoes. After the assault case against him was dropped in 2004, Bryant was paired with Nike's chief basketball designer Ken Link. The two began to work together on what would be his 'official' signature shoe, the Zoom Kobe 1. Prior to the 2005/06 season Bryant had gone through a training regime that bulked him up to 225lb. His extra weight meant he needed a more cushioned, supportive and durable design, which made the shoes heavier than his previous Huarache models but the added benefits made the increased weight worth it.

Arguably the finest moment of Bryant's career came when he was wearing his new signature shoes and he scored 81 points in the Lakers' 122-104 victory against the Toronto Raptors in January 2006, the second highest single game score and second only to Wilt Chamberlain's 100 pointer in 1962. His performance is still regarded as one of the greatest individual performances in sports history. After uncertainty caused by his off-court troubles, his performances confirmed Nike had made the right decision and their relationship with Bryant went on to flourish and produced a long line of Kobe signature shoes that have proved influential beyond Nike's basketball range and will continue to be beyond Bryant's retirement.

MICHAEL SCHUMACHER'S SHOE MAKER
2004 FIA FORMULA 1 WORLD CHAMPIONSHIP

PUMA SPEED CAT/FUTURE CAT

When Peter Schmid first designed a bespoke motor racing shoe for Puma he might have imagined a pair of them on the feet of a Formula 1 world champion, but probably never imagined that they would also become a fashion icon.

In 2000, Sparco, the renowned Italian motorsports clothing manufacturer, approached Puma with the idea of collaborating on producing a shoe designed specifically for professional motor racing drivers. The result was the Speed Cat: a streamlined, low-profile boot with a snug fit, a rounded heel suited to driving and a thin sole that maximized pedal feel, but was comfortable enough for everyday wear.

Released in 2001, the Speed Cat made its debut on the feet of the Jordan Formula 1 team and was worn by driver Jean Alesi and the team's pit crew in black suede with a Jordan yellow formstripe. Just as Formula 1 cars continually evolve, so too did the Speed Cat and it was soon being made in different materials, colours and versions.

The Speed Cat made its next evolution when, after Michael Schumacher won his unprecedented seventh Formula 1 world championship in 2004, Puma announced that they would be the German's official racing shoes supplier. In collaboration with Schumacher, Puma evolved

the Speed Cat into the Future Cat. It featured asymmetrical lacing to improve blood circulation and a re-designed forefoot for retaining the snug fit but improving its comfort. The midsole was made from a dual-density material to dampen vibrations while driving but maintain pedal feel. It also had an embroidered leaping cat on the forefoot that proved to be a very popular feature, and seven stars – one for each of Schumacher's world championships – on an external carbon-fibre patterned heel counter. Continuing its F1-like evolution, Schumacher wore a number of different hi- and low-top versions and special editions for different races during his 2005 campaign.

Despite being originally designed as a motor racing shoe, the low-top Future Cat unexpectedly began to gain a following as streetwear. Its aerodynamic and low-profile looks appealed to many who were jaded with an era of shoes that looked more like armour than sports equipment. With Puma one of the first brands to recognize the potential of the lifestyle sector, the Future Cat was soon made available in a wide range of styles and colours, but all

Right Seven-time F1 World Champion Michael Schumacher walks down the pit lane in his Puma Speed Cats during practice for the Chinese Grand Prix in 2004.

retained the sleek silhouette and the popular leaping cat on the forefoot that were now synonymous with it. Its continuing popularity led to the third evolution of the Speed Cat, the Drift Cat. While remaining inspired by motor racing, it was designed as a lifestyle shoe and was lighter and more comfortable than the Future Cat.

The Speed Cat and its evolutions remain one of the most popular and best-selling products in Puma's history. Although now better known as a lifestyle shoe, it can still be found in pit lanes in racing categories from karts to Formula 1 and after Lewis Hamilton won his second and third world championships in them in 2014 and 2015, its popularity has shown no sign of slowing down.

Below Puma Future Cat Hi-Top, signed by Michael Schumacher (Puma Archive).

NO LIMITS
2006 DEVELOPMENT OF THE NIKE SOLE

OSSUR/NIKE FLEX RUN NIKE SOLE

When Sarah Reinertsen had her left leg amputated it was to inspire a life that saw her overcome many challenges to become one of the world's leading female para-triathletes and the first woman with a prosthetic leg to finish the Hawaii Ironman Championship.

Born in May 1975, Reinertsen was diagnosed with proximal femoral focal deficiency, a disorder that meant she didn't have the tissues needed to stimulate the growth of her left leg, resulting in it being much shorter than her right leg. This caused her difficulty in walking. Leg braces failed to improve her condition, and at the age of seven she and her parents elected to have her leg amputated above the knee. Rather than allow it to get her down or to feel sorry for herself, she was determined to live as normal a life as possible and to focus on what she had, not what she had lost.

Life wasn't easy being the only child in her school with a physical disability and Reinertsen was often left frustrated when she was not included in school sports activities. When her parents signed her up for the local soccer league and the coach told her to go and kick a ball against the wall on her own, the experience of exclusion caused something to snap. Having been brought up by her parents to pick herself up and to defy those who told her she

couldn't do something because of her disability, Reinertsen determined to find a way to prove that having a prosthetic limb was no more disabling than having to wear glasses.

Aged 11 she saw amputee runner Paddy Rossbach compete in a 10k race. Reinertsen was struck by how fluid, graceful and powerful she was, and in that moment her life changed. She felt running could empower her to do anything she wanted and realized that she too could run a marathon or one day go to the Paralympics. By the age of 13 she was ready to compete and attended her first international track meet, where she broke the 100m world record for female above-knee amputees. She went on to become a member of the US Disabled Track and Field team for seven years and represented the US at the 1992 Barcelona Paralympic Games. Between 1997 and 2004, Reinertsen also competed in seven marathons including New York, Los Angeles, the Millennium New Zealand, London and Boston.

In 2004, Reinertsen decided that she wanted to make history and become the first female para-triathlete to

Right Sarah Reinertsen, one of the world's most successful para-athletes, running with her Össur Flex Run and Nike Sole

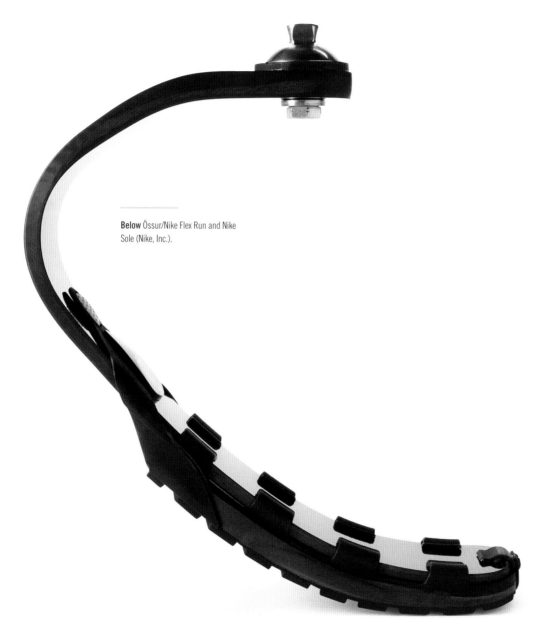

Below Össur/Nike Flex Run and Nike Sole (Nike, Inc.).

complete one of the toughest endurance races in the world, the Ironman World Championship in Hawaii. Comprising a 2.4-mile swim, a 112-mile cycle and a 26.2 -mile marathon run, it is among the most challenging tests for any athlete. After a good performance in the swimming stage, she was almost stopped in her tracks 20 miles into the cycling stage when she encountered strong headwinds and she was disqualified from the event when she reached the end of the stage 15 minutes after the cut-off time.

The following year she trained even harder and completed the race inside the required time to become the first woman in history to finish the Ironman Hawaii on a prosthetic leg.

In 2006, Reinertsen began a relationship with Nike that brought about a collaboration between Nike and Össur, one of the world's leading orthopaedics manufacturers and makers of prosthetics and running blades. Founded in Iceland in 1971 by prosthetist Össur Kristinsson, their products had become the choice of many of the world's most successful para-athletes. The Össur Flex Foot running blade used by Reinertsen was made from carbon fibre, a light but very strong material with excellent shock absorption and flexing qualities, which are critical for amputee athletes. Previously, Reinertsen would turn cobbler herself, stripping the outsole from a regular running shoe and attaching it to her prosthetic leg. But being an athlete and not a shoemaker, the results could often be both unstable and unreliable. Of course, this was the norm, not just Reinertsen but for many para-athletes.

The first prototype sole developed by Nike was made by Tobie Hatfield, Nike's innovation director and brother of

Tinker Hatfield, the company's revered shoe designer. It was based on a Nike Free 5.0 Trail outsole and glued to a plastic-based sleeve that would slide on to the blade. Nike worked closely with Reinertsen to design and tweak the next set of prototypes based on her feedback and testing.

The end result was simply named 'Nike Sole' and was an integrated layered sole consisting of an outsole, midsole and thermal plastic urethane called Aeroply, made of recycled Nike Air capsules, which served as an interface between the Nike Sole and the Flex-Run carbon fibre blade. Nine nylon plastic tabs served as fingers that wrapped securely around the Flex-Run to lock it in place but facilitated easy installation and removal too. It also featured a rubber leash for easy placement over a medallion fastener to provide extra security.

Reinertsen felt the new sole improved her performances and meant she and other para-athletes could now leave the cobbling to Nike. The sole was also another step forward in allowing para-athletes greater choices in footwear. Just as able-bodied athletes have a huge range of options open to them as to the most appropriate shoes to wear for different sports, future versions of the Nike Sole would offer para-athletes the same choices by allowing them to attach Nike Soles with different tread patterns and constructions.

Reinertsen continues to be a prolific triathlon competitor and has broken the women's above-knee amputee marathon record several times. Seeing her disability as a gift, she strives to support and inspire those with physical challenges so they can pursue active lifestyles through sport and live fulfilling lives beyond the barriers they face.

FROM CLOWNING TO CROWNING
2008 BEIJING OLYMPIC GAMES

PUMA COMPLETE THESEUS II

When Usain Bolt first burst on to the world scene it was seemingly out of nowhere. Most people outside athletics had never heard of the young Jamaican sprinter and yet at Beijing he ripped up records in the 100m and 200m to the amazement of the whole world. But what made his achievements all the more incredible is that in the early days of his career, not only did it all seem so easy for him, but fast cars, fast food and having fun seemed much more important than winning gold medals.

Born in August 1986, Usain Bolt grew up in Trelawny, Jamaica, with his parents, brother and sister. Feeling that his young son was too lazy for his own good, his disciplinarian father gave him chores to do. The one he hated the most was carrying heavy buckets of water from the river up to the house. It was backbreaking work but began to develop his physique. One of his teachers, Devere Nugent, noticed his latent speed while playing cricket at school. Nugent suggested that his speed would be better put to use in sprinting rather than cricket. The young Bolt had his doubts. He loved playing cricket, and also felt that his height was a disadvantage in running because it prevented him from starting as quickly as some of his classmates. But Nugent soon realized that all Bolt needed was a reason to win, so he bribed him with the one thing he knew Bolt would

run for. Food. It worked and Bolt won his first 100m with ease, enjoying not just the juicy jerk chicken he won as his reward but also the buzz he got from winning.

After he entered and won more competitions it became obvious to all that he was quick, and he was soon offered a scholarship to William Knibb High School, the school responsible for many of Jamaica's best athletes. The school's only proviso was that he focused on running rather than on his beloved cricket. Being an individual sport rather than a team sport, athletics put him in sole charge of his own destiny, which was something that appealed to him and so he agreed. He settled on the 200m and 400m, as they allowed him to make the most of his combination of speed and stamina. Ironically, in hindsight, he did not choose the 100m, as the consensus in the sport was that it was unsuited to tall athletes. Winning came easily to him and he immediately dominated his schoolmates. While others seemed to have to try extra hard to win, for Bolt it was a breeze and he even began to enter other events like the high jump and long jump just for fun, winning those too. He was in such a different league that his teachers began to arrange sports day when he was away at competitions just to give everybody else a chance.

At the age of 14 he began running for Jamaica. In his first

Caribbean regional event he won silver in the 200m and 400m and then made his international debut at the 2001 World Youth Championships in Hungary. Despite his talent, Bolt still wasn't taking running seriously. He just couldn't see it as his future and especially didn't like the hard work that was involved. He would occasionally skip training, causing his coach to search for him and haul him back to school. His love of pranks also got him into trouble. When he sneaked out of the school van on the way to the Carifta Trials and hitched a ride with a friend, his coach panicked and called the police. When Bolt arrived at the stadium the police and the coach were waiting for him and angrily sat him down to give him a good talking to. Although a reluctant runner, Bolt's coaches refused to let him waste his talent. Desperate to drop the 400m, he faked an injury at the World Youth Championships so that he would miss the semi-final, but his coaches saw right through it and made him race. In 'defiance', he won the gold medal in the 200m and set a new record.

It was aged 15 that Puma first noticed Bolt's talent and approached his manager Norman Peart about signing him.

Opposite Usain Bolt proudly presents his Puma Complete Theseus II shoes to the world following his record-breaking 100m win at the 2008 Beijing Olympic Games (Olympic Multimedia Library)

Below Puma Complete Theseus II,
worn by Usain Bolt (Puma Archive).

Pascal Rolling, Puma's head of running marketing, had been enthralled by his charisma and had witnessed first-hand the effect he could have on a crowd at the 2002 Carifta Championships. An obvious, if reluctant, star in the making, he was being called the next Michael Johnson (despite running better times than Johnson had at the same age) but unlike many athletes, he was also a natural entertainer and so Puma signed him to a modest deal and provided him with all the shoes and equipment he needed. But it wasn't long before Puma started to have their doubts when he failed to live up to expectations at the 2004 Olympic Games in Athens and was criticized by some in Jamaica, who said he had an unprofessional attitude. Many in his home country blamed his love of partying and fast food. If he even ventured near a KFC or Burger King it was likely to appear in the press and Puma were now so concerned by his lifestyle that they began to consider dropping him. 'Well, he's a young guy, but he doesn't really want to train as hard as he should. He has all the potential but he does get injured. If he doesn't practise he's never going to be great,' said Puma's CEO Jochen Zeitz. After discussions, Zeitz and Puma's other top brass decided it was time to drop him. But a few weeks later they had a change of heart. 'Let's just stick with him,' said Zeitz, 'I'm sure he can pull it off. He's a great guy and if he gets a good coach he can do miracles, let's just stand by him.'

Bolt began working with Glen Mills, one of Jamaica's most successful coaches. Shaking hands on their partnership proved to be the moment Bolt decided athletics was going to be his life and that he needed to get serious if he was going to be an Olympic gold medal winner. Mills encouraged him to embrace training and to find a hunger for success. Whenever he succumbed to temptation and went partying, Mills calmly reminded him how much hard work was needed to get where they both wanted him to be. It proved

to be the start of wonderful relationship. Although injuries prevented him from going to the 2006 Commonwealth Games in Melbourne, Bolt won bronze in the World Athletics Championships in Stuttgart the same year and a week later took silver in the IAAF World Cup in Athens. Despite Bolt's desperation to run the 100m, Mills was sceptical of his chances and felt he would do better in the 400m. However, he made an agreement with him that he could race in the 100m if he broke the Jamaican 200m record, which had been set 36 years ago. At the Jamaican Championships he did just that, running 19.75. Fulfilling his side of the bargain, Mills entered Bolt in the 100m at the Vardinoyiannia meeting in Crete where he won gold and, probably more importantly, confirmed his ability in the distance and raised his expectations.

Bolt continued to develop in the 100m and at the 2008 Jamaica Invitational ran a time of 9.76, the second fastest in the history of the event. Watching the race was Michael Johnson, who said that he was shocked at how quickly Bolt had improved in the 100m. Just three months before the Beijing Olympic Games Bolt improved further when he ran 9.72 in New York ahead of Tyson Gay. 'It looked like his knees were going past my face,' Gay said after the race. By allowing Bolt to race in the 100m, Mills had inadvertently found a distance that made him focus on practice. The lazy, mischievous clown in him appeared to have largely, if not completely, been exorcised. In Beijing, despite his inexperience, he announced that he would enter the 100m as well as the 200m. For both distances Puma had provided Bolt with their Complete Theseus II model but in gold. Reminding many of Michael Johnson's gold Nikes from the Atlanta Games, what was special about Bolt's shoes was that, apart from the gold paint job, they were essentially the same model as those on sale in the high street.

In round one of the 100m heats, despite a terrible start, he easily caught up and jogged across the finish line in first place. The public's anticipation increased. In the second round, he won in 9.92 despite looking around for the last half of the race, and in the semi-final he pulled ahead at 60m, but again slowed up to finish 9.85. Just like in high school, it all seemed too easy for him. In the final, despite another poor start, he was leading by 50m, and by 80m began thumping his chest before crossing the line to finish in an incredible world record time of 9.69. Many, including the IOC president, criticized him for showboating and slowing before the line, but Jamaican Prime Minister Edmund Bartlett defended him, saying, 'We have to allow the personality of youth to express itself'. The fact was Bolt had seen the 100m as just 'a kick, a race for fun', but two days later, in the 200m, which he called 'the Real Deal', there were no finish line antics and he sprinted hard all the way, even dipping his chest to improve his time. Still not done, as third leg of the Jamaican 4x100m team he won his third gold medal in Beijing and with his teammates set a new Olympic and world record. Marvelling at his feats, the whole world seemed to be talking about Bolt after Beijing.

Bolt's victories were hailed as a new beginning for a sport that had been lacking in big characters and mired in drug scandals. While there was no doubt he had vastly improved his attitude and approach to his sport, there was still enough of the clown to endear him to the world. Puma and Jochen Zeitz could also look back with satisfaction. Not only had their relationship become a close one, but the decision to stick with him had paid off. After his wins he had proudly displayed his gold spikes to a global audience, earning Puma tens of millions of dollars' worth of publicity and, perhaps more importantly, had allowed them to claim that they made the fastest shoes in the world.

THE MASTER BLASTER'S CENTURY OF CENTURIES
2012 INDIA VS BANGLADESH

ADIDAS 22YDS LITE IV

It's said that in India they worship many gods, but when it comes to sport there is only one: Sachin Tendulkar. When he walked on to a cricket pitch he was never alone, because he carried with him the weight of the hopes and dreams of over a billion people. Despite that burden he played like no other batsman before him.

When Tendulkar began playing cricket, it was as if he was born to it. Born in April 1973 in Mumbai, he first picked up a cricket bat after his elder brother Ajit introduced him to the sport to help curb the mischievous bullying streak that got him into fights at school. He also introduced him to Ramakant Achrekar, a well-known club cricketer and coach at Shivaji Park. Impressed with his talent, Achrekar advised his parents to move him to Sharadashram Vidyamandir High School, a school with a reputation for producing excellent cricket players, and continued coaching him at Shivaji Park. He ensured Tendulkar was never short of matches, starting him in one match where he would often score 50 runs, retiring him, then sending him on a scooter to another

ground, where he would score another 50. Practising relentlessly, he was soon being described by many as a child prodigy. When, just short of his 15th birthday, he was part of an incredible record-breaking unbroken 664-run partnership with his friend and teammate Vinod Kambli in an inter-school game, he appeared destined for greatness.

Aged just 14 he began playing club cricket for Bombay, scoring 100 not out in his first game, making him the youngest Indian to score a century on his first-class debut, and he finished the 1988/89 season as Bombay's highest run-scorer with 583 runs at an average of 67.77. His more seasoned teammates began to speak widely about the young prodigy and it seemed obvious to all that he should make his international debut, despite being only 15 at the time. When he wasn't selected for India's 1989 West Indies tour for fear of being injured by the Windies' fast bowlers, he was devastated, but when told why, showed maturity beyond his years, saying, 'But if I get hit, I'll grow faster.' When he did make his international debut it was against India's great rivals, Pakistan. Laughing at his youth, the Pakistanis teased him, asking, 'Have you got permission to play from your teacher?' When a bouncer from Waqar Younis struck his head, leaving him dazed, he refused medical assistance, leaving the Pakistanis in no doubt that he was no mere

child. In his second Test, during the 1990 tour of England, the 17-year-old confirmed aility beyond his years when he almost single-handedly rescued his more experienced teammates from defeat with his first Test century, scoring 119 not out. He was so impressive in England that two years later he was asked to join Yorkshire, becoming the county's first ever player to be selected from outside Yorkshire. While his time in England didn't see him performing to his full potential, it boosted his confidence enormously, which became apparent when, during a tour to New Zealand, he replaced an injured teammate at the top of the batting order and scored 82 to cement his opening position.

As India's economy grew in the 90s and its media became more widely accessible, Tendulkar's fame began to spread beyond cricket, as did his role as India's talisman. At the 1996 Cricket World Cup he was the leading run scorer with over 500 and when India lost to Sri Lanka there was rioting in the stands, illustrating that a side featuring Tendulkar was increasingly expected to win. Those expectations were never higher than in 1998 when, in his batting prime, he took up the much-anticipated challenge of facing Shane Warne during Australia's tour of India. It was to be a true clash of the titans, with the world's number one batsman facing the world's number one spin bowler. The first clash, during a warm-up match between the tourists and Mumbai, saw Tendulkar victorious after making an unbeaten 204 runs as Warne conceded 111 runs in 16 overs. Mumbai won by 10 wickets and it was all over by lunchtime on the third day. Against spinners Warne and Robertson Tendulkar showcased his signature drive straight down the pitch and right over their heads, a shot that was also instrumental in defeating Australia in the Test series that followed. Legends of the game waxed lyrical about Tendulkar's batting, describing it as an 'art form' and marvelled at the Bruce Lee-like punch he delivered to a ball that meant sixes came from what seemed like the merest of strokes.

In the early 2000s, despite injuries and a loss of form, he continued to impress, equalling Sir Donald Bradman's record of 29 Test centuries during the 2002 West Indies series, and being named Player of the Tournament at the 2003 World Cup. In his 14th international year and still under constant scrutiny in India, many predicted his decline and after a disappointing start to India's 2003 Tour of Australia, it appeared that his many years of Test cricket might be coming to an end. However, in the fourth and final Test, Tendulkar gave a superb display of batting that reminded many that he was still the master, scoring 241 not out to ensure India retained the Border-Gavaskar trophy. However, it was to be the only highlight in a bad spell for India and Tendulkar and it wasn't until 2008 that his old form returned. His comeback began with the breaking of Brian Lara's record for most Test runs with 11,953 and following the Mumbai terror attacks he scored possibly his most important century against England, helping India to win the Test and the series, providing the nation with an important lift. He dedicated his century to the victims of the tragedy.

Despite having been a brand ambassador for adidas since 1997, in 2009 Tendulkar began a relationship with the company that launched the Three Stripes into India's collective consciousness when, as well as on his feet and clothing, they appeared on his hallowed bat in a match against New Zealand in the Compaq Cup Tri-series in Sri Lanka. The deal also saw Tendulkar extending his relationship with adidas to become a lifetime ambassador.

In 2011, India co-hosted the Cricket World Cup and with Tendulkar now approaching the final years of his career he had the extra pressure of wanting to deliver India's first World Cup since 1983 before his retirement, despite the fact that no hosting side had ever won it. As always, he led by example, scoring 53 to help India defeat holders Australia. Against old rivals Pakistan in the semi-finals he scored 85 to take India through. In the final, played at his home town ground, all of India's eyes and expectations were on him after Sri Lanka set a target of 275. India got off to a terrible start when Lasith Malinga dismissed Virender Sehwag, and the trophy appeared to be slipping away when Tendulkar, the man most believed had got India to the final, was caught behind by Sri Lanka's Kumar Sangakkara. It was left to captain M.S. Dhoni to keep his side in the match and when India recovered and pulled through to win, the Wankhede Stadium erupted with joy. In celebration, Tendulkar's teammates carried him on their shoulders and Virat Kholi summed up the feelings of all of India when he said, 'He has carried the burden of the nation for 21 years. It is time we carried him on our shoulders.' In recognition of his achievement Tendulkar was awarded the Bharat Ratna, India's highest civilian award, only presented to those deemed to have given the highest degree of national service.

In the same year adidas created the 22YDS Lite (named after the length of a cricket pitch), the shoes that Tendulkar would wear during his moment of crowning glory. With a low foot-bed and wide mid-foot, they were designed with a focus on stability, providing cricket players with a solid foot position when facing fast bowling and featured a mesh upper to allow breathability and protection from dust. Unusually, this design meant the three stripes had to be placed at the front of the shoe. Made with adiPrene inserts, adidas's cushioning technology, in the heel and in the forefoot, the shoes offered greater impact cushioning than had previously been seen in a cricket shoe. It placed adidas in a market traditionally dominated by smaller specialist cricket brands and soon became a favourite for international players, especially fast bowlers. The moment that the 22YDS would go down in history came when Tendulkar wore them to become the first person in history to achieve a century of centuries in international cricket, a remarkable achievement that many believed would never happen and even more believe will never be beaten. It came after a wait of a year during which time even Tendulkar himself was unsure if he would reach the landmark. His historic hundred came in an ODI against Bangladesh in March 2012. To celebrate his feat adidas released a limited 'Century of Centuries' 22YDS model that became an instant collector's item.

Tendulkar retired in 2013 after an amazing 24 years, 663 Tests and ODIs, over 34,000 runs and a hundred centuries, to the lament of many. His performances united rich and poor alike in his country and many believe that India's rise as a nation went in tandem with Tendulkar's as a cricketer. His appeal was by no means restricted to India and he was undoubtedly cricket's first superstar, causing even legends of the game to pause and watch watch when he came to the crease. But his godlike status in India never changed his view that he was but a servant of his country. The mischievous boy, introduced to cricket as a bully had become a paragon of modesty, a perfect ambassador for his sport and adidas, and an inspiration to over a billion people.

Below adidas 22YDS Lite IV, worn by
Sachin Tendulkar (adidas Archive).

To
Herbert
Thanks for a wonderful
Partnership and all
the support.
Best wishes,

th July 2012

SEVENTH HEAVEN
2012 WIMBLEDON CHAMPIONSHIPS

NIKE ZOOM VAPOR 9 TOUR

Ahead of the 2012 Wimbledon Championships, even Roger Federer's most ardent fans believed that his best days were behind him. Not having won a Grand Slam since 2010, the prevailing opinion was that now that he had hit his 30s and had a young family to worry about, his game had lost some of its edge and that over five sets he was beginning to lack the endurance he once had. But when he took on Andy Murray in the final, the Fed Express showed all the doubters that he could still deliver.

In 2012, Federer was celebrating 10 years with Nike. When he first signed he was a promising but Grand Slam-less young player and had negotiated the deal himself. Earning him $1 million a year, it was a bargain deal for Nike, given what he would go on to achieve. When a 10-year extension was agreed in 2008 after he had won 12 Grand Slam titles it was believed to be worth as much as $13 million a year, showing that Nike fully recognized how much Federer's stock had risen in the interim and making him one of Nike's highest paid athletes.

For the 2012 season Federer and Nike's Tinker Hatfield collaborated on a new tennis shoe that would be Nike's most advanced model ever. Federer was keen for Hatfield to create a design that brought some of the benefits of a running shoe to tennis, resulting in a shoe that was close to the ground but with less weight, added comfort and breathability. It also needed to be a platform that Nike could adjust to allow for the change in playing surfaces during the course of a season. The result was the Zoom Vapor 9. The model featured a new 'Dynamic Fit' system, with fingers through which the laces pulled together like a pulley to mould to the shape of the wearer's foot. It allowed Federer to create the custom fit that he was looking for, tighter at the front but with room for movement everywhere else. To enhance support a frame was added to the bottom edge of the upper. The frame, made from a lightweight but strong and flexible TPU (thermoplastic polyurethane), provided stability and protection during fast directional changes. The design also integrated 'Zoom', a development of Nike's Air system that included high tensile fibres in the Air capsule to deliver a more responsive and springy feel.

During the year Federer's Vapors went through many colourways but for Wimbledon they were respectfully white, although danced close to the edge of the 'all white' uniform rules by featuring the All England Club's purple on

Right Roger Federer on his way to Wimbledon title number seven wearing Zoom Vapor 9s, the most advanced tennis shoe Nike had ever made.

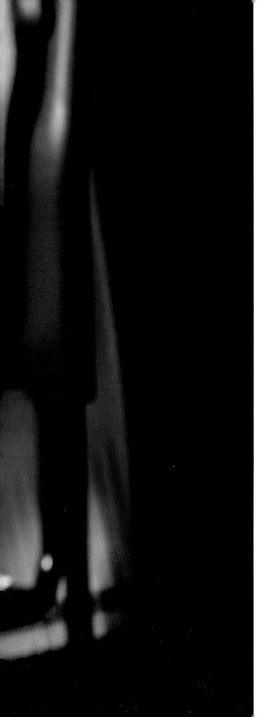

the Nike Swoosh and green on the TPU frame. Celebrating Federer's Wimbledon titles they also featured a gold Wimbledon trophy emblazoned with a '6'.

Journalists and spectators found it hard to choose between the two challengers for the 2012 Wimbledon men's title. While Federer couldn't be discounted, it did appear that he was past his best. On the other hand, the younger Andy Murray, while showing the potential, still hadn't developed into a Grand Slam winner, but many believed he might finally do it and become the first British man to win Wimbledon for over 70 years.

As soon as the match started, predictions of Federer's demise looked like they could be accurate, as Murray broke his serve in the first game. He looked uncomfortable with the pace Murray was setting and to slow things down began playing sliced groundstrokes. When Murray drove a ball straight at him from close range, a move echoing the aggression displayed by his coach Ivan Lendl in times past, it forced Federer to duck to avoid it hitting him. Federer appeared slightly rattled, resulting in some uncharacteristic errors that allowed Murray to serve out for the set, taking it 6-4.

With the sun still shining on Murray in the second set he continued to serve well and out-harried Federer, but when four break points came his way, the difference between him and the Swiss Maestro started to become clear after he failed to convert them. Sensing weakness, Federer realized

Left Nike Zoom Vapor 9 Tour, worn by Roger Federer (Wimbledon Museum).

that he needed to be aggressive on Murray's second serves and it paid dividends, with some amazing backhand drop volleys helping him hold for 6-5 and then take the set after coming from 40-15 down.

As the weather changed in the third set, so too did Murray's fortunes and when rain came, with Federer 40-0 up in the third game, the closing of the Centre Court roof seemed to seal Murray's fate. In contrast, for Federer it appeared to create a stage that not only confirmed the doubters were wrong, but proved he had lost nothing of his previous majesty. While Murray slipped and slid around the court, Federer was calm and imperious, coming back to win game eight from 40-0 down and then serving to win the set 6-3.

In the fourth set Federer often appeared to be just toying with Murray, shaping himself for one shot but playing another. He was at his most creative once again, crafting winning returns and forcing Murray into committing errors. While Murray looked like a broken man, Federer was gliding around majestically. Once again he had turned Centre Court into his royal court and, despite making the crowd's home favourite look like a jester, they couldn't help but bow down to him as he took his seventh Wimbledon singles title: 4-6, 7-5, 6-3, 6-4.

Defying those who had written him off, Federer had equalled the record of his hero Pete Sampras with seven Wimbledon Championships and confirmed, even in the minds of those who had said it was now beyond him, that he was the greatest player the sport had ever seen. As a tearful Andy Murray said in his gracious runners-up speech, 'Not bad for a 30-year-old.'

THE PROJECT
2012 LONDON OLYMPIC GAMES

NIKE ZOOM VICTORY ELITE

When Mo Farah failed to qualify for the final of the 5,000m of the 2008 Olympic Games in Beijing it was one of the lowest points in his life. His disappointment with himself was so great that he had doubts about his own ability, but after much soul-searching he made a vow to transform himself from an also-ran into a gold medal winner in just four years.

Mohamed Farah and his twin brother Hassan were born in March 1983 in Mogadishu, Somalia, to Muktar and Amran Farah. When fighting between rival clans turned Mogadishu into a war zone, their parents sent the boys and their sister to live with their grandmother in Djibouti while their elder brothers went to live in their mother's home village. When their father sought asylum in England he was told he could only bring three of his children with him, forcing his parents to make the painful decision to split Mo and Hassan until the whole family could eventually be reunited.

Aged only eight, Farah began a completely new life in England. Unable to speak a word of English, at first he found it hard to integrate at school in Isleworth, London, but

when his teacher Alan Watkinson spotted his athletic ability he found his place on the sports field. However, it wasn't athletics that Farah dreamed about, it was football, so much so that to get him to come to the running club Watkinson had to allow him to play half an hour of football beforehand. When Watkinson entered him in the 1996 English schools cross-country at the age of 13 he finished ninth but when Watkinson said to him a year later, 'Win this year and I'll buy you a football shirt', Farah did win. With an Arsenal shirt as his reward, he went on to win four more English school titles, leading to his first major title in the 5,000m at the European Junior Championships in 2001.

When Farah decided to commit his life to athletics he soon realized he wasn't as disciplined as he could be in terms of his social life. Determined to become world class, at 21 he moved in with a group of Kenyan runners living in nearby Teddington and began to follow their completely dedicated and disciplined approach to training. It worked. The following year, in 2006, he won silver in the 5,000m at the European Championships and gold in the 2006 European Cross-Country Championships. Just as he was finding form, a disappointing sixth at the 2007 World Championships and then failure to reach the finals at the Beijing Olympic Games left him wondering if world class was a level he couldn't achieve.

Deciding to put the disappointment of Beijing behind him, he set his sights on the 2012 Games in his home city of London. Ian Stewart, newly appointed head of the UK Athletics' endurance team, encouraged him to consider more carefully how he trained, advising him to cut back on his mileage so that he would be more rested for races. He also encouraged him to train at altitude and so during the winter of 2008 Farah spent time in Kenya and Ethiopia training in the thin air at a height of 8,000m. Stewart's advice paid off. In 2009, he broke the British indoor record in the 3,000m in Glasgow and then again at the UK Indoor Grand Prix in Birmingham shortly afterwards with a performance Steve Cram hailed as 'the best performance by a male British distance runner for a generation'. Seventh place at the 2009 World Championships was disappointing but Farah bounced back to win silver at the European Cross-Country Championships. More altitude training helped him to prepare for a great 2010 in which he set a new British record in the London 10,000m and won gold in both the 5,000m and 10,000m in the European Athletics Championships in Barcelona.

With Farah now Great Britain's number one distance runner and the London 2012 Games on the horizon, he looked to America to further boost his performance. In 2001, disturbed by the United States' lack of elite long-distance runners, Nike's

Thomas Clarke had founded the Oregon Project. Run by Alberto Salazar, multiple New York City and Boston marathon winner, its aim was to promote long-distance running by providing elite level training and performance facilities funded by Nike. It wasn't a new idea. Nike's famed Athletics West team had benefitted from the company's support and funding in the 1970s and '80s but the Oregon Project was very much Salazar's baby and in him Farah saw a coach who could take him to a new level. However, when he had previously approached Salazar, the fact he wasn't American and was sponsored by adidas, having signed with them in 2006, meant they simply couldn't work together. But with his adidas contract nearly up and Farah willing to consider a move to Oregon, things were different. Seeing it as also a way to escape the intensifying media speculation as the London Games approached, Farah signed with Nike and moved with his family to Oregon in early 2011.

The move attracted criticism. The Oregon Project had come under scrutiny from both the US and World Anti-Doping Agencies due to its use of a 'high altitude house', which, they claimed, could be equivalent to blood doping, but ultimately no action was taken. There was no disputing Salazar's training worked, however, when Farah had his best year to date in 2011, setting a European record in the 5,000m in Birmingham, winning gold in the 3,000m at the European Indoor Championships, the NYC Half Marathon, the Prefontaine Classic 10,000m and setting a British record in the 5,000m at a Diamond League meeting in Monaco. At the 2011 World Championships in Daegu, South Korea, Farah made history when he won the 5,000m and silver in the 10,000m, making him the first Briton to win international medals in both distances.

In the run-up to London 2012, Farah was talked up as one of Great Britain's top medal hopes and was the focus of intense media coverage. As part of the Oregon Project, Nike also had high hopes for him. Specifically for the Games the company had launched the 'Volt' range, a collection of 16 specialized shoes that gave Nike athletes a number of options to choose from depending on their event, including the Flyknit Racer, the world's first 'knitted' high performance shoe. Farah's choice was the Zoom Victory Elite, the lightest running spikes that Nike had ever made, and which featured the company's Flywire technology. The idea behind Flywire was to provide maximum support to the foot while minimizing weight. By using threads made of Vectran, a super-light but super-strong polyester, support could be placed precisely where necessary, similar to the way a suspension bridge works. Without needing to rely on layers of material to provide support, the shoes only needed a thin external layer, resulting in them weighing only 93gms, even lighter than the famous gold spikes that Michael Johnson wore in 1996, which weighed 112gms.

As Farah lined up for the 10,000m in the Olympic Stadium in his home town it was with the weight of expectation on his shoulders. Before and during the Games, Great Britain's athletes were achieving in every sport. On the evening that became known as 'Super Saturday', Jessica Ennis and Greg Rutherford had both delivered gold for the home crowd and Farah didn't want to be the first to break the Olympic fever that was gripping the host nation and its athletes. Buoyed by his home crowd, Farah appeared happy and confident. At the start Kenenisa Bekele, the reigning champion, led, with Farah second and despite slipping back into the middle of the pack, Farah appeared calm and in control. With 12 laps left, he began making his way back to the front. The lead changed constantly between the Kenyan, Ethiopian and Eritrean runners and with five laps left Farah moved into third, with his Oregon training partner Galen Rupp close behind. With two laps left, he was second behind Bekele, ready to pounce. As tensions mounted in the stadium and the leaders jostled for position on the last lap Farah made his move, hit the front and kicked all the way to the finish line to the deafening roars of approval of the home crowd. With Rupp in second it was a 1-2 for Nike and Salazar's Oregon Project.

Ahead of the 5,000m Farah was only too aware that just six men had won the 'double' before, but he remained undaunted. Whatever happened he was already an Olympic gold medallist. The race began at a slow pace and he ran comfortably at the back. Two laps in, he headed towards the front and settled into the middle of the pack. Just like the 10,000m the Kenyans and Ethiopians jostled for the lead until with three laps to go, Farah moved forwards into second. With two laps left, he took the lead and when the final lap bell went began his surge, fending off the challenge from the Kenyan Thomas Longosiwa. With 600m remaining, Farah kicked and the entire stadium roared, almost carrying him across the finish line.

As he celebrated his first double, Farah could look back on the disappointment of the Beijing Games and reflect on his remarkable journey from non-qualifier to double Olympic champion in only four years. Crediting Alberto Salazar for his role in his transformation, the relationship was a perfect example of how a sports brand could play a major part in enabling an athlete to improve his performance beyond just the equipment it provided him with. While by no means the first, the successful partnership between Farah and Nike set a benchmark that other athletes and sports brands now look to emulate in their quest for victory, taking the relationship between brand and athlete to a level beyond mere endorsement.

Below Nike Zoom Victory Elite spikes (Nike).

ACE OUTTA COMPTON
2015 THE SERENA SLAME

NIKE NIKECOURT FLARE

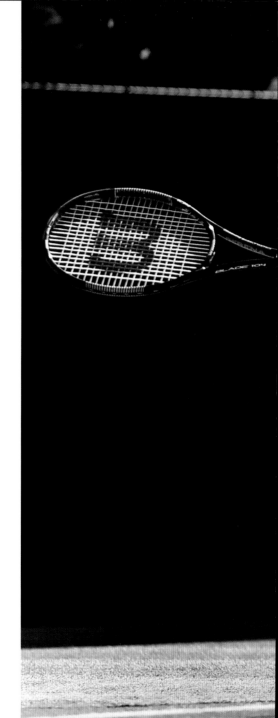

Life for Serena Williams has never been easy. Major health scares, seemingly irrecoverable dips in form, family problems, tragedy and frequent injuries would have greatly curbed the careers of most tennis players, but not Williams. Growing up in Compton, Los Angeles, she was the youngest of Richard and Oracene Williams' five daughters. Compton had once been a desirable neighbourhood for the city's black middle class, but had suffered a period of economic decline and become one of the toughest areas in California, and the Williams sisters were occasional witnesses to gang violence on the streets around their house.

A big tennis fan, Richard Williams had envisioned his daughters as Grand Slam champions before they were even born. He made no bones about the fact that he saw tennis as a way of making money and getting his family 'out of the ghetto' and avidly read books and watched instructional videotapes so that he and his wife could teach their children. As soon as they were old enough to hold tennis rackets, Richard began coaching his daughters on public tennis courts in and around Compton where he and the girls became a familiar sight with their shopping trolley full of used balls that Richard had pleaded LA's country clubs to donate. Despite learning in

an environment that was as far removed from a country club as could be (both recall frequently ducking when they heard gunfire), both Venus and Serena showed a talent for the game, and Richard began to put into action the 78-page plan he had mapped out for them.

Jumping forward to 2014, the sisters from Compton had executed their father's plan to perfection, winning an incredible 25 Grand Slams between them. Serena, in particular, had overcome numerous injuries only to come back stronger than ever. Had it not been for those, one can only contemplate how much more complete her domination of the women's game would have been.

As Serena and Nike discussed concepts for her new signature shoe in 2013, her design ideas centred on tackling her injuries and, in particular, her troublesome ankles. Ankle problems had frequently plagued her and had resurfaced during the 2013 Australian Open when she sprained an ankle while serving for the match. As a result, greater stability was key and Serena was keen for Nike to design a shoe that was bigger and more built up.

....

Right Serena Williams stretches for the ball in her NikeCourt Flares on the way to defeating Garbiñe Muguruza 6-4, 6-4 during the 2015 Championships final, earning her a sixth Wimbledon singles title.

Aaron Cooper, one of Nike's most talented designers, had other ideas in mind, however, and felt that there was a way to achieve stability by using a much more minimal design. Drawing inspiration from fellow Nike designer Eric Avar's work on Kobe Bryant's Zoom Kobe VI, Cooper was sure that a similar ankle support would address Serena's concerns. He also drew inspiration from working with a kung-fu master from whom he gained an insight into what he described as 'unencumbered flexibility' and the idea of creating a product that became an extension of the athlete when worn, almost as if the athlete was competing barefoot. The result was named the NikeCourt Flare and it was to play a small part in one of the most exciting chapters of Serena's career.

The end of 2014, a year to forget for Serena, saw the beginning of one of her greatest achievements. For the first eight months of the year many of her performances had been affected by injuries to her back and thigh. She crashed out in the second round of the French Open, beaten by Garbiñe Muguruza, who only lost four games in the match. At Wimbledon, losing in the third round, Serena made her earliest exit since 2005 and was forced to withdraw from the doubles event alongside sister Venus after becoming disorientated. She bounced back, however, winning 19 out of her next 20 matches and her sixth overall and third consecutive US Open singles title. Her victory meant she had drawn level with Chris Evert for the most singles titles won by a woman at the US Open in the Open Era and that she equalled Evert and Martina Navratilova's 18 major singles titles. While many were already calling her

the greatest female player of all time, by equalling Evert and Navratilova, her claim to the title was unequivocal. Further evidence came from the fact that she had held the No. 1 ranking for the entire year, a feat that hadn't been achieved since Steffi Graf in 1996.

Opening the 2015 Grand Slam season at the Australian Open Serena defeated Maria Sharapova for the 16th consecutive time and took her sixth Australian Open title and 19th Grand Slam title, only three behind Steffi Graf on 22. As she prepared for the clay court season, the week of 20 April marked Serena's 114th consecutive week as the world No. 1, the third longest run in WTA history. However, she suffered her first defeat of the season in the semi-finals of the Mutua Madrid Open to Petra Kvitová, ending a 27-match winning streak.

Serena's French Open looked over before it began, as she played through a bout of flu. Managing to reach the semi-final she coughed and spluttered her way to victory but on the eve of the final she was suffering enough to consider pulling out. Looking better when she came on court for the final against the Czech Lucie Safarova, Serena took the first set 6-3 after her huge forehand helped to earn her a break in the fourth game. Leading 6-5 in the second and two points from the title, Safarova forced a tiebreak, which she won 7-2 to set up a decider. Clearly unsettled, Serena let rip and turned the air blue, her anger increasing when she was broken by Safarova in the second game to go 2-0 down. Despite a warning for swearing, Serena broke back, established a lead and two more breaks gave her a third French title, a 20th Grand Slam singles title and made her

only the third person to win each major three times.

Having won the last three Grand Slams, Serena was now on the verge of achieving her second 'Serena Slam' by winning four consecutive majors in a row. But to do that she needed to win Wimbledon and when Britain's Heather Watson ran her close in the first round it looked like Serena might find it more difficult than she had before. The win qualified her for the WTA Finals, the earliest a player had qualified since 2003. Serena then faced three former No. 1s to reach the final: defeating her sister Venus, Victoria Azarenka and Maria Sharapova. In the final she faced Garbiñe Muguruza, the 21-year-old who had been responsible for the worst defeat in her career.

Muguruza would test her once again, particularly when taking a 4-2 lead in the first set before Serena came back to win 6-4. In the second set Serena cruised to a 5-1 lead before wobbling again. Muguruza fought back to make it 5-4 before Serena broke her serve to love with a wide forehand on her second match point. She had achieved her 21st Grand Slam, her second Serena Slam and, at 33, was the oldest woman in the Open Era to win a Grand Slam singles title.

The moment Wimbledon was over the question that Serena didn't want to answer was asked: could she win the US Open and add a calendar year Grand Slam to her achievements? Sadly the answer was no. Her attempt came to an end in the semi-finals when she lost to Roberta Vinci in three sets. Disappointed, Serena called an end to her season. It had been an amazing year filled with incredible achievements and also one minor one: it had been completely ankle injury free.

Right Nike NikeCourt Flare, worn by
Serena Williams (Wimbledon Museum).

BLOOD, SWEAT & CLEATS
2015 TOUR DE FRANCE

SIDI WIRE CARBON AIR VERNICE

When Chris Froome crashed out of the 2014 Tour de France it marked the beginning of a remarkable 12-month comeback that saw him battling not just his rivals, but injury, a French media made paranoid by a decade of doping and hostile fans who had been turned against him and his team. Dogged by insinuations that his performances could only be achieved with performance-enhancing drugs, his 2015 Tour proved to be as much a test of mental resilience as it was physical.

Froome's preparations for the 2015 Tour de France had begun a year previously after he was forced to abandon the defence of his 2013 victory when he crashed for the third time in two days and suffered a fractured left wrist and a broken bone in his right hand. Hoping to become the first British man to win back-to-back Tours, it was a cruel blow, but he quickly picked himself up and focused on winning the Vuelta a España in August 2014 as the first step in his quest for a second Tour win. With little over a month to prepare, he and Team Sky had to work fast and a team of nine was hastily put together. Unsure of how well he would

be able to perform, it was something of a leap into the dark for Froome, but he and Team Sky put in a performance that Team Principal Sir Dave Brailsford felt was one of their best and Froome was able to push his rival Alberto Contador all the way, finishing second overall. The victory made him even hungrier to win the 2015 Tour.

For 2015 the famed Italian cycling shoe maker Sidi had equipped Froome and Team Sky with the most advanced shoes it had ever made. Founded in 1960 by Dino Signori (from whose initials the company takes its name), Sidi began as a small manufacturer of mountain trekking boots but as cycling boomed in popularity in Italy in the 1970s, began to make cycling footwear. The company developed a reputation for incorporating the latest technology into its shoes that allowed cyclists to fine-tune the fit and performance of their footwear to almost microscopic levels of detail, making them a favourite among pros. Froome's shoes were the latest example of this and featured micro adjustable ratcheting dials, an adjustable heel cup supporting the ankle, a binding system on the upper that distributed pressure evenly over the instep and vents and air channels to allow airflow and heat dissipation, but which were sealable in cold conditions. The sole was made of braided carbon fibre weaved in opposing directions to optimize stiffness while allowing a flex in the

toe area. If Q from James Bond had designed shoes, he would have designed these.

When the route of the 2015 Tour's 21 stages was announced, some were already writing Froome off. With 13km of cobbled sections, more mountain passes and fewer time trials than 2014, it didn't appear to suit him at all and was far more suited to one of his main rivals, the Columbian Nairo Quintana. The first nine days would involve closely fought and punchy racing during which, as had happened in 2014, Froome could find himself crashing out and potentially ending his Tour. Froome felt that it was the rigorous and punishing mountain section of the route that would decide the eventual winner. When announcing it race director Christian Prudhomme said, 'If you do not climb, you will not win the Tour in 2015', as if to confirm Froome's thoughts.

The opening stages took place in the Netherlands and Belgium and were characterized by wet weather and strong crosswinds but, after a team effort and careful race planning, by the end of Stage 2 Froome had put a valuable minute and a half between himself and Quintana. In Stage 3 Froome came second, giving him the overall lead and the yellow jersey, for which Sidi provided accompanying yellow shoes. However, he had to hand the jersey back just one stage later when German rider Tony Martin took the lead during Stages 4 to 6. When Martin was forced to withdraw from the race after a crash, the lead was handed back to Froome. However, he refused to wear the yellow jersey for the following stage, saying, 'Out of respect for Tony I would never have worn it in any case. That's not the way to get the yellow jersey, due to someone else's misfortunes.'

By the time the Tour reached the Pyrenees for Stage 10, Froome led his two main rivals: Contador by just over one minute and Quintana by two, but knew that the hard work was about to begin and that only now would the real contenders emerge. After winning the stage he increased the gap to Contador by over four minutes and to Quintana by three. But Froome was to find that his competitors and the mountain climbs were not the only challenge he would face for the rest of the Tour.

With the sport still wounded by years of doping, paranoia over blood and mechanical doping surrounded the Tour from the start and had led to insinuations by former competitors now in the media that Froome's performances were not clean. Using words such as 'super astonishing', 'phenomenal' and 'verging on the ridiculous', the former Vuelta a España winner Laurent Jalabert was widely interpreted to be insinuating that Froome was doping, an opinion echoed in the French media. Although not outright, the accusations, along with a long-standing perception of Team Sky as 'new money', provoked hostility from the French fans leading to Froome and his team being spat at, punched, receiving threats of broken legs and even having urine thrown at them.

However, Froome and his team would not allow the damaging accusations to distract them and he successfully maintained his lead throughout the Tour's final week in the French Alps. As expected it was Quintana who had emerged as his main rival. But, despite making major inroads into Froome's lead, he was unable to catch him in the penultimate Alpe D'Huez stage, leaving Froome with an overall lead of 1 minute and 12 seconds, too great for Quintana to make up in the final stage in Paris and making Froome the champion elect. He was duly crowned 'King of the Mountains', becoming the first British rider to earn the title since 1984 and one of a rare group of riders to have won both the mountain stage and the overall race in the same year. With tradition making the final stage in Paris little more than a procession for the leaders, Froome finished the race side by side with his teammates and became the first British rider to win the Tour de France twice. In celebration of his achievement, Sidi released a limited edition replica of Froome's Yellow Jersey shoes, which sold out almost immediately.

In his victory speech, he addressed the insinuations against him and his team while also remaining gracious, saying, 'The Maillot Jaune is special, very special. I understand its history, good and bad, and I will always respect it, never dishonour it and I'll always be proud to have won it.' While the media speculation and malevolent behaviour of some of the fans might have destroyed the confidence of some of the most seasoned competitors, Froome's victory was testament not just to the power of his legs, but also to his strength of mind.

Below Sidi Wire Carbon Air Vernice,
Chris Froome Edition (SIDI SpA).

MESSI'S MIDAS TOUCH
2016 LIONEL MESSI'S FIFTH BALLON D'OR

ADIDAS MESSI 15

Always looking awkward in anything other than his Barcelona strip, when Lionel Messi received his fifth Ballon d'Or in January 2016, he confirmed that not only was he the best football player in the world, but also one of the most modest. Clearly far more at home on a football pitch, in an age when players often seem to seek the spotlight more than the ball, the bashful Argentinian looked dazed and uncomfortable in it.

Born in Rosario, Santa Fe, Argentina in June 1987, Lionel Messi has always shied away from attention. Growing up in a football loving family he joined his favourite club, Newell's Old Boys, aged only six and was part of a youth side that won 500 matches and lost just one in four years. Despite winning trophies at such a young age, when his proud mother wanted to show them off, he was embarrassed and would plead with her not to. While shy off the pitch, on it he was a different person and transformed into a leader that his teammates loyally followed.

By the age of 10 Messi's signature was chased by Newell's and rivals River Plate but when he was diagnosed with a growth hormone deficiency that needed treatment costing $1,000 per month, unable to afford it, they reluctantly withdrew. With his father's health insurance only covering two years of treatment, his future in football looked in jeopardy. Fearing for his health and potential career, his family asked relatives in Catalonia, Spain, to arrange a trial with FC Barcelona. When a tape of him reached a club scout, he was amazed. He couldn't believe a boy so young possessed such skills and, although initially hesitant to sign a foreigner so young, it was eventually arranged for the 13-year-old to join Barcelona's youth academy La Masia, with the club agreeing to pay for his treatment. Being a foreigner, the rules stated he could only play in Catalan League and friendly games and the lack of playing time made it difficult for him to integrate. It also didn't help that he was so shy that his teammates thought he was mute. But after completing his treatment and learning the Barcelona way, he made a number of friends who starred alongside him in later years including Fàbregas, Piqué and Iniesta.

In contrast to arch-rivals Real Madrid, who had built a team of 'Galacticos' by buying-in success, club President Joan Laporta made Barcelona's priority the nurturing of its own talent, making La Masia its priority. After signing a contract, Messi was now eligible to play in all competitions, and he and his teammates rewarded the club's focus in 2002/03 when the youth team won Barça's first youth treble. With Messi the core of the team and top scorer with 36 goals, he was already attracting foreign attention and at the end of the season received an offer to join Arsenal. While teammates Fàbregas and Piqué headed abroad, Messi believed his loyalty belonged to Barcelona and stayed in Catalonia.

With first team players often coming to watch Messi on the youth team, it wasn't long before he was rising up the ranks and in October 2004 manager Frank Rijkaard selected him for the first team after lobbying by senior players. Aged 17 years, 3 months and 22 days, he made his debut against Espanyol, becoming the youngest ever player to represent the club. When he scored his first senior goal, set up by his mentor Ronaldinho, against Albacete in May 2005 he set another record, becoming the youngest player to score for the club. Having signed with them a year earlier, the brand that had the honour of being on his feet for his first senior goal was Nike. But, by the end of his first season Messi was soon being courted by all the major sportswear brands. When adidas offered an estimated €400,000 per year for five years, far more than the €100,000

Below adidas Messi 15, 5th Ballon d'Or,
Platinum Edition (adidas AG).

Nike had offered, he signed and joined David Beckham and Zinedine Zidane in the brand's line-up of star footballers.

In 2005, Messi's performances earned him a place in the Argentina squad for the FIFA World Youth Championship. He did not disappoint, scoring six goals during Argentina's march to the title. However, injury brought a downturn in his fortunes in 2006 causing him to miss Barcelona's Champions League win over Arsenal and, at the World Cup in Germany, he was denied a chance to shine when Argentina went out in the quarter-finals. It was in the run up to the World Cup that year that he had started wearing adidas's famed F50 boots. He began playing with the F50.6 Tunit boot that was the first to allow players to customize the upper, outsole and sock liners. However, he wasn't a fan of its stiff interchangeable sole plate, instead opting to wear the F30 boot, which was technically a less advanced and heavier boot, but much more to his liking. Keen for him to be seen in their flagship model, adidas made custom soled F50s just for him.

Despite Barcelona's decline in form during the 2006/07 season, Messi's game-changing abilities frequently led to comparisons to countryman Diego Maradona. Never more so than when he scored two goals in three weeks that replicated Maradona's famous 'Goal of the Century' and 'Hand of God' goals. This, along with increasingly taking on Ronaldinho's mantle as the Brazilian lost form, earned him the nickname 'Messiah'. In 2008, when Ronaldinho and Frank Rijkaard were dismissed after two poor seasons, Pep Guardiola was appointed and his presence had an immediate effect on Messi. To prevent his frequent injuries he was given new training, nutrition and lifestyle routines that kept him almost injury free and in the 2008/09 season he was instrumental in Barcelona winning the Copa del Rey, La Liga and the Champions League (when he famously kissed his F50 boot) making the club the first treble champions in Spanish history. The treble became a sextuple when they went on to win the Supercopa de España, the UEFA Super Cup and the FIFA Club World Cup. Messi duly won both the Ballon d'Or and the FIFA World Player of the Year award by the biggest voting margins in each trophy's history. adidas celebrated by creating two exclusive F50i colourways for Messi to go along with his signature silver +f50.9, both of which featured the Sun of May, the national emblem of Argentina.

Despite the adulation and his superstar status, Messi remained the shy and humble boy from Rosario and as his success continued in the 2010/11 season, he became the lynchpin of the team, scoring a total of 53 goals in all competitions and helping Barcelona win La Liga with only one defeat. For the 2010 World Cup, adidas produced their lightest boot ever, the F50 adiZero, which weighed just 165g, but despite demonstrating his usual pace and creativity in them, Messi was criticized for Argentina's lacklustre performance, although his individual performance still contributed to his second Ballon d'Or win. By the time he won his fourth in a row in January 2013, at just 24 years of age, Messi was the top goalscorer in Barcelona's history having scored 68 goals in a single season. In 2012, he had surpassed Gerd Müller's 40-year-old record of 85 goals in a calendar year by scoring 91. Confirming the fact that Barcelona were the greatest club side in the world was the fact that his teammates Iniesta and Xavi came second and third in the race for the coveted 'golden boot'. Despite being plagued with injuries, 2013 saw Messi finishing the season with a total 60 goals, making him the top scorer in Europe for a second year. The 2013/14 season, however, proved one to forget as Barcelona finished the season trophy-less. In December 2014, to celebrate 10 years of adidas's partnership with Messi, the company released the Mirosar10, the last of his F50-based boots and a tribute to his home town of Rosario, it featured the 'M' shield logo that adidas had begun using on his boots and signature colourways from 2012 onwards. They came at a time that Barcelona appeared to be heading for another disappointing second half of the season and speculation that Messi would be leaving the club. However, the team's attacking trio: Messi, Neymar and Suarez finally began to gel when Messi returned to his old position on the right wing and found arguably the best form of his career. With the team no longer so dependent on him, Messi enjoyed greater freedom and scored 58 goals, helping secure Barcelona another La Liga, Copa del Rey and Champions League treble. Ahead of the Champions League final adidas released a brand new signature boot created specifically for Messi called the Messi 15. It featured a number of new technologies including an upper made with MessiTOUCH, a new material that provided extra grip on the ball and an external frame on the mid and rear giving it a secure 'locked-in' feel.

When Messi was awarded his fifth Ballon d'Or in 2016 in recognition of his 2015 achievements, it came as no surprise. In celebration adidas released a platinum version of his boot featuring pearlescent Argentinian leather and platinum Messi and adidas logos. On the insole of the boot was the Spanish phrase, 'el más grande de todos los tiempos' meaning 'the greatest of all time'. While most players have to retire, or even die, to achieve such a title, there are very few who have seen him play that would deny the claim. His extraordinary skill, selfless attitude and great modesty have made the game of football all the richer for his presence and made him a paragon for all those who will try to follow in his footsteps.

UNDER ARMOUR CURRY II

The opening decade of the 21st century was great for Nike and adidas. Between them the rivals utterly dominated the sports business and although challengers snapped at their heels, their hold seemed unassailable. But when a former high school failure started making sweat resistant t-shirts for American football players, he set himself on a path that would see him deposing one giant and causing the other to look anxiously over its shoulder. Born in August 1972 in Baltimore, Maryland, Kevin Plank was a self-described 'hustler' from a young age and as early as his teens had a mind for entrepreneurship. Despite being a promising football player his poor academic performance at Georgetown Prep and a brawl with some football players resulted in him being kicked out of the school. Fortunately, his football prowess had been noticed by the coach at nearby St. John's College and it earned him a place there. It proved to be the making of him. Taking his education seriously with a view to playing college football, he joined Fork Union Military Academy in Virginia to improve his chances of a football scholarship. It paid off when he enrolled at the University of Maryland and became a special team player.

It was while at Maryland that Plank came up with an idea that would change not just his own destiny but that of the entire sports business. Noticing that the cotton t-shirts he and his teammates wore would become heavier as they soaked up sweat, Plank reasoned that there must a material that would wick away perspiration. Not only was cotton uncomfortable when wet, but its weight increased by potentially two to three pounds as it absorbed sweat, reducing a player's performance. He realised the answer was under his nose when he noticed that the compression shorts he wore in practice remained sweat free. Made from a synthetic stretchy material, it remained dry throughout training. Plank visited nearby Minnesota Fabrics and found a similar material and asked a tailor to make some t-shirts with it. Armed with seven prototypes, he handed them out to some of his teammates and to baseball and lacrosse players. At first they were reluctant, feeling the shirt's silky texture felt like women's wear, but when they wore them during games, their feedback was universally positive.

Ever the entrepreneur, Plank sensed an opportunity. Already pursuing business side-lines including selling bootleg concert t-shirts and Valentine's roses, the chance to develop a business that combined an innovative new product with his love of sport was too good to miss. Feeling sure it had potential he put together a business plan and after graduating May 1996, despite a job offer from Prudential, he took a gamble and used $15,000 he had made from his side-lines and cash advances from credit cards to launch his new business, based in his grandmother's house in Washington D.C.

When deciding on a name Plank had intended to call his company 'Heart', but when his trademark application was refused he instead tried 'Body Armor', but that too was denied. The name he eventually chose was the result of pure serendipity. Unable to remember it, his brother asked him "How's that company you're working on, uhh … Under Armor?" It was perfect. When needing to choose a sales hotline number, rather than the American spelling he chose the British, 'armour', because he felt that 888-4RMOUR was more memorable than 44ARMOR, and so Under Armour Athletic Apparel was born.

Using his contacts in college and pro sports leagues, Plank built a customer base and hit the road with a trunk full of samples, visiting colleges across the USA, and soon won his first contracts, with Georgia Tech and Arizona State. By the end of 1996 Under Armour had sold 500 of its sweat resistant HeatGear shirts, earning $17,000 in sales, but it was the following year when things really began to take off.

Right Kevin Plank, CEO and founder of Under Armour (Dcavalli).

After introducing a range of products for different sports and uses, athletes took an interest in the brand because its products appeared to offer real performance benefits. By the close of 1997 Under Armour had sold over 7,500 products, but more importantly, had grown a core group of loyal customers.

After the nascent brand appeared on the cover of USA today and had prominent screen time in two Warner Bros football themed movies, *Any Given Sunday* and *The Replacements*, Plank decided to take Under Armour's first ever print advertisement in ESPN Magazine. It was credited with boosting sales by $750,000. Incredible, especially given that Plank hadn't paid a penny for the *Any Given Sunday* endorsement. Under Armour's growth was almost unprecedented and after only three years, Plank could boast clients including twelve NFL teams, eight Major League Baseball teams and four NHL teams. Plank's ability to connect with customers and a product that improved their performance was a winning combination. With revenue now over $1m, he was finally able to start paying himself a wage.

By 2003 the company and Plank were winning awards for innovation and leadership and had won a legion of young fans who saw Under Armour as a cool alternative to the established brands. So cool in fact, that despite Plank having a 'no endorsement fee' policy at the time, athletes would forego their fee and appear in Under Armour advertising in return for product. The brand's success had not gone unnoticed by its much larger rivals however and others began to produce similar ranges. Nike's Pro Compression and adidas' Clima Tech were direct responses to the growing performance product market that Under Armour had pioneered and were also a sign that they recognised they were an emerging threat.

Under Armour's response to the incursion came in 2006

when the brand moved into the footwear. Just as they had with clothing, Under Armour made an impression with a range of football cleats that captured 23% of the market in its debut year. Encouraged by their first foray into the heart of enemy territory, it wasn't long before ranges were expanded to include lacrosse, softball and baseball cleats, but it was in 2008 that the brand really went for the jugular, launching a range of training shoes. Although by now a global brand, footwear helped to launch Under Armour into the stratosphere and just 14 years after its founding, the company passed the $1 billion annual revenue mark. Under Armour's rise had been so rapid that from their lofty positions, Nike and adidas could never have envisioned a threat coming from outside of their traditional competitors. If they weren't already worried, they would be when Under Armour's partnership with an unlikely NBA superstar helped them lay even more claim to Nike and adidas's positions.

Born in March 1988, Wardell Stephen Curry's physical stature made him appear unlikely to ever make history in the NBA. At 'only' 6 ft 3 in and 160 lbs, he was well below the average stats of players who traditionally dominated the game. The son of Dell Curry of the Charlotte Hornets, 'Steph' Curry hoped to follow in his father's footsteps and begin his career at Virginia Tech but because of his size, Virginia failed to offer him a scholarship and instead he headed to Davidson College, whose head coach Bob McKillop had seen something special in him. When Curry helped Davidson to win the Southern Conference regular season title and led in scoring with 21.5 points per game, McKillop's recruitment of him despite his smaller frame proved prescient and was born out when Curry finished college with a string of scoring,

....

player of the year and All American awards.

Curry began his pro career with the Golden State Warriors in 2009 and ended his debut season as runner up in NBA Rookie of the Year voting. Injury blighted his 2011-12 season but able to shake it off the next season, he began to earn a reputation for scoring three-pointers, ending the year with a new league record for three-pointers scored in a single season. To this point Curry had been a Nike player. His godfather worked for the brand and so he had grown up wearing Swooshes, but when it came to re-signing his contract, Nike appeared apathetic. When he and his father met with Nike the absence of Lynn Merritt, Nike's senior director of basketball appeared to confirm this. Instead, a director of less stature attended and began by mispronouncing Curry's name. Another faux pas occurred when Kevin Durant's name appeared in the presentation rather than Curry's. To cap it all, Nike had no plans to give Curry a much prized player's training camp, which was important to him as a way to give back to the younger generations. It was clear that in Nike's eyes he was only a second tier player. Curry senior's advice to his son was to head in a different direction, after all, he had spent much of his career doing that to prove people were wrong about him.

The moment that Curry decided on that direction didn't happen after a presentation or over a negotiating table, but typically, at home with his family. After a year of negotiations, it was time to decide and Curry enlisted the help of Riley, his one-year-old daughter. He presented three shoes to her, a Nike, an adidas and an Under Armour. The first one, the Nike, was quickly thrown over her shoulder. The second shoe made a similar exit. The third, she handed to her father. It was the Under Armour shoe.

When Nike passed on their right to match Under Armour's offer, it only served to confirm to Curry their indifference

towards him. It was a decision both they and ironically adidas would regret when Curry's 2014-15 season went down in legend. The fast pace that new coach Steve Kerr had introduced to the Warriors' game suited Curry and his ability to score almost supernatural three-pointers. The Warriors won their first title in 40 years and reached the Finals with 67 wins, earning Curry the MVP title with an average of 23.8 points per game. Hailed for being the herald of a 'three-point revolution', Curry broke or closed on all the three-point records in existence. Curry and the Warriors' title meant his signature shoes began flying off the shelves and in 2014 his success directly played its part in Under Armour achieving the previously unimaginable when the company unseated adidas to become the second largest sports wear brand in the United States. Despite missing the title in the 2015-16 season, Curry proved he and the Warriors were no one hit wonders when he again led the team to the Finals with 73-9 game win record, surpassing the 72-10 record set by Michael Jordan's Chicago Bulls during the 1995-96 season.

Just as Curry helped eclipse Jordan's record, many now wonder if Under Armour might one day eclipse Nike. Many sneakerheads say the brand will never be as cool and lacks heritage but when you consider that in 2016 Under Armour boasted an unprecedented MVPs in five different sports in the form of Curry, Cam Newton (NFL), Bryce Harper (MLB), Carey Price (NHL) and Jordan Spieth (PGA Player of the Year), it appears to be gaining heritage quickly. In only twenty years, Under Armour has grown from an idea on a football field to challenging the world's number one sports brand. While the gulf between Under Armour and Nike is immense, just as a skinny point guard went from being rejected for being too small, to taking on and beating the giants of the NBA, Under Armour may too be the David that topples the Goliath Nike.

BIBLIOGRAPHY & SOURCES

PUBLICATIONS

ASICS – The History, Asics Europe B.V., 2015

ASICS Tiger – An Evolution, Asics Europe B.V., 2015

Boris Becker – The Player, Boris Becker with Robert Lübenoff and Helmut Sorge, Bantam Press, 2004

Bowerman and the Men of Oregon, Kenny Moore, Rodale, 2006

Catch Up, Puma Newsletter (various issues)

Cathy – My Autobiography, Cathy Freeman with Scott Gullan, Highdown, 2004

The Design of Sports, edited by Susan Andrew, Laurence King Publishing, 1999

Gold Rush, Michael Johnson, Harper Sport, 2011

Just Do It – The Nike Spirit in the Corporate World, Donald Katz, Adams Media Corporation, 1994

Mo Farah – Twin Ambitions, Mohamed Farah with T.J.Andrews, Hodder & Stoughton, 2013

Out of Nowhere – The Inside Story of How Nike Marketed The Culture of Running, Geoff Hollister, Meyer & Meyer Sport, 2008

Out of the Box – The Rise of Sneaker Culture, Elizabeth Semmelhack, Skira Rizzoli, 2015

The Puma Story, Rolf-Herbert Peters, Marshall Cavendish Business, 2008

The Man Who Could Fly – The Bob Beamon Story, Bob Beamon and Milana Walter Beamon, Genesis Press, 1999

Serious, John McEnroe with James Kaplan, Sphere, 2002

Shoe Dog, Phil Knight, Simon & Schuster, 2016

Silent Gesture, Tommie Smith with David Steel, Temple, 2007

Sneaker Wars, Barbara Smit, Ecco, 2008

Sneakers – The Complete Collectors' Guide, Unorthodox Styles, Thames & Hudson, 2005

The Sports Shoe – A Social and Cultural History c.1870 – c.1990 (PhD Thesis), Thomas Turner, 2012

The Story as Told by Those Who Have Lived It and Are Living It, Keith Cooper, adidas, 2010

Usain Bolt – Faster Than Lightning, Usain Bolt with Matt Allen, Harper Sport, 2013

Swoosh – The Unauthorised Story of Nike And The Men Who Played There, J.B. Strasser and Laurie Becklund, HarperCollins, 1993

Trainers, Neal Heard, Carlton Books, 2003

Winners In Action – The Complete Story of the Dunlop Slazenger Sports Companies, Brian Simpson, JJG Publishing, 2005

Where'd You Get Those? 10ᵗʰ Anniversary Edition – New York City's Sneaker Culture 1960-1987, Bobbito Garcia, Testify, 2013

ONLINE SOURCES

adidas archive, adidas-archive.com

adidas Group Blog, blog.adidas-group.com

adidas news stream, news.adidas.com

BBC, bbc.co.uk

Bleacher Report, bleacherreport.com

Business Insider, businessinsider.com

Classic Kicks, classickicks.com

Converse News Archive, media.converse.com

Complex, complex.com/sneakers/

The Daily Mail, dailymail.co.uk

Deadspin, deadspin.com

ESPN Go, Kobe's Masterpiece article by Arash Markazi, espngo.com

Foster's Famous Shoes, article by Rachael Foster, boltonrevisited.org.uk

Funding Universe, fundinguniverse.com

Getty Images, gettyimages.com

The Guardian, theguardian.com

High Snobiety, highsnobiety.com

Independent, independent.co.uk

International Olympic Committee, olympic.org

Kicks On Fire, kicksonfire.com

Le Coq Sportif Blog, blog.lecoqsportif.com

Los Angeles Times, latimes.com

The New York Times, nytimes.com

Nice Kicks, nicekicks.com

Nike News, news.nike.com

Out of the Box, riseofsneakerculture.org

Sneaker News, sneakernews.com

Sneaker Freaker, sneakerfreaker.com

Sole Collector, solecollector.com

The Telegraph, telegraph.co.uk

Wikipedia, wikipedia.org

EXPERTS

Claire Afford, Archive Specialist, Reebok International

John Boulter, former adidas and Reebok Marketing Director

Rod Dixon, Olympian, New York Marathon winner and Kids Marathon founder

Helmut Fischer, 'Mr.Puma', Puma SE

Dr. Martin Gebhardt, Manager of History Communication, adidas AG

Jordan Geller, Nike collector and historian, owner of ShoeZeum

Johannes Hackstette, Manager Corporate Communications, Puma SE

Martin Herde, Collection Manager, adidas AG

Alixandria Ogawa, Public Relations, Vans Inc.

Anna Renton, Museum Curator, Wimbledon Lawn Tennis Museum

Patricia Reymond, Collections Manager, The Olympic Museum

Pascal Rolling, Head of Sports Marketing for Running, Puma SE

Chris Severn, 'Father of the adidas Superstar'

Stan Smith, Former World No.1, Wimbledon and US Open Champion

Huub Valkenburg, CEO, Karhu

MUSEUMS AND ARCHIVES

adidas AG Archive, Herzogenaurach, Germany

Fondazione FILA Museum, Biella, Italy

Puma SE Archive, Herzogenaurach, Germany

Reebok International Ltd Archive, Boston, MA, United States

Northampton Museums & Art Gallery, Northampton, UK

The Olympic Museum, Lausanne, Switzerland

The Wimbledon Lawn Tennis Museum, London, UK

PHOTO CREDITS

INDEX

A

Abdul-Jabbar, Kareem 62, *63*, 116
Abrahams, Harold 14, *14–15*, 16
adidas 8, 9, 12, 16, 33, 39, 40, 49, 54, 56, 61, 69, 215, 217
    All Blacks168, 170, *170–1*
    Argentinas 40, *41*
    Azteca Golds 49
    Boris Becker 120
    Copa Mundials *108*, 108–9, *109*
    French subsidiaries 62, 64, 76, 86, 89
    Kareem Abdul-Jabbar *63*, 64
    Kobe Bryant 176, 178
    Le Coq Sportif 86, 89
    Lionel Messi *212*, 213
    LA Olympic Games (1984) 112, 115
    Matchplays 86, *87–8*, 89
    Michael Jordan 116, 117, 118
    Muhammad Ali *74*, 74–5, *75*
    Originals 144
    Orions 96, *96*, *97*
    Pelé Pact 71, 72
    Predators 109, 143–4, *144–5*
    Sachin Tendulkar *190*, 191, 192, *193*
    Special *60–1*
    sportswear 86, 89
    Stan Smith 62, 76, *76–7*, 77, *77–8*, 89
    Steffi Graf 128, *129*, *130–1*, 131
    Supergrips and Promodels 62, 64
    Superstars 64, *65*
    Weltrekords 54, *55*, *57*
    see also Dassler, Adolf 'Adi'; Dassler, Armin; Dassler, Horst; Dassler, Rudolph 'Rudi'; Puma
aerobics *104*, 105, 107
Air Force 1s, Nike *102*, 102–3, *103*, 179
Air Jordans, Nike *117*, 117–18, 120, 139, 176, 179
Air Ships, Nike 118, *119*
Air Trainer 1s, Nike *124–5*, 125, *126–7*, 127, 133
Air Zoom M9s, Nike 166, *167*
Akron Firestone Non-Skids 10
Ali, Muhammad *74*, *74*
All Blacks, New Zealand 168, *169*, 170
All England Lawn Tennis and Croquet Club 18, 21, 194–5
All Star, Converse 10, *11*, 12, *12–13*
Alva, Tony 'Mad Dog' *90–1*, 93
American Athletics Union (AAU) 47, 69
American Basketball Association (ABA) 28, 64
American Football 214
Anastasio, Angelo 64
A.R. Hyde & Sons 111
Argentinas, adidas 40, *41*
Argentine Football Club 213
Ashe, Arthur 86, *87*, 89
ASICS 9, 47
    Gym Ultras 156, *157*, *158–9*, 159
    see also Onitsuka Tigers
Association of Tennis Professionals (ATP) 86, 89
Athens Olympic Games (2004) 189
Atlanta Olympic Games (1996) 156, *157*, 159, *160*, 161, 163, 166
Australian Aboriginals 173, 175
Australian Cricket Team 192
Australian Tennis Opens 128, 204

B

b-boys 84
Ballon d'Or 8, 211, 213
Bannister, Roger *34*, 35–6
Barcelona Football Club 211, 213
Barcelona Olympic Games (1992) 140–1, 156, 161, 173
Barry, Rick 64
Bartlett, Edmund 189
basketball
    adidas 62, 64, 116, 118, 176, 178
    Allen Iverson *152*, 153–4
    Converse All Star 10, *11*, 12, 62
    George Mikan and Pro-Keds Royal 26–7, *27*
    Grant Hill 146–7, *147*
    Kobe Bryant 176, 178
    Michael Jordan and Nike 116–18, *117*, *119*
    Nike Air Force 1s *102*, 102–3
    Reebok Pump *132*, 133–4, *135*
    Shaquille O'Neal and Shaqnosis 148, *149*, 150, *150*, *151*
    Walt 'Clyde' Frazier 82, *82–3*, 84, *84–5*
    Wardell Stephen Curry 217
Beamon, Bob 54, *55*, 56, 115
Beastie Boys 84
Becker, Boris 120, *120–1*, 122
Beckham, David *142*, 143, 144, 213
Beconta 82, 84
Beijing Olympic Games (2008) 186, *187*, 189, 199
Benoit, Joan 112, 115

Dassler, Horst; Dassler, Rudolph 'Rudi'; Puma

Berlin Olympic Games (1936) 8, 10, 22, *23*, 24
Biddulph, Samuel 14
Blue Ribbon Sports (BRS) 49, 69, 80–1
    see also Nike
Bolt, Usain 186, *187*, 189
Bonavena, Oscar 74, *74*
Bones Brigade 136
Borg, Björn 98, *99*, 101
Boston Celtics 10, 64, 134
Boston, Ralph 56
Bowerman, Bill 9, *46*, 47, 49, 66, 69, *80*, 80–1
boxing boots, Muhammad Ali's *74*, 74–5, *75*
Bragg, John 74, 75
Brasher, Chris 35–6
Brown, Dee *132*, 133, 134
Brown, Larry 154
Brown, Paul 133
Bryant, Kobe 176, *177*, 179

C

Caballero, Steve 136, *137*
Camuset family 86, 89
Carlos, John 50, *51*, 52, 54
Carter, Jimmy 24
Caruthers, Ed 61
Chamberlain, Wilt 10, 12, 179
Chang, Michael 134
Charity, Ron 86
Charlton, Jack 143
Chataway, Chris 35–6
Chicago American Gears 26
Chicago Bulls 118

Christie, Linford 140

Clydes, Puma 84, *84–5*

Collins, John *142*, 143, 144

Commonwealth Games (1990) 173

Complete Theseus, Puma 186, *187*, *188*, 189

Connors, Jimmy 86, 89, 122

Contador, Alberto 208

Converse 112, 116, 118, 179

    All Star 10, *11*, 12, 64

    All Star II 12, *12–13*

    Basketball Yearbook 10

Converse, Marquis Mills 10

Cooper, Aaron 202–3

Copa Mundials, adidas *108*, 108–9, *109*

Corsairs, Onitsuka Tiger *48*, 49

Cortez, Nike *48*, 49

Court Flares, Nike 202, *202–3*, 204, *205*

Cracks, Puma 50, *51*, 52

Cram, Steve 199

Cramm, Gottfried von 21

Crawford, Jack 'Gentleman' 18

cricket 14, *190*, 191–2, *193*

Curren, Kevin 122

Curry, Wardell Stephen 217

cycling *206*, 207–8, *208–9*

Czechoslovakia 30, 33

D

Danieli, Marcelo 98

Dapper Dan Roundball Classic 116

Dassler, Adolf 'Adi' 8, 9, 22, 24, 33, 38–40, 54, 61, 62, 74, 86, 108, 112, 118

Dassler, Armin 54, 56, 71, 72, 120, 121, 140

Dassler, Horst 8, 54, 56, 62, *63*, 64, 71, 72, 74, 76, 86, 89, 112, 115, 118, 120, 128, 131, 144

Dassler, Käthe 38–9, 62, 112

Dassler, Rudolph 'Rudi' 9, 22, 38–40, 54

Davidson, Carolyn 49

Davies, Lynn 56

Deas, Gerald 64

Decker, Mary 112, 115

Dell, Donald 78, 89

Diadora 98, *99*, *100–1*

disabled athletes *96*, 96–7, 182, *182–3*, 185

Discs, Puma *140*, 140–1, *141*

Dixon, Ron 110–11, *111*

Dorrance, Anson 164

Drechsler, Heike 140–1

Dunlop Green Flash 18, 76

E

Edberg, Stefan 120, 121

Ellis, Frampton 176

Empire Games (1954) 36

England Cricket Team 191, 192

England Football Team 40

England Rugby Team 168, *169*

Era, Vans *92–3*, 93

Euro 2000 144

Evert, Chris 128, 204

F

Falk, David 117–18

Farah, Mo *198*, 199–200

Federer, Roger 194, *194–5*, 197

FIFA Women's World Cup Championships 164, 166

Fila Grant Hills *146*, 147, *147*

Fireman, Paul 105, 107, 133, 148

First World War 10, 21, 22

football/soccer

    adidas Copa Mundials *108*, 108–9, *109*

    adidas Predators 143–4, *144–5*

    J.W. Foster & Sons 14, 16

    Lionel Messi *210*, 211, 213

    Mexico World Cup (1970) *70–1*, 71, 72

    Mia Hamm 164, *165*, 166

World Cup final (1954) 38, *39*, 40

Ford, Chris 154

Formula 1 180

Fosbury, Dick 58, *58–9*, 61

four-minute mile, breaking the 35–6

Fox, Terry *96*, 96–7

Frazier, Walt 'Clyde' 82, *82–3*, 84–5

Fredericks, Frankie 163

Freeman, Cathy *172*, 173, 175

Freestyles, Reebok *104*, 105, *106–7*, 107

French Rugby Team 170

French Tennis Opens 128, 204

Froome, Chris *206*, 207–8

G

Galieva, Roza 159

Gay, Tyson 189

Gebrüder Dassler Sportschuhfabrik 22, 24, *24–5*, 38–9

Golden State Warriors 217

Graf, Steffi 128, *129*, 131, 204

Grand Slams, adidas 128, *129*, *130–1*, 131

G.T. Law & Son running spikes *34*, 35, *37*

Guelfi, André 89

gymnastics 156, *157*, *158*, 159

H

Haillet, Robert 76

Half Cabs, Vans 136, *138–9*, *139*

Hall, Arthur 42, 44

Hamilton, Lewis 181

Hamm, Mia 164, *165*, 166

Hary, Armin 50

Hatfield, Tinker 102, 125, 127, 194

Hatfield, Tobie 185

Helsinki Olympic Games (1952) 30–1, *31*, 33, 35

Hennigan, Hans 71–2

Herberger, Josef 'Sepp' 38, 40

high jump 58, *58–9*, 61

Hill, Grant 146–7, *147*

hip hop 64, 103, 153

Hitler, Adolf 8, 22, 24, 38

Hohental, Arno 30

Hollister, Geoff 80

Holzman, William 'Red' 82

Hulatt, Tom 35

Hungarian Football Team 38, 40

Hyde, Abraham 111

I

Indian Cricket Team 191, 192

Ingrova-Zátopková, Dana 31

International Lawn Tennis Federation (ILTF) 21

International Olympic Committee (IOC) 50, 52, 94–5, 189

Ironman Championship, Hawaii 182, 185

Italian Football Team 108

Iverson, Allen *152*, 153–4, 179

J

Jackson, Colin 140, *140*, 141

jogging 81, 112

Johnson, Jeff 49

Johnson, Michael *160*, 161, 163, 189

Johnston, Craig 143–4

Jordan, Michael 116–18, *117*, 134, 148, *152*, 153, 154, 166, 217

Joyner, Al 112, 115

J.W. Foster & Sons 14, *14–15*, 16, *16–17*, 35, 105

K

Karhu 30, 31, *31*, *32–3*, 33

Károlyi, Béla 156, *157*

Keds *see* Pro-Keds

Kholi, Virat 192

Kidd, Eleanor and Paul 44

Kilgore, Bruce 102
Kings, Puma *70–1*, 71, 72, *72–3*
Knight, Phil 9, *46*, 47, 49, 69, 81, 112, 116, 148
Kriek, Johan 120

L

Landy, John 36
Larrabee, Mike 74
Le Coq Sportif 86, 89
Lewis, Carl 112, *113*, 115
Liddell, Eric 14, 16
Litchfield, Paul 133–4
Lomu, Jonah 168, *169*, 170
London Olympic Games (1948) 10, *11*, 30
London Olympic Games (2012) *198*, 199, 200
Long, Carl 'Lutz' 24
long jump *55*, 56, 141
Lopes, Carlos 94–5
Los Angeles Lakers 176, 179
Los Angeles Olympic Games (1932) 30
Los Angeles Olympic Games (1984) 112, *113*, 115, 156

M

Malone, Moses 102, *102*
Martin, Tony 208
Matchplays, adidas 86, *87–8*, 89
McEnroe, John 98, 101, 115, 122, *124–5*, 125, 127
McWhirter, Norris 36
Melbourne Olympic Games (1956) 33
Messi, Lionel 8, *210*, 211, 213
Mexico Olympic Games (1968) 49, 50, *51*, 52, 54, *55*, 56, 61, 71
Meyer, Ray 26
Mikan, George 26–8, *27*
Mills, Glen 189
Milwaukee Bucks 64, 118
Minneapolis Lakers 26–8

Moceanu, Dominique 156
Montreal Olympic Games (1976) *94*, 94–5, 156
Moon Shoes, Nike 80–1
Moore, Peter 117, 118, 144
Muguruza, Garbiñe 204
Munich Olympic Games (1972) 61, 67, 69, 94
Murray, Andy 21, 194, 197

N

NASA 111
National Basketball Association (NBA) 12, 26, 27, 28, 64, 82, 84, 116, 118, 134, 146–7, 148, 153–4, 176
National Invitation Tournament 26, 82
Navratilova, Martina 128, 131, 204
Nazi Germany 22, 24, 38, 40
NCAA Championships 10, 66, 80, 161
New Balance 9, 42, *42–3*, 44, *44–5*
New York Knicks 82, 84
New York Marathon 96, 110–11
New York Rens 10
Nike 9, 12, 21, 47, 49, 105, 107, 148, 213, 215, 217
    Air Force 1s *102*, 102–3, *103*, 179
    Air Pressures 133, 134
    Air Trainer 1s *124–5*, 125, *126–7*, 127
    Cathy Freeman 173, *174*, 175
    Cortez *48*, 49
    Gold Zytel running spikes *160*, 161, *162*, 163
    John McEnroe 98, 115, *124–5*, 125, 127
    Kobe Bryant *178*, 179
    LA Olympic Games (1984) 112, *113*, 115
    Mia Hamm *165*, 166
    Michael Jordan 116–18, *117*, 134
    Mo Farah 200
    Roger Federer 194, *194–5*
    Sarah Reinertsen and the Sole 182, *182–3*, *184–5*, 185
    Serena Williams 202, *202–3*, 204, *205*

Steve Prefontaine *68*, 69
    waffle soles 80, 81, *81*, 112
    see also Blue Ribbon Sports (BRS);
        Bowerman, Bill; Knight, Phil
Norman, Peter 50, *51*, 52
Norwegian Women's Football Team 164, 166
Nottinghamshire County Cricket Club 14
Nugent, Devere 186
Nurmi, Paavo 30

O

Olympic Works 16
O'Neal, Shaquille 28, 148, *149*, 150
Onitsuka, Kihacharo 9, 47
Onitsuka Tigers 47, 49
    Corsair *48*, 49
    Runsparks *94*, 94–5, *95*
Oregon Project 200
Oregon Waffles, Nike 81
Originals, adidas 144
Orions, adidas 96, *96*, 97
Orlando Magic 147, 150
Ossur Flex Run *182–3*, 183, *184–5*, 185
Ovett, Steve 115
Owens, James 'Jesse' 8, 22, 24, 56, 115

P

Pakistan Cricket Team 191, 192
Paralympic Games 182
Paris Olympic Games (1924) 14, *14–15*, 30
Pelé *70–1*, 71–2, *72–3*, 164
Peralta, Stacy 93, 136
Perec, Marie Jose 173, 175
Perry, Fred 18, *19*, 21
Peters, Jim 31, 33
Philadelphia 76ers 102, 154
Plank, Kevin 214–15, *215*, 217
plimsolls 18, 76, 105

Prague Spring (1968) 33
Pre Montreal Racers, Nike *68*, 69
Predators, adidas 109, 143–4, *144–5*
Prefontaine, Steve 66–7, *68*, 69
Pro-Keds 26, *27*, 28, *29*, 103
Promodels, adidas 62, 64
Puma 9, 16, 39, 40, 54, 56, 71–2
    Boris Becker 120, *121*, *122–3*
    Cat motor racing shoes *180*, 180–1, *181*
    Cracks 50, *51*, 52
    Discs *140*, 140–1, *141*
    Kings *70–1*, 71, 72, *72–3*
    Suedes 52, *52–3*
    Usain Bolt 186, *187*, *188*, 189
    Walt 'Clyde' Frazier 82, *82–3*, 84, *84–5*

Q

Questions, Reebok *152*, 153, 154, *155*, 176, *177*, 179
Quintana, Nairo 207, 208

R

racism 24, 50, 52, 86, 153, 173
Rahn, Helmut 40
Raveling, George 116
Reebok 9, 16, 21, 105, 215, 217
    Freestyles *104*, 105, *106–7*, 107
    Pump and InstaPump 21, *132*, 133–4, *135*, 148
    Questions *152*, 153, 154, *155*, 176, *177*, 179
    Shaqnosis 148, *149*, 150, *150*, *151*
Reinertsen, Sarah 182, *182–3*, 185
Retton, Mary Lou 156
Riley, William 9, 42, 44
Rio Olympic Games (2016) 141
Rollins, Tree 12
Rome Olympic Games (1960) 50
Ronaldhino 211, 213
Rossbach, Paddy 182

rugby 168, *169*, 170
Run DMC 64, *65*
running shoes
    G.T. Law & Son *34*, 35, *36–7*
    Jesse Owens and the Dasslers 22, *23*, 24, *24–5*
    J.W. Foster & Sons 14, *14–15*, 16, *16–17*, 35
    Karhu Helsinki Spikes 30, 31, *31*, *32–3*
    New Balance Tracksters 44, *44–5*
    Nike 47, *48*, 49, *68*, 69, 80–1, *81*, 112, *113*, *114–15*, 115, *160*, 161, *162*, *173*, *198*, 199, 200, *201*
    Onitsuka Tiger Runsparks *94*, 94–5, *95*
    Puma *140*, 140–1, 141, 186, *187*, *188*, 189
    Saucony *110*, 111, *111*
Rush, Eric 168
Russian gymnastics team 156, 159
Ruth, Babe 27–8

S

Sabatini, Gabriela 131
Safarova, Lucie 204
Salazar, Alberto 112, 115, 200
San Diego Rockets 64
Saucony *110*, 111, *111*, 118
Schumacher, Michael 180, *180*
Second World War 24, 30, 38
segregation/civil rights 24, 50, 52, 86
Seoul Olympic Games (1988) 131
Severn, Chris 62, *63*, 64
Shaqnosis, Reebok 148, *149*, 150, *150*, *151*
Sharp, Isadore 96–7
Sidi 207–8, *208–9*
Simburg, Art 54, 56
skateboarding *90–1*, 93, 136, *137*, 139
Slam Dunk Contest, NBA *132*, 133, 134
Smith, Geoff 111
Smith, Stan 8, 76, *76–7*, 77
Smith, Tommie 50, *51*, 52, 54

Soles, Nike 182, *182–3*, *184–5*, 185
Specials, adidas *60–1*
Speed Cat and Cat series, Puma *180*, 180–1, *181*
Speer, Albert 24
Spot-Blit 118
Strasser, Rob 107, 116, 117, 118, 144
street wear, sports shoes as 9, 12, 21, 28, 64, *65*, 77, 84, 103, 144, 180–1
Strug, Kerri 156, *157*, *158*, 159
Suedes, Puma 52, *52–3*
Supergrips, adidas 62, 64
Superstars, adidas 64, *65*
Sydney Olympic Games (2000) 163, 173, 175

T

Tardelli, Marco 108, *108*
Tarmak, Juri 61
Taylor, Charles Hollis 'Chuck' 10, 12
Team Sky 207, 208
technology, sport shoe
    adidas 22YDS Lites 192
    adidas Argentinas 40
    adidas Grand Slams 128, 131
    adidas KB8s and Kobes 176
    adidas Predators 143–4
    adidas Supergrips and Promodels 62, 64
    Under Armour 217
    Chuck Taylor All Star II 12
    New Balance Arch Support Company 42
    New Balance Trackster 44
    Nike Moon Shoes 80–1
    Nike Air Force 1s 102
    Nike Zoom Vapor 9s 194
    Nike Zoom Victory Elites 200
    Puma Discs 140
    Puma Speed Cats 180
    Reebok's Pump systems 21, 133–4, *135*, 148
    Sidi cycling shoes 207

Tendulkar, Sachin *190*, 191–2
tennis
    Arthur Ashe 86, *87*, *88*, 89
    Borg *vs* McEnroe Wimbledon (1980) 98, *99*, 101
    Boris Becker and Puma *120*, 120–1
    Dunlop Green Flash 18, *19*, 20, 21
    John McEnroe and Nike Air Trainer 1s *124–5*, 125, *126*, 127
    Roger Federer 194, *194–5*
    Serena Williams 202, *202–3*, 204
    Stan Smith 62, 76, *76–7*, 77, *77–8*
    Steffi Graf 128, *129*, 131
Thompson, John 153
Thorn, Rod 118
Tiriac, Ion 120
Tour de France *206*, 207–8
Tracksters, New Balance 44, *44–5*
Traum, Dick 96

U

Under Armour Athletic Apparel 214–15, *216*, 217
US military 10, 24, 38–9, 111
US Tennis Opens 131, 204
US Women's Soccer Team 164, *165*, 166

V

Vaccaro, Sonny 116–17, 118, 179
Van Doren, Paul 91, 93
Vans 91, *92–3*, 93, 136
    Half Cabs 136, *138–9*, 139
    Style # 44s and # 95s *92–3*, 93, 136
Villas, Guillermo 120
Virén, Lasse 67, 69, *94*, 94–5
Volvo Invitational (1986) 125, 127

W

waffle soles, Nike 80, 81, *81*, 112

Wagner, Berny 61
Waitzer, Josef 24
Walter, Fritz 40
Warne, Shane 192
Watkinson, Alan 199
Watts, Quincy 163
West German football team 38, 40, 108
Wilkins, Dominique 134
Williams, Serena 202, *202–3*, 204
Williams, Venus 202, 204
Wimbledon Championships
    Arthur Ashe 86, 89
    Borg *vs* McEnroe (1980) 98, *99*, 101
    Boris Becker 120–1
    Fred Perry 18, *19*, 21
    Navratilova *vs* Graff (1988) 131
    Roger Federer 194, *194–5*, 197
    Serena Williams 202, *202–3*, 204
    Stan Smith 76, *76–7*, 77
World Championships, IAAF 140, 161, 163, 175, 189, 199
World Cup Championship, Football 213
    Hungary *vs* Germany Final (1954) 38, *39*, 40
    Mexico (1970) *70–1*, 71, 72
    Spain (1982) 108
World Cup Championship, Cricket 191–2
World Cup Championship, Rugby 168, *169*, 170

Z

Z-Boys 93
Zátopek, Emil 30–1, *31*, 33
Zeitz, Jochen 189
Zidane, Zinedine 144, 213
Zoom Kobe 1s, Nike *178*, 179
Zooms, Nike 112, *113*, *114–15*
Zoom Vapor 9s, Nike 194, *194–5*, *196–7*
Zoom Victory Elites, Nike *198*, 199, 200
Zvereva, Natasha 128

ACKNOWLEDGEMENTS

Writing *Golden Kicks* was a real team effort and would not have happened without the following people, to whom I would like to express my deep felt thanks:

Babe and our Babes, my reasons for being, it's all for you. Mum, for all the love, support and encouragement. Dad, for the genes, definitely a chip off the old block. Mr. T.P.D. Sarjoo, truly 'Golden', for teaching me everything worth knowing, this book is named for you. To my uncle and aunt and other mum and dad, Judy and Hassan, for being my other mum and dad. To Michael, Arash and Nene, Amir and Deepali, Anoush and Sharon, Alison, Deanne and Louise for your love and encouragement. To Shirish, Aruna, Geeta, Anita and Priya-Nisha for everything that you do for us. To Raj, Amit, Anisha and Ayesha for your enthusiasm. To the Chavdas, Dipak and Anjna, Sherrick, Vidya and Jay who have been eagerly awaiting this book. Thanks for the ride to Manchester! Thank you Ansuya, never forgotten and always missed.

Charlotte Croft and Sarah Connelly at Bloomsbury, I can't thank you enough for your vision and enthusiasm, for bringing me into the Bloomsbury family and for being such a pleasure to work with, I hope we can do it again!

John Ly, my old mate and photographer par excellence, you've made this book look amazing. Cushty!

Yeshpal Sharma, the Prince of Smethwick, big brother, human encyclopaedia of sport and comic relief.

Barry Cullen, much missed friend and mentor, I know you'd be proud.

Stan Smith, a true legend, for your help, feedback and of course, the much treasured foreword.

Jan Runau, Martin Gebhardt, Martin Herde and Terrell Clark at adidas. I can't express my gratitude enough for your invaluable help, enthusiasm and for the privilege of access to your archives and use of your images.

Helmut Fischer, Pascal Rolling, Johannes Hackstette, and Robin Lootz at Puma for your time, support the interviews and the wonderful archive photos.

Claire Afford at Reebok for your help and enthusiasm, and for going to the trouble of getting the shoes photographed.

Alixandria Ogawa at Vans for your support, the images and for answering my queries.

Huub Valkenburg at Karhu for all your help and the Helsinki three stripes images.

Christopher Mak at ASICS for the books, much appreciated.

Grayson Palmer at Saucony for tracking down the DXN and Rod photos.

Alanna Hollings at Nike for permission to use the Nike images and for trying to get those archive photos, I did appreciate it!

Simon Wainright at Converse for permission to use the All Star II image.

John Boulter, I so enjoyed our conversation and hearing your memories. Thanks also for answering my multitude of questions!

Chris Severn, Father of the Superstar, for all your advice, memories and the Kareem and Horst photo. I know this will be just the start of a long friendship.

Rod Dixon at KiDSMARATHON, our conversation was literally a marathon (2:08:59) and was the most inspiring conversation I've ever had with anyone, what you are doing to get kids active is amazing.

Yasmin Meichtry and Patricia Reymond at The Olympic Museum, Lausanne, for the honour of allowing us access to your wonderful collection and giving us our own private tour!

Anna Renton, Audrey Snell and James McCann at the Wimbledon Lawn Tennis Museum for your help, enthusiasm and for allowing us access to your collection and library.

Rebecca Shawcross at Northampton Shoe Museum for all your help and the archive photos.

Jordan Geller at ShoeZeum for answering my Nike questions, nobody knows the Swoosh like you!

Robert Brooks, the greatest adidas fan of all, it was great to spend a morning talking three stripes with you. Big thanks also for the lift and introducing me to Henry.

Henry Davies, The Other Side of the Pillow, the best Vans shop in the world, big thanks for the photo of the Style #95s.

Solveig Fuentes at Always Tri for the photos of Sarah.

Jamie Lilly at Motonation for the Sidi Froome shoes photo.